Brazil

Brazil

Neoliberalism Versus Democracy

Alfredo Saad-Filho and Lecio Morais

First published 2018 by Pluto Press
345 Archway Road, London N6 5AA

www.plutobooks.com

British Library Cataloguing in Publication Data
A catalogue record for this book is available from the British Library

ISBN   978 0 7453 3675 6   Hardback
ISBN   978 0 7453 3670 1   Paperback
ISBN   978 1 7837 1785 9   PDF eBook
ISBN   978 1 7837 1787 3   Kindle eBook
ISBN   978 1 7837 1786 6   EPUB eBook

This book is printed on paper suitable for recycling and made from fully managed and sustained forest sources. Logging, pulping and manufacturing processes are expected to conform to the environmental standards of the country of origin.

Typeset by Stanford DTP Services, Northampton, England

Simultaneously printed in the United Kingdom and United States of America

Contents

Tables and Figures

Acknowledgements

We are grateful to many friends, colleagues and students who have generously contributed to our understanding of Brazil. Special thanks are due to Alice Kinghorn-Gray, Armando Boito, Ben Fine, Bruno Höfig, Charlotte Hübner, Juan Grigera, Leda Paulani, Lucas Bertholdi-Saad, Maria de Lourdes Rollemberg Mollo, Neil Coleman, Pedro Loureiro, Sam Gindin and Sila Demirors for their helpful comments and suggestions. Lena Lavinas read the entire manuscript and offered detailed comments, for which we are immensely grateful.

We are indebted to Anne Beech for her continuing support for the publication of this book.

Acronyms

ARENA	*Aliança Renovadora Nacional* (National Renewal Alliance).
BA	Bureaucratic-authoritarian state or political regime.
BNDE	*Banco Nacional de Desenvolvimento Econômico* (National Bank of Economic Development).
BNDES	*Banco Nacional de Desenvolvimento Econômico e Social* (National Bank of Economic and Social Development).
BPC	*Benefício de Prestação Continuada* (benefit paid to the elderly and disabled).
BRICS	Brazil, Russia, India, China and South Africa.
CBA	*Comitê Brasileiro pela Anistia* (Brazilian Committee for Amnesty).
CCTs	Conditional cash transfer programmes.
CEO	Chief executive officer.
Cofins	*Contribuição sobre o Faturamento das Empresas* (Contribution on Company Revenues).
CPMF	*Contribuição Provisória sobre Movimentações Financeiras* (Provisional Contribution on Financial Transactions).
CSLL	*Contribuição sobre o Lucro Líquido* (Contribution on Net Profits).
CUT	*Central Única dos Trabalhadores* (Confederation of Trade Unions linked to the PT).
DIEESE	*Departamento Intersindical de Estatística e Estudos Socio-economicos* (Joint Trade Union Department of Statistics and Socioeconomic Studies).
DPD	Domestic public debt.
FDI	Foreign direct investment.
FIESP	*Federação das Indústrias do Estado de São Paulo* (Industrial Federation of the State of São Paulo).
FSE	*Fundo Social de Emergência* (Social Emergency Fund).
GDP	Gross domestic product.
IBGE	*Instituto Brasileiro de Geografia e Estatística* (Brazilian Institute of Geography and Statistics).
IMF	International Monetary Fund.

ISI	Import-substituting industrialisation.
LRF	*Lei de Responsabilidade Fiscal* (Fiscal Responsibility Law).
M&As	Mergers and acquisitions.
MBA	*Movimento Brasileiro pela Anistia* (Brazilian Movement for Amnesty).
MCMV	*Minha Casa Minha Vida* (My Home My Life housing programme).
MCV	*Movimento Custo de Vida* (Movement Cost of Living).
MDB	*Movimento Democrático Brasileiro* (Brazilian Democratic Movement).
MFA	*Movimento Feminino pela Anistia* (Women's Movement for Amnesty).
MPL	*Movimento Passe Livre* (Free Fare Movement).
MST	*Movimento dos Trabalhadores Rurais Sem Terra* (Landless Peasants' Movement).
NEM	*Nova Matriz Econômica* (New Economic Matrix).
NGO	Non-governmental organisation.
OECD	Organisation for Economic Cooperation and Development.
PAC	*Programa de Aceleração do Crescimento* (Growth Acceleration Programme).
PBF	*Programa Bolsa Família* (Family Grant Programme).
PCB	*Partido Comunista Brasileiro* (Brazilian Communist Party).
PCdoB	*Partido Comunista do Brasil* (Communist Party of Brazil).
PCO	*Partido da Causa Operária* (Party of the Workers' Platform).
PDT	*Partido Democrático Trabalhista* (Democratic Labour Party).
PGR	*Procuradoria Geral da República* (Attorney General's Office).
PIL	*Plano de Investimento em Logística* (Plan of Investment in Logistics).
PL	*Partido Liberal* (Liberal Party).
PMDB	*Partido do Movimento Democrático Brasileiro* (Party of the Brazilian Democratic Movement).
PND	*Plano Nacional de Desenvolvimento* (National Development Plan).
PSB	*Partido Socialista Brasileiro* (Brazilian Socialist Party).
PSDB	*Partido da Social Democracia Brasileira* (Brazilian Social Democratic Party).
PSOL	*Partido Socialismo e Liberdade* (Socialism and Freedom Party).

PSTU   *Partido Socialista dos Trabalhadores Unificado* (Unified Workers' Socialist Party).
PT   *Partido dos Trabalhadores* (Workers' Party).
QE   Quantitative easing.
SoA   System of accumulation.
SOE   State-owned enterprise.
SUS   *Sistema Único de Saúde* (National Health System).
TNC   Transnational company.
UK   United Kingdom.
URV   *Unidade Real de Valor* (Unit of Real Value).
US   United States.
USA   United States of America.
USSR   Union of Soviet Socialist Republics.
WTO   World Trade Organisation.

Presidents of Brazil, 1930–2017

Getúlio Vargas (3 November 1930 – 29 October 1945)
José Linhares (29 October 1945 – 21 January 1946)
Eurico Dutra (21 January 1946 – 31 January 1951)
Getúlio Vargas (31 January 1951 – 24 August 1954)
Café Filho (24 August 1954 – 8 November 1955)
Carlos Luz (8 November 1955 – 11 November 1955)
Nereu Ramos (11 November 1955 – 31 January 1956)
Juscelino Kubitschek (31 January 1956 – 31 January 1961)
Jânio Quadros (31 January 1961 – 25 August 1961)
Ranieri Mazzilli (25 August 1961 – 7 September 1961)
João Goulart (7 September 1961 – 2 April 1964)
Ranieri Mazzilli (2 April 1964 – 15 April 1964)
Humberto Castelo Branco (15 April 1964 – 15 March 1967)
Artur da Costa e Silva (15 March 1967 – 31 August 1969)
Military Junta (31 August 1969 – 30 October 1969)
Emilio Garrastazu Médici (30 October 1969 – 15 March 1974)
Ernesto Geisel (15 March 1974 – 15 March 1979)
João Figueiredo (15 March 1979 – 15 March 1985)
José Sarney (15 March 1985 – 15 March 1990)
Fernando Collor (15 March 1990 – 29 December 1992)
Itamar Franco (29 December 1992 – 1 January 1995)
Fernando Henrique Cardoso (1 January 1995 – 1 January 2003)
Luiz Inácio Lula da Silva (1 January 2003 – 1 January 2011)
Dilma Rousseff (1 January 2011 – 31 August 2016)
Michel Temer (31 August 2016 –)

Preface

Our academic collaboration began in the late 1990s. Several articles and book chapters later, we decided to consolidate our understanding of Brazilian political economy by writing this book together. The tragedy of the Workers' Party (*Partido dos Trabalhadores*, PT), the impeachment of President Dilma Rousseff, and the unprecedented economic and political calamities engulfing the country added urgency to this project. They also brought our arguments into sharper relief.

The certainties that underpinned the democratic New Republic (*Nova República*), founded in 1985, have disintegrated. At the time of writing, Brazil's constitutional order lies in shreds, and the country's democracy is being stress-tested as never before.

The high hopes with which political democracy was achieved against an almost universally detested dictatorship remained alive after the death of President-elect Tancredo Neves, in 1985. Democracy was consolidated despite the petty manoeuvring and robbery of public assets under President José Sarney (1985–90). Democracy provided an exit route from the thieving megalomania of gangster-President Fernando Collor, in 1992. Democracy held the country together during the tenure of Vice-President Itamar Franco (1992–4), a shallow man who never missed an opportunity to embarrass the Republic. Democracy resisted the arrogance and plunder of the national patrimony orchestrated by the Marxist sociologist-turned-neoliberal-guru, Fernando Henrique Cardoso (1994–2002). The democratic consensus seemed to flourish under the presidencies of Luís Inácio Lula da Silva (2003–10) and Dilma Rousseff (2011–16), but only too briefly in what turned out to be its swansong. Lula, the trade union leader, was pragmatic, intuitive and charismatic. He was also detested by the traditional elites, but they could do business with him. Lula was also fortunate, as global economic circumstances favoured his years in power.

It was different with Dilma Rousseff. A former left-wing guerrilla under the dictatorship, she was an excellent manager but lacked the talent, experience, inclination and nous to lead a divided country with a political system vulnerable to deadlock and underpinned by pernicious and powerful elite interests. Then the economy began to fall apart. The stage was set for an epic drama culminating in Dilma Rousseff's impeachment, in 2016, by an 'alliance of privilege' fronted by a larcenous political mob, pantomimic judges, police officers masquerading as national saviours, self-interested media moguls and a rabid and vengeful middle class. Their rebellion anointed the sinister Michel Temer as President, whose tenure offered the world a calamitous spectacle of greed and incompetence. Readers can be certain of much entertainment in what is, at heart, a sad, even tragic, story with a gloomy ending: the (hopefully temporary) exhaustion of a young democracy.

This book refutes the facile claim that the Brazilian disaster is due to the contamination of economic life by political corruption and fiscal irresponsibility driven by the PT. In these pages, we offer an alternative interpretation of the overlapping crises in Brazil. Our approach cannot be summarised within a slogan but, then, neither can the complexities of reality. Understanding Brazil's predicament since the political transition from dictatorship to democracy, and the economic transition from import-substituting industrialisation to neoliberalism, requires a full account of global patterns, structural forces and relations, unique conjunctures and historically-specific detail.

Brazil is a complex country struggling with almost intractable problems and, it seems, a stubborn inclination to falter and to fail. The country has enormous potential set against huge social needs. It would be easy to prescribe solutions to Brazil's dilemmas; many analysts have done so with abandon and greater or lesser contact with underlying realities. This book offers nothing of the sort. Instead, it proposes an innovative framing of the country's predicament, with a view to supporting new forms of social organisation and political contestation, coupled with the targeting of socially-inclusive economic alternatives. These are, ultimately, the challenges confronting any work in applied political economy.

Alfredo Saad-Filho and Lecio Morais
London and Brasília, November 2017

Introduction

Overview

Brazil is the world's fifth biggest country in area and in population; its economy is the largest in Latin America, and one of the ten largest in the world. Between the late 1940s and 1980, GDP growth rates approached 7 per cent per annum (4 per cent per capita), which was outstanding even during the postwar 'golden age' of global capitalism. The country was transformed. A poor economy that, until the early twentieth century, specialised in the production of coffee for export, became a large, industrialised and fast-growing powerhouse, exporting durable consumer goods to China, construction services to the Middle East and, eventually, aeroplanes to the USA.

Rapid economic growth is not unproblematic, but it has two potentially redeeming features: domestically, it opens up the possibility of satisfying everyone's basic needs; externally, it can support a rebalancing of the global political economy. Brazil squandered these transformative possibilities. Regardless of the changes in the economy and the extraordinary growth of productive capacity through import-substituting industrialisation (ISI), Brazil was, and continues to be, one of the world's most unequal countries, with wholly avoidable poverty stunting the lives of tens of millions of people; it has also often failed to contribute significantly to global diplomacy. In the meantime, a minority has devoured the gains from growth, gorging on consumption levels that are both morally unconscionable and impossible to generalise: they are, by definition, incompatible with a common citizenship.

In laying claim to the wealth of the nation, the elites disregarded the Other. In order to achieve their material ambitions, they plundered the natural environment. To secure their position, they monopolised political power.[1] Brazilian growth was *perverse* because it increased economic and social inequalities. Specifically, it strengthened elite command of the country's resources and political institutions, and their control of the level, composition and distribution of investment, employment, trade, finance and the national output.

The Brazilian state was dominated by an oligarchic republic until 1930, a right-wing populist dictatorship between 1930 and 1945, and a military dictatorship between 1964 and 1985. In the interval, a precarious democracy was caught between landed interests, various strands of populism and, threatening their uneasy balance, emerging forces on the political left. A more successful democracy was built in the 1980s, but the judicial-parliamentary coup of 2016 shows that political freedom remains fragile, and that the pursuit of equality is not universally welcomed. Despite the veneer of an integrated and cordial society, where rich, poor, women, men, black and white enjoy samba, cold beers and football together, Brazilian society has been forged by 500 years of racism, exclusion, inequality, violence and authoritarianism. Their imprint has persisted, regardless of changes in the political regime.

Growth faltered in the 1980s, and the economy was overcome by a prolonged stagnation lasting into the 2000s. In the meantime, inflation accelerated from around 20 per cent per year, in 1972, to an annualised peak above 5,000 per cent, in mid-1994. That scourge was eliminated by the Real plan, named after the currency introduced in its wake, the *real*.[2] The stabilisation of the currency was not an unproblematic achievement, since the Real plan was used instrumentally to consolidate Brazil's transition to neoliberalism. However, neoliberalism did not bring growth, sustained improvements in living standards or a less divided society. On the contrary, GDP growth rates and job creation declined even further, and the pattern of employment deteriorated even in comparison with the so-called 'lost decade' of the 1980s.

Luís Inácio Lula da Silva, founder of the PT, was elected President in 2002, partly as a reaction against the inequities and inefficiencies of neoliberalism. Yet, his victory meant little until the favourable winds of the global commodity boom gave the government enough freedom to expand citizenship, raise wages and implement successful but invariably marginal distributional policies, without antagonising too many interests. At the end of his first administration, elite reaction against the creeping democratisation of the economy and society pushed Lula into a political corner from which escape seemed impossible. But escape he did, and with flair. Under growing pressure from the right, Lula shifted left, *ma non troppo*. He built a social and political coalition supporting mildly heterodox economic policies and a stronger push for the distribution of income. In the unprecedentedly favourable global context of the mid-2000s, these policies triggered a mini-boom; Lula's achievements were crowned with international glory, expressed by the rise of Brazil among the BRICS and the award of the 2013 Confederations Football Cup, the 2014 FIFA World Cup and the 2016 Olympic and Paralympic Games. The good times did not last.

The global economic environment turned hostile in 2008, and repeated policy mistakes and unrelenting elite hostility bedevilled the administration led by Lula's successor, Dilma Rousseff. Eventually, her government collapsed amidst the most severe economic crisis in Brazil's recorded history. By 2016, the Brazilian economy was ruined. Successive contractions of national output reduced per capita income back to its level in the early 2000s, eliminating the gains under the PT administrations. The open unemployment rate shot up from 4 per cent to 14 per cent between 2014 and 2016, with the loss of millions of jobs. The fiscal deficit and the domestic public debt mounted, and large firms in the oil, shipbuilding, construction, nuclear, food-processing and other industries were seriously affected.

On the political side, the Constitution was ripped to shreds. President Rousseff was overpowered by a coalition of privileged social groups whose leaders were implicated in a seemingly endless sequence of corruption scandals. The judiciary went rogue, disabling both the economy and the political system in the guise of 'fighting corruption'. Congress was demoralised and the Executive was disorganised. The elite's palpable hatred of the PT, the left and the poor eventually hardened into indifference to the social consequences of the coup.

At the time of writing, policy-making has become erratic, except for the dogged attempt by the administration led by Michel Temer to impose an excluding form of neoliberalism. The main point of the coup is to attack workers' rights, protections, pensions; all the rest – corruption included – is accessory. Surprising as it may seem, this excluding variety of neoliberalism is not simply elite retribution against the social gains in the previous period. Instead, it builds upon policies maintained, reinforced or imposed by the Rousseff administration, especially but not exclusively in its desperate final months, when the PT overturned its earlier achievements and abandoned even recent commitments as part of its struggle to survive. Yet even in the good times, the PT had never really broken with the neoliberal system of accumulation inherited from previous administrations; the party never tried to build an alternative economic system or social structure, and had deliberately alienated the social forces that might support a transformative project. It is ironic but not surprising that the crisis of the PT would be due, in part, to the inconsistencies in its own power project. These are reviewed in detail in what follows.

This book analyses the trajectory of the Brazilian economy, society and political system in recent decades. They are examined from the point of view of the limitations in (and contradictions between) the *political transition from military dictatorship to democracy*, and the *economic transition from ISI to neoliberalism*.

The transition to democracy, between 1974 and 1988, was predicated on a socially *inclusive* logic that fostered the expansion of citizenship and aimed to build a Scandinavian-style welfare state in a peripheral economy. In contrast, the transition to neoliberalism, between 1988 and 1999, was based on an *excluding* logic fostering financialisation, the deterioration of the living and working conditions of the majority and the concentration of income.

This book reviews these transitions in order to shed an original light upon the enduring features of Brazil's political economy, its recent metamorphoses and emerging fragilities. These features and fragilities include shifting but entrenched social and economic inequalities, seemingly irresolvable political fractures, balance of payments vulnerability, persistent weaknesses in the manufacturing sector and severe fiscal and financial constraints. The book also shows that the tensions due to the incompatibility between democracy and neoliberalism have limited the scope for distribution and social integration. They have produced political crises and impasses, culminating in the obliteration of the federal administrations led by the PT.

Method and Analytical Framework

This book is grounded on Marxist political economy. It examines the relationship between the political transition from dictatorship to democracy and the economic transition from ISI to neoliberalism through the prism of the *systems of accumulation* (SoA) in Brazil. The use of a grand theoretical framework is necessary for reasons of internal consistence; it also helps to avoid incoherent policy analysis and excessive focus on description at the expense of insight.[3] Only grand theories can illuminate long-term patterns, structures, systemic contradictions and historical shifts that may be difficult to discern, hard to understand or obscured by countless events of fleeting relevance. Yet, it is those patterns and structures that frame the trajectory of the concrete over time; that is, the making of history.

The SoA is the instantiation, configuration, phase, form or mode of existence (these terms are used interchangeably) of capitalism in a given conjuncture. It is determined by the class relations encapsulated in the mode of extraction, accumulation and distribution of (surplus) value and the institutional structures and processes through which those relations reproduce themselves (including the political forms of representation of interests and the patterns of social metabolism, see below).[4] Since the SoAs express the form of the capital relation relatively concretely, at a specific time and place, they are intrinsically variegated.

Examination of the SoA should include, first, the forms of the state, property, law, labour, exploitation, markets, technology, credit, money, distribution and competition, and the relationships between capital accumulation, social structure, the natural environment and the rest of the world. Second, it should consider the forms of political representation and the hegemonic ideology legitimising the SoA and stabilising incompatible interests. These historically constituted structures and processes can only be examined concretely through the political regimes, policy choices and institutional histories in which they are embedded.

Accumulation within each SoA is limited by *constraints* expressing the contradictions of capital in specific contexts and setting limits to economic and social reproduction. These constraints are contingent and historically specific, rather than permanent or logically necessary. They must be identified empirically, and they are usually addressed by public policy. While the existence of constraints to accumulation is widely recognised in the literature, each constraint is usually examined in isolation, as if they were unrelated elements blocking an otherwise undifferentiated process of 'growth'. This is misguided. The constraints are embedded within the SoA, and they help to define it. Since the SoA and the constraints are inseparable in reality, they must be analysed together.

Identification of the constraints to accumulation can usefully start from the circuit of industrial capital as outlined in Karl Marx's *Capital* Volume 1, that is, $M–C<^{MP}_{LP} \ldots PC'–M'$, where M is money, C and C' are (different) commodities, MP is means of production (land, buildings, machines, material inputs, and so on), LP is labour power, …P… is production, and M' is greater than M. This suggests that typical constraints include (but are not limited to) labour, finance and resource allocation, the balance of payments and the institutional setting (the property structure, mode of competition, role of the state and so on).

The *accumulation strategy* includes the spectrum of economic, social and other policies securing the reproduction of the SoA, managing, dislocating or transforming the constraints, and shaping the restructuring of capital in a specific conjuncture.

Systems of Accumulation in Brazil

Brazil has experienced three SoAs since gaining its independence in 1822. First, primary export-led growth with an oligarchic state and different political regimes, especially a centralised, authoritarian and exclusionary Empire, and a decentralised but similarly authoritarian and excluding First Republic (*República Velha*, Old Republic), overthrown in 1930 (this period is not examined in what follows).[5] Second, ISI with a developmental state, between 1930 and 1980. This period included a plethora of political forms, especially populist and military dictatorships and populist democracies, and it was punctuated by political crises and *coups d'état*. Third, after a long transition, a neoliberal economic system with political democracy, since the late 1980s.

While shifts between *varieties* of SoAs are normally driven by domestic imperatives, transitions *across* SoAs are usually triggered by exogenous transformations in global capitalism: this is one of the manifestations of the peripheral (dependent) character of the Brazilian economy. Global shifts tighten up the constraints on the Brazilian SoA, with pressures usually being relayed by the balance of payments. They reduce the policy space available to the government and limit its capacity to address other constraints, compromising economic performance. As the crisis spreads across the political-economy divide, the traditional modalities of reproduction can become dysfunctional. A transition to a new SoA follows.

The key economic tasks of the Brazilian state include the reproduction of the dominant SoA, addressing the constraints, implementing consistent accumulation strategies and driving systemic transitions. In doing this, the state must negotiate the tensions between two key roles. The *conservative role of the state* derives from the imperatives to secure the relations of domination, reproduce the mode of exploitation and preserve the existing patterns of inequality of income, wealth and privilege, regardless of economic performance.[6] This role is compatible with distinct political forms, from dictatorship to formal democracy. Attempts to challenge the conservative role of the state have triggered political turbulence in Brazil,[7] for example, in the 1920s, 1944–5, 1953–5, 1961–4, 1977–84, 1985–8, and between 2013 and the time of writing. The *transformative role of the state* concerns the use of public policy to enforce the primitive accumulation of capital, drive the expansion of capital(ism) through diverse SoAs, and hothouse the emergence of a capitalist class across primary export-led growth, followed by manufacturing and, later, finance. In this sense, heavy state intervention does not imply any form of 'state capitalism'. Rather, it merely shows that public policy responds to the imperatives of accumulation.[8]

Tensions between its conservative and transformative roles help to explain why the Brazilian state has generally been strong 'vertically', acting decisively to subdue native populations, slaves, poor immigrants, peasants and wage-workers, while it has been weak 'horizontally', with only limited capacity to manage conflicts among domestic elite groups and between them and their external counterparts.[9] Those elites include large and medium-sized capitalists (especially manufacturing, financial and agricultural capitalists, exporters and traders), large landlords, regional and local political chiefs, the technocracy, top civil servants, military officers, the Catholic hierarchy (and, more recently, the leaders of the main evangelical sects), the mainstream media and their hangers-on.[10] Disputes between them tend to be addressed through bargains, corruption or political capture. Historically, *pragmatism* has been one of the principles of formulation and implementation of economic policy in Brazil.

The tensions induced by economic growth and restructuring have created fissures within the elite. One of the implications of these tensions has been the disorderly development of the institutions of the state and the emergence of a bureaucracy that has often been divided between the implementation of policies narrowly defined by sectional interests, including those of the bureaucracy itself, and the pragmatic pursuit of policies determined by minimum common denominators (see above).[11] Since the Brazilian state has rarely been cohesive, the concept of 'state autonomy' – grounded upon a solid institutional bloc – is analytically inappropriate.[12]

The Brazilian state is, then, strong but fragmented, and it has often been unable to address consistently the constraints to the dominant SoA, and either unwilling or unable to limit inequality and support a common citizenship. By the same token, the state has generally been unable to plan the expansion of capacity, provide infrastructure, develop new competitive advantages and secure the provision of long-term finance for industry. Because of that, and the nature of the external constraints, Brazilian growth has tended to be volatile rather than planned or stable, with constraints being addressed haphazardly by poorly coordinated policies, changing configurations of the state and shifting political systems. This has raised the costs and limited the efficacy of state action, in contrast with more successful examples of accumulation in, e.g., East Asia, North America or Scandinavia.

Despite these limitations, Brazilian growth has been supported by the plunder of the natural environment, heavy reliance on cheap labour, a relatively large internal market, globally integrated export agriculture and an internationalised manufacturing sector. Finally, and unsurprisingly, accumulation has tended to be more successful in periods of stronger hegemony, when governments were more likely to follow coherent policies; for example, under Presidents Juscelino Kubitschek (1956–61), Emílio Médici (1969–73), Ernesto Geisel (1974–9), and in the second administration of Luís Inácio Lula da Silva (2006–10).

Structure of the Book

This book includes this introduction, nine chapters and a conclusion. Chapter 1 reviews the main features and limitations of the system of accumulation driven by ISI between 1930 and 1980. Even though Brazil developed an advanced manufacturing sector through ISI, this sector remained excessively fragmented and inefficient, and it was limited by balance of payments, financial and fiscal constraints. They affected the provision of inputs, availability of infrastructure and external balance. The macroeconomic disruptions induced by the two oil shocks and the international debt crisis weighed heavily upon the SoA, and the fragilities of ISI surfaced through a permanent slowdown in Brazil's GDP growth rate and a gradual slide into hyperinflation. Social tensions escalated because of distributional conflicts and mounting demands for democracy. Even though the transition to democracy, in 1985, satisfied the political aspirations of the emerging mass movements, it did not directly resolve the growing distributional conflicts, address the tightening constraints on the economy or improve macroeconomic management. The economic paralysis that afflicted the dictatorship in its later years and that gripped the first democratic administrations was symptomatic of the exhaustion of ISI and the weakening of the structures of social domination associated with that SoA.

Chapter 2 reviews the transition from dictatorship to democracy, focusing on the mass movements that led to the demise of the military regime. These movements drew upon an inclusive logic promoting political freedom, economic equality and the construction of a democratic welfare state. However, the transition was limited by an elite pact that delivered a shallow democracy, expanding citizenship while, at the same time, securing the reproduction of economic privilege. In this sense, the 1988 Constitution created a stunted democracy and a constrained welfare state. These limitations worsened because of the weakness of the economy and the pressures emerging in the transition from ISI to neoliberalism. As it included severe contradictions, not least between democracy and neoliberalism, the Brazilian political transition created a *democracy fragile by design.* Finally, this chapter reviews the rise of the PT as a left party of a new type. The party was formed as a genuinely working-class organisation, committed to (a poorly specified) democratic socialism. However, the pressures of functioning in a democracy eroded the PT's radical edge while, simultaneously, boosting its ability to acquire political office.

Chapter 3 examines neoliberalism as a system of accumulation (that is, the contemporary stage of global capitalism), as the prelude to a review of the transition to neoliberalism in Brazil. The neoliberal reforms in the late 1980s and early 1990s were justified by the presumed exhaustion of ISI, the need to improve economic efficiency and the imperative to control inflation. These challenges provided ideological cover for the economic transition from ISI to neoliberalism. This chapter examines the macroeconomic changes in the Brazilian economy due to the neoliberal transition, focusing on the internationalisation and financialisation of the economy, the changes to the balance of payments, the vicious circles created by the Real inflation stabilisation plan and their implications for growth. It is shown that, after the transition, Brazil remained an unequal, dependent and poverty-generating economy but, in contrast with the previous period of ISI, the country became a *low-growth* economy, where economic performance was permanently limited by the threat of balance of payments and exchange rate crises. Swings in international capital flows triggered the crisis of the *real,* in 1999, but the ultimate cause of the crisis was the fragilities created by the neoliberal transition. These shortcomings were addressed, in part, by the 'neoliberal policy tripod' introduced in 1999 (including inflation targeting and Central Bank independence, free capital movements and floating exchange rates, and contractionary fiscal and monetary policies).[13] Since then, the tripod has ruled Brazilian macroeconomic policy.

Chapter 4 reviews the structural changes in the Brazilian economy during the 1990s, focusing on the implications of the new SoA for production, the industrial structure and the level and patterns of employment. Import liberalisation and greater international integration hollowed out Brazil's manufacturing base, fostered the reprimarisation of the economy,[14] and increased the country's dependence on foreign trade, investment and technology. Manufacturing employment declined and productive capacity fell in key sectors, especially the more technologically sophisticated branches of industry. While the economy lost dynamism and capacity to create 'good' jobs, the state became less able to address the problems of growth, restructuring and policy coordination. Meanwhile, the neoliberal reforms were gradually embedded into the Constitution, especially through fiscal rules justified by the imperatives of inflation stabilisation and 'good governance'. In doing so, neoliberalism acquired legitimacy and tightened its hold on the institutional fabric of the country, undermining the democratic aspirations embodied in the Constitution.

Chapter 5 outlines the successes and limitations of the first administration of Luís Inácio Lula da Silva. Lula's election, in 2002, was the outcome of two mutually reinforcing processes. On the one hand, there were the tensions between the inclusive logic of democracy and the exclusionary consequences of neoliberalism (including poverty, inequality and precarious employment). On the other hand, there was the endogenous development of the PT, that led it to position itself primarily as an 'honest' party committed to 'fairness' and 'development', at the expense of its earlier commitment to some form of socialism.[15] On this basis, the PT built an 'alliance of losers', including groups with only the experience of *losses* under neoliberalism in common. This alliance underpinned the PT's attempt to govern within the established rules, that is, accommodating neoliberalism and the policy tripod. Continuity was tempered by changes in the social composition of the state through the appointment of thousands of popular leaders to positions of power, and the distribution of income at the margin through faster economic growth and federal transfers. This virtuous circle was limited by the government's political fragility. Lula was repeatedly attacked by the neoliberal elite and the middle class, until the *mensalão* corruption scandal led to the collapse of the 'alliance of losers', in 2005. Lula responded with a new 'alliance of winners', bringing together the groups that had benefitted the most during his first administration. They supported his successful bid for re-election, in 2006.

Chapter 6 reviews the achievements of 'developmental neoliberalism' during the second Lula administration (2007–10) and the first administration led by Dilma Rousseff (2011–14). This hybrid variety of neoliberalism included neodevelopmental economic policies, in addition to the neoliberal policy framework expressed in the tripod.[16] Developmental neoliberalism had positive implications for economic growth, employment, distribution and social welfare, and it supported Brazil's impressive recovery after the global economic crisis. High commodity prices and abundant liquidity alleviated the balance of payments constraint, while the appreciation of the *real* reduced inflation. However, private investment failed to pick up, there were no significant transformations in the productive structure, public investment was insufficient to sustain broad-based growth, and no attempt was made to reduce the inequality of wealth. Moreover, the disintegration of ISI in the 1980s and the imposition of neoliberalism in the 1990s entrenched a tendency towards deindustrialisation, the elimination of skilled jobs and the creation of low-paid jobs, and the concentration of income. They eroded the tax base, expanded needs, imposed financial and other stresses on the public sector, and enforced tight budgetary limitations on Brazil's emerging welfare state. Limited counter-tendencies prevailed for a time, during the PT administrations, but they were eventually overwhelmed by economic decline and the neoliberal reaction.

Chapter 7 reviews the achievements and insufficiencies of the administration led by Dilma Rousseff. Her coalition had a commanding position in Congress and, for a short time, the PT was close to achieving political hegemony. Rousseff was committed to faster economic growth and income distribution through the incremental strengthening of neo-developmentalism and the erosion of the neoliberal tripod. To do this, the government introduced a 'new economic matrix' aiming to support a private-investment-driven cycle of growth focusing on infrastructure and basic goods, boosting productivity and reconstituting strategic production chains. The administration also pushed for the reduction of interest rates in order to support production at the expense of financial interests. However, these initiatives failed. Private capital did not respond, and the government's fiscal and monetary policies contributed to a growth slowdown that worsened the fiscal imbalance and reduced the scope for distribution. Rousseff's difficulties were compounded by the fragmentation of the government's base in Congress. These troubles led to a policy drift, culminating in inconsistent fiscal, tax, public-investment, labour-market and transfer policies. As the economy slowed down, the government shifted towards neoliberal orthodoxy in a vain attempt to reach an accommodation with the bourgeoisie. However, contractionary policies stalled demand, employment and distribution, plunging the economy into a deep crisis and eroding the PT's support among the workers and the poor.

Chapter 8 surveys the economic, political and distributive shifts associated with the transitions to democracy and to neoliberalism, focusing on the changes in Brazil's class structure and their political forms of expression. The chapter examines two fractions of the bourgeoisie (the internal and the internationalised bourgeoisie), the middle class and the formal and informal proletariat. The changes in the class structure are described, and these insights inform an original interpretation of the protests against Rousseff, which started in 2013. These protests were significant for four reasons. First, they were the largest mass demonstrations in Brazil in a generation. Second, they signalled an irreversible break in the base of support for the PT and paralysed Rousseff's administration. Third, they were symptomatic of the emergence of a new type of political protest under neoliberalism, explained by the notion of 'lumpenisation of politics'. Fourth, the protests started from the left but were captured by the right, which signalled the recomposition of a mass base for the far right for the first time in half a century.

Chapter 9 analyses the collapse of Rousseff's administration as the outcome of a confluence of revolts led by an 'alliance of privilege'. This alliance included most of the elite, especially the mainstream media, finance, industrial capital, the middle class, the judiciary, the Federal Police and large sections of the government's base in Congress. A range of dissatisfactions was brought together by the deterioration of the economy since 2011. They were intensified by corruption scandals focusing on the PT, especially the *lava jato* (carwash) operation. In order to contextualise these events, this chapter reviews the PT's involvement in corruption, the role of the middle class in corruption scandals and the way in which corruption was used as a tool to destroy Rousseff and the PT. In this sense, the impeachment was more than the tortured end to a government, or a savage attack against the PT. Rousseff's impeachment expressed the contradictions between *neoliberalism as system of accumulation* and *democracy as its political form*. They include the rupture of the fragile equilibrium between citizenship and privilege embedded in the Constitution, the shrinkage of the space for hybrid economic policies and the collapse of the PT's political project. These contradictions have evolved into a (temporary) historical impasse in which no configuration of political forces can establish hegemony, secure political stability or restore economic growth.

1

A Troubled Path to Development

Overview

This chapter reviews the main features of the Brazilian system of accumulation driven by ISI between, approximately, 1930 and 1980. The chapter focuses on the development policies implemented in this period, their constraints and limitations, and the reasons why the crisis of ISI was expressed through faltering economic growth and rising inflation.

Despite significant achievements, including some of the fastest GDP growth rates in the world over five decades, extraordinary economic diversification and the remarkable development of the manufacturing sector, Brazilian ISI was severely limited. These limitations included several economic constraints, and the continuing inability of the state to coordinate investment and secure the provision of infrastructure, even though they were essential to support growth, urbanisation and welfare improvements in a rapidly changing society.

These limitations became apparent in the wake of the two oil shocks in the 1970s, and the international debt crisis in the early 1980s. They showed that ISI was based on monetary, financial, fiscal, tax and exchange-rate policies incompatible with internal and external balance. Brazil's macroeconomic troubles culminated in a gradual slide into hyperinflation, revealing the limitations of the SoA. High inflation would be overcome only in the mid-1990s, as part of the transition to a new neoliberal SoA (see Chapter 3). In the meantime, political instability increased, social conflicts escalated and a mass campaign for democracy forced the military government to transfer power to a civilian administration (see Chapter 2).

The achievements and limitations of Brazilian ISI must be examined in the context of the transformations in global hegemony during the twentieth century. Despite localised tensions, examined below and in Chapter 2, Brazil embedded itself peacefully in the US-led global order (unlike Argentina, say, where conflicts about that country's appropriate place in the world fuelled political crises and relative economic decline).

In exchange for joining World War II on the side of the Allies, Brazil obtained US resources and technology, allowing the internalisation of the production of steel;[1] the US also supported the creation of the Brazilian Development Bank (*Banco Nacional de Desenvolvimento Econômico*, BNDE) in the early 1950s.[2] Brazil's natural resources and minerals became increasingly important for US industry and military effort during the Cold War, while Brazilian exports posed no direct challenge to US producers. In addition, Brazil's internal market and supportive government policies attracted many US-based transnational companies (TNCs). In the postwar years, Brazil was a successful case of internationalising manufacturing-led growth, at the expense of earlier aspirations for 'autonomous' development. By and large, the Brazilian bourgeoisie was only too happy to orbit around US capital.[3]

The crisis of Brazilian ISI was closely associated with the turbulence facing US hegemony in the wake of the crisis of Keynesianism and defeat in Vietnam.[4] Worldwide inflation, the oil shocks, political instability and the 'dollar crisis' tightened up the balance of payments constraint in most developing economies, but also in the UK, Italy and the USSR. Many poor countries would be overwhelmed by the international debt crisis, and accumulation strategies based on ISI collapsed almost everywhere. The USA became less inclined to accommodate large emerging powers, unless they were in the imperial borderlands. In these adverse circumstances, the growth, diversification and increasing sophistication of Brazil's manufacturing exports triggered a competitive backlash from the US state and US-based producers. The global ambitions of Brazil's military government also met stiff resistance, symbolised by unbending US opposition to Brazil's nuclear programme and instrumental support for human rights (see Chapter 2). Instability grew both at home and abroad, culminating in an economic impasse expressed by falling growth rates and escalating inflation.

These processes are considered in what follows, in five parts. The first describes the process of ISI in Brazil. The second examines the political forms associated with import-substitution, and the reasons for the collapse of democracy. The third focuses on the economic policies of the military regime, and the fourth looks at the expression of the crisis of ISI through rising inflation. The fifth reviews the distributional implications of inflation, the efforts at stabilisation, and how they contributed to the economic transition to neoliberalism.

ISI in Brazil

ISI is a system of accumulation driven by the internalisation of the production of (previously imported) manufactured goods and ancillary services, in order to alleviate the balance of payments constraint, create employment and incorporate new ('modern') technologies and cultural values.[5] The expansion of manufacturing includes both 'horizontal' diversification and 'vertical' deepening of productive capacity, supported by the expansion of economic infrastructure, especially essential inputs (oil, chemical products, capital goods and so on) and public services (electricity, water, sanitation, transportation, etc.).

Typically, manufacturing growth under ISI is sequenced. It generally begins with the production of non-durable consumer goods (e.g. processed foods, beverages, tobacco products and cotton textiles). It later deepens to include durable consumer goods (especially household appliances and automobile assembly), simple chemical and pharmaceutical products (for example, oil refining and certain pharmaceutical products) and non-metallic minerals (especially cement). In a small number of countries, including Brazil, ISI can reach a third stage, including the production of steel, capital goods (e.g. industrial machinery and electric motors) and technologically complex goods (electronic machines, aircraft design and assembly, shipbuilding).[6]

Brazilian ISI was associated with a peculiar structure of property relations, effectively a 'macroeconomic division of labour'. Briefly, the production of non-durable goods was dominated by small domestic firms, durable goods were typically produced by TNCs and capital goods were produced by large domestic oligopolies. Infrastructure and basic goods (steel, electricity, telecoms, oil, gas and air, road, rail and sea links, and so on) were generally supplied by state-owned enterprises (SOEs). State-owned banks played a dominant role in the provision of credit for economic growth (see below).[7]

The Brazilian economy grew rapidly, if unevenly, for several decades under ISI. Agriculture declined from well over 30 per cent of GDP in the early years of the twentieth century to a little over 10 per cent in the early 1980s, while manufacturing increased almost exactly in the opposite direction, from under 15 per cent of GDP to well over 30 per cent.[8] Large-scale economic changes drove demographic, sociological, cultural and political transformations leading to new patterns of behaviour and the emergence of new industries, social classes and interest groups.[9]

Despite these transformative outcomes, Brazilian ISI was limited in four ways. First, even though ISI generally followed the sequence outlined above, on closer inspection it was a haphazard process of industrial diversification propelled by short-term profitability that tended to run ahead of the availability of inputs and the provision of infrastructure and public services. These mismatches were symptomatic of the unwillingness or inability of the state to address the strategic requirements of accumulation, not to mention welfare improvements, social cohesion and the material conditions for citizenship.[10]

Second, despite the attempt to alleviate the balance of payments constraint through ISI,[11] Brazil became increasingly dependent on foreign resource inflows to finance a spiralling demand for imported machinery, industrial inputs and technology, which expressed the disproportions, gaps and inefficiencies in the production structure built by the SoA.[12] The balance of payments also had to contend with the weight of loan repayments and TNC royalties and profit remittances. In this sense, far from 'closing' the economy, ISI *increased* the country's external dependence.[13] The fact that, under ISI, the value of imports and exports declined relative to GDP is immaterial: it merely indicates the weakness of Brazil's export sector and, separately, the fact that output tended to grow faster than the country's external trade.

Third, the Brazilian financial sector was always fragile, inefficient and averse to lending for industrial development.[14] The country's private financial system emerged in the late nineteenth century, focusing primarily on lending for export agriculture, and it kept its focus on trading and speculating with primary products and lending to the rich, which normally involves short loan terms and readily-available collateral. This shallow financial system eventually expanded into the provision of consumer credit for the urban middle class. During ISI, manufacturing investment was funded primarily by foreign direct investment (FDI), foreign loans, government subsidies, state-owned banks (especially BNDE), directed credit[15] and firms' retained earnings.[16] Generally speaking, Brazil's financial structures were highly dependent on external resources and associated with high interest rates and activist monetary policy (i.e. the manipulation of the currency). They helped to make the economy vulnerable to high inflation

Fourth, the state was weak, but it had to play a key role in ISI.[17] Government agencies influenced production and investment decisions, subsidised capital accumulation through cheap credit, infrastructure and inputs provided by SOEs, and drove technological development, for example, in agriculture and in the energy, construction, aerospace, computer, defence and nuclear industries. The state also had to mediate conflicts between local and foreign capitals and between rival domestic groups. However, public policy was permanently hampered by political disputes and by the tax system, which was never robust enough to support that level of state activism. Central and local governments tended to accumulate substantial liabilities, and fiscal deficits and inflation became persistent features of the economic landscape (see below).[18]

For all these reasons, despite rapid GDP growth and the expansion and diversification of manufacturing, ISI contributed directly and indirectly to the concentration of income and wealth and the reproduction of mass poverty. It also failed to alleviate the balance of payments constraint, and the financial system remained dysfunctional. The state was interventionist but financially weak, institutionally disarticulated and unable to enforce consistent priorities.[19] These limitations help to explain industrial fragmentation, poor infrastructure and the feebleness of the national system of innovation, and the vulnerability of the currency, volatility of GDP growth rates and bouts of political instability under ISI. The impressive successes in the (state-led) mining, steel, telecoms, aircraft and defence industries, and in (heavily state-supported) automobile and ethanol production serve to highlight the shortcomings in the (state-led) nuclear and IT industries and the (private) textile, plastics, toy, wood, beverage and food industries.[20]

Political Structures of ISI

Brazilian ISI was associated with a state ideology and policy practice based on nationalist developmentalism. This was deployed unevenly and often instrumentally in support of industrialisation in different political regimes, including populism, limited forms of democracy and long periods of dictatorship.[21] Nationalist developmentalism also helped to maintain social cohesion and quash dissent, despite the powerful centrifugal forces unleashed by ISI.

We noted above that ISI unleashed profound demographic, sociological, cultural and political changes that created new (mostly urban) groups with conflicting interests. Often, these groups were antagonistic towards the agrarian ruling classes that were attached to the 'old liberal' (Victorian) ideology of *laissez-faire* and glorified Brazil's 'agrarian vocation' and its place in the pre-World War I, UK-led global order. They also suggested that the agrarian elites ought to keep control of the state.[22] Stripped of their rich complexity, these conflicts between 'old' and new' elite groups centred on the extent and modes of transfer of resources from the primary export sector to the rest of the economy, and where and how these resources should be allocated – for example, into manufacturing industry, infrastructure or welfare provision – and, at a further remove, which industries, regions and groups should benefit.

The disputes were intensified by balance of payments, fiscal, financial and institutional constraints that, the developmentalists claimed, derived from the political hegemony of the landowners and foreign interests. These groups were 'holding back' the country, but their grip could be loosened by an energetic state-driven ISI supplemented by democratic reforms and the distribution of income and wealth, especially land. Although this progressive impulse gradually found its way into the political system and public administration, state-led reformism was constrained by the conflict between the developmental role of the state in supporting accumulation, and its conservative role in maintaining social cohesion and preventing conflicts from escalating into challenges to the social hierarchy.[23]

In the economic domain, nationalist developmentalism was used to justify state economic intervention and public ownership of basic industries on behalf of 'the nation as a whole'. This imperative was especially prominent in infrastructure and in industries requiring high investment and complex technologies, and with long lags and low returns. However essential, these investments were often shunned by domestic and foreign capital, for example, in oil, steel, electricity generation, shipbuilding and transport links. Interestingly, nationalist arguments rarely interfered with the penetration of foreign capital in easier, simpler and more profitable sectors. In general, the Brazilian state and the elite welcomed FDI with few restraints, leading to a whole range of industries being controlled by external brands, especially in the durable goods sector, with automobiles and household appliances at the forefront. In summary, the main economic role of the state under ISI was to support private accumulation through regulation, credit, subsidies, infrastructure and cheap inputs, fostering a capitalist, US-centred, uncoordinated, polluting and urban-based vision of manufacturing-led development.

Nationalist developmentalism was closely associated with political populism.[24] Across Latin America, populism was a political system of transition, constructed around a 'leader', that is, a prominent figure (usually the President or dictator) with popular appeal and embodying a nation-building programme centred on the opposition between the 'people' and the 'elite'. In this context, the 'people' includes, primarily, the deprived masses of newcomers to the cities and the manufacturing-led urban economy. The 'elite' is usually represented by the alliance between traditional primary exporters (large landowners, mineral interests, financiers) and foreign capital. The leader has a dual role; on the one hand, he (the leader was generally male) expresses the national project; on the other hand, he personifies the people, articulates their demands and delivers material improvements. In return, the people provide him with personal adoration and, if necessary, votes.

The leader routinely bypasses the apparatus of the old agrarian state, builds new institutions and manipulates the rules both for short-term advantage and to align society and the state with his vision for the country. This vision usually involves the construction of a 'modern' economy, a degree of national autonomy, greater social cohesion through the state-led accommodation of popular demands for citizenship, employment, income growth and distribution, and – importantly – the preservation of social hierarchy. Across Latin America, political repression under populism was often brutal, regardless of the democratic façade of the state. In attempting to square this circle, populism normally delivered much less than its florid discourse might have suggested. In this fluid social and institutional context, the leader had considerable discretion to steer growth and distribute the gains through the developmental apparatus of the state and the incipient welfare institutions, backed up by the institutions of coercion. Potential channels of distribution included public ownership, subsidies, regulation, new institutions, patronage, clientelism and corruption.[25]

In sum, the Latin American variety of populism is, generally, both economically transformative *and* socially conservative.[26] The prominence of the leader forestalls the consolidation of institutions based on citizenship and mass protagonism, and populist practices tend to reproduce rather than transcend the undemocratic features of the oligarchic state.[27] Populist states also tend to pursue contradictory goals, for example, rapid manufacturing development *together* with the protection of the agrarian elite, democratisation *simultaneously* with bourgeois control of the state, mass social and economic inclusion *and* the reproduction of traditional patterns of subordination, and nationalism *alongside* the internationalisation of the economy.

The inevitable tensions and conflicts, and the impossibility of finding stability under adverse external circumstances, triggered frequent crises of accumulation and political gridlock. Across Latin America, this was epitomised by chronic macroeconomic volatility, recurrent balance of payments difficulties, inflation and frequent political crises, intensified by the emergence of mass movements contesting the existing patterns of inequality.[28] Those irresolvable contradictions led to the collapse of populist, nationalist and developmentalist regimes in Brazil and almost everywhere else in Latin America between the mid-1960s and the mid 1970s.[29]

A Developmental Dictatorship

Populism was replaced by bureaucratic-authoritarian (BA) regimes across Latin America between the mid-1960s and the mid-1970s.[30] In Brazil, the Second Republic, a limited and unstable democracy inaugurated in 1946, was overthrown by a military coup in 1964. At an immediate level, the coup brought to an end the reformist administration of President João Goulart, which had embodied a national development project inspired by nationalism, left-wing populism and Latin American structuralist economics (see below).

Goulart attempted, bravely but clumsily, to lead a coalition of the state bureaucracy, domestic capital and organised workers in support of 'basic reforms', intended to transform the social and property relations responsible for external dependence and the reproduction of poverty, improve the distribution of income and wealth, and consolidate a common citizenship. The proposed SoA would include ISI-led man-ufacturing growth, nationalisation of essential services, controls on transnational capital and finance, rescheduling or non-payment of the external debt, land reform centred on the takeover of low-productivity 'semi-feudal' estates, reform of public administration and the expansion of democracy.

It was expected that the new SoA would support a virtuous circle of growth, in which the expansion of mass demand would drive investment and technical progress and bring rapid gains in productivity and wages.[31] The appeal of these reforms responded to, and fed, the rise of a mass left led by the (pro-USSR) Brazilian Communist Party (*Partido Comunista*

Brasileiro, PCB), which had been illegal since 1947 but by the 1960s operated relatively openly. The rising tide of mass struggles trapped the agrarian and conservative interests into a tight political corner.

At the same time, Goulart's administration was beset by fiscal, monetary and balance of payments crises.[32] They were intensified by the hostility of the US administration,[33] the intransigence of a conservative Congress, the bitter antagonism of the landed oligarchies and most industrial capitalists (who, Goulart had hoped, would support his reform programme), and the vitriolic opposition of the Catholic Church, the mainstream media and the urban middle classes.[34] Goulart's administration was paralysed gradually, until it was overthrown by a right-wing coalition fronted by the military.[35]

The 1964 coup did not represent merely the capture of the Executive by conservative forces threatened with reformist dislocation. The coup derived from an emerging alliance between internal manufacturing capital, foreign capital, traditional landed interests and the urban middle class.[36] They converged around the belief that the reproduction of the established patterns of domination was incompatible with Goulart's reforms. The elite chose, instead, a deeper integration with foreign capital and the US-led global economy, managed by a 'strong' BA regime. After the coup, the military leaders of the regime and the technocratic cadres in public administration implemented an authoritarian accumulation strategy based on a concentrating and internationalising ISI.[37] This variety of ISI included much greater penetration of foreign productive and financial capital, state support for a new agribusiness sector, an incipient financialisation and the concentration of income and wealth, sustained by variable levels of repression.[38]

Most forms of social organisation and political contestation were outlawed and the trade unions were brought under state control.[39] The traditional political parties were abolished, with only two new parties accorded legal status, on condition that they did not call themselves a 'party': the mouthpiece of the military government, ARENA (*Aliança Renovadora Nacional*, National Renewal Alliance), and the tame opposition MDB (*Movimento Democrático Brasileiro*, Brazilian Democratic Movement). Both operated under severe constraints.[40]

The military government imposed an accumulation strategy based on an orthodox economic policy mix centred on inflation control.[41] The rate of inflation had touched on 90 per cent per annum before the coup, and the right-wing rebellion had made huge political capital out of Goulart's economic tribulations. However, the new administration's contractionary strategy was only partially successful. Even though real wages declined by 25 per cent between 1964 and 1967, inflation fell much more slowly than had been expected. Instead of declining to 25 per cent in 1965 and 10 per cent in 1966, inflation fell to 28 per cent in 1965, then rose to 37 per cent in the following year. Economic growth, which had been expected to reach 6 per cent per annum, was 3.9 per cent in 1965, and 4.4 per cent in the next year.[42]

The government introduced an ambitious reform to reorganise the financial system and support the emergence of a capital market-based system inspired by the US-UK model.[43] To this end, the administration reformed the tax system[44] and introduced new financial institutions and regulations[45] in order to deepen the capital markets, promote new private-based financial structures, boost long-term private investment and support FDI.[46]

The growth slowdown and the government's apparent inability to control inflation damaged the administration politically, and mass discontent triggered a policy shift. In 1967–8, the regime intensified political repression, changed its inflation policy to a loose target of around 20 per cent per annum, and embarked on a strongly expansionary strategy centred on externally-funded public investment in energy and infrastructure and the credit-led expansion of the consumer durables sector, aiming at the higher income brackets.

The economy responded immediately, due to its large spare capacity (up to 40 per cent in 1965),[47] high unemployment, greater labour 'flexibility' and the compression of real wages imposed by the dictatorship. The expansion of demand was reinforced by the rapid income growth of the upper strata, as a result of wage increases and housing and other subsidies newly available to the better off.[48] The growth impulse was boosted further by a domestic credit boom, generous export subsidies and the liberalisation of FDI and external borrowing.[49] Public expenditure rose rapidly, and the country's foreign debt started to escalate. From a very low base, under Goulart, it reached US$10 billion in 1972.[50] The so-called 'Brazilian economic miracle' was underway. GDP growth rates rose above 10 per cent per annum between 1968 and 1973.

The pattern of demand changed significantly.[51] The automotive and electrical goods industries expanded, respectively, by 19 and 14 per cent per annum between 1968 and 1971, pulled by domestic demand; productivity growth in these sectors was very rapid.[52] In contrast, the textiles and foodstuffs sectors grew by less than 8 per cent per annum, and then only because of export subsidies (since wages and the domestic mass market were stagnant).[53] This pattern of growth was replicated across the manufacturing sector (see Table 1.1).

Table 1.1   Growth rates of production and exports, 1964–74 (per cent per annum)

	Growth rate of production		Growth rate of exports	
	1964–68	*1968–74*	*1964–68*	*1968–74*
Non-metallic minerals	5.1	11.3	66.7	18.5
Metals	11.3	8.6	40.7	13.4
Machinery	2.8	18.2	11.1	78.0
Electrical and communications	17.1	14.8	40.0	50.6
Transport equipment	7.8	20.7	11.1	78.0
Paper	7.0	6.3	4.3	59.4
Rubber	10.4	14.6	−39.2	60.5
Chemicals	7.5	14.3	7.0	16.4
Textiles	−1.6	4.5	5.5	29.4
Food products	4.6	8.7	35.4	17.5
Wood products	0.7	16.9	5.0	−3.5
Leather	10.1	5.8	52.6	26.1
Clothing and footwear	2.5	6.0	15.8	118.8
Beverages	5.7	10.1	19.9	36.1
Tobacco products	0.4	6.7	21.2	34.6
Unweighted average	6.1	11.2	19.8	42.3

Source: Coes (1994, p. 449).

The government introduced further reforms to the capital markets to encourage the expansion of the stock market and the development of industrial-financial conglomerates. These reforms failed. The tax rebates and the fiscal and regulatory incentives triggered a mini-stock market boom that ended in a crash in 1971. The irrelevance of both the financial boom and the crisis to the rhythm of economic growth suggests that the regime's strategy of financial development did not achieve its goals. Despite the rapid growth of credit, the private financial institutions and the capital markets remained dysfunctional,[54] that is, short-termist and speculative, albeit in more sophisticated forms, and were either unable or unwilling to fund economic development.[55]

The period of accelerated growth between 1967 and 1973 ended with the first oil shock. Brazil imported 80 per cent of its oil, and was the largest oil importer among the developing countries; the oil shock implied a direct loss of 3–4 per cent of national income (the current account deficit rose, in one year, from US$1.7 billion to US$7.2 billion).[56] Worse still, the Brazilian economy had been booming for many years. There was little spare capacity, several large projects were close to completion, private financial institutions showed signs of fragility, and the regime feared political instability in case of a sharp economic slowdown or a contractionary adjustment.[57] Moreover, oil prices were widely expected to decline, lending weight to the view that the dictatorship should press for growth funded by external borrowing.[58]

The government launched the ambitious Second National Development Plan (PND2) in 1974, ostensibly to 'bridge the gap between underdevelopment and economic development',[59] through a range of SOE-led mega-projects. Brazil would build a new energy infrastructure, including the world's largest hydroelectric dam, new road, rail and air links, nuclear power stations and a brand new telecommunications network.[60] PND2 would also expand, integrate and decentralise geographically the country's manufacturing base through the development of a new generation of high-tech industries, focusing on chemical and metallurgical products, information technology, aeronautics, shipbuilding, energy and oil. These ventures would generally be led by SOEs in association with domestic and foreign capital.[61] This accumulation strategy promoted the integration of domestic, foreign and state capital both within and across sectors, eroding further the economic independence of the internal bourgeoisie (see Chapter 8).

Given the global turmoil and the limitations of the Brazilian financial system, large-scale funding for PND2 had to be provided directly by the government through taxation, or by large SOEs through external loans. Pressure on the SOEs to seek funds abroad was intensified by government-imposed tariff caps and restrictions on their domestic borrowing, which helped to reduce inflation and released loanable funds for the private sector. In this way, SOEs were deliberately used as political (and external borrowing) tools.[62] As domestic capital gradually withdrew its commitment to PND2, the government and the SOEs picked up the slack. The sprawling expansion of the SOEs and the state bureaucracy during PND2 altered the balance of power within the elite. Increasingly, domestic capital felt that the government was 'too big', and that its 'size' and 'interventionism' infringed upon the rights of capital. The consequences of this political shift in the bourgeoisie would be felt in the ensuing decades.

Faced with the prospect of significant shortfalls in financing PND2, the government's accumulation strategy relied, increasingly, on external loans.[63] This was arguably unproblematic at that time, because interest rates were exceptionally low during the 1970s and, on completion, PND2 projects would either generate (through additional exports) or release (through ISI-led reductions in the country's import bill) foreign currency to pay off the loans.[64] Brazil's external debt grew from US$10 billion in 1972 to US$26 billion in 1976, while inflation rose from under 20 per cent per year to over 40 per cent, because of the adverse impact of the oil shock and the emerging bottlenecks in domestic productive capacity. Still, the economy continued to grow.[65]

This uneasy balance would not last. The second oil shock, in 1979–80, had a severe impact on the Brazilian balance of payments. Higher prices raised the oil import bill from under US$4 billion in 1978 to almost US$11 billion in 1982. In 1980, the current account deficit reached US$12.4 billion, and the external debt touched US$54 billion.

Rising global interest rates following the Volcker shock, in the USA,[66] pushed Brazil's debt service from US$2.7 billion in 1978 to US$11.4 billion in 1982, while the debt stock reached US$70 billion (rising to US$100 billion in 1986).[67] The rate of inflation reached 100 per cent in 1980. Under growing domestic and external pressure, the government imposed a sharp adjustment strategy inspired by IMF policies, but without IMF support. The currency was devalued by 30 per cent, and the administration imposed a severe economic contraction to limit domestic consumption and investment, cut imports and stimulate exports. In 1981, Brazil experienced negative GDP growth rates for the first time since 1930. This was ineffective. No elite sector was willing to accept losses, and the emerging workers' movement (see Chapter 2) was already strong enough to prevent a significant decline in real wages.

The international debt crisis arrived in 1982, when Mexico declared itself unable to service its loans.[68] Global credit markets froze, at least for the developing countries. The situation in Brazil was extremely delicate, as the country had already exhausted its currency reserves, and the weight of the debt was pushing several large SOEs towards bankruptcy. Powerless, the government agreed an orthodox macroeconomic adjustment programme with the IMF. The currency was devalued again, an export-led economic strategy was put in place, and much higher interest rates were imposed to repress domestic demand and attract foreign capital. In the meantime, the adverse shocks and cost pressures pushed the rate of inflation to 200 per cent in 1983.

The debt crisis posed a severe threat to Brazilian firms and banks that had borrowed abroad. Their liabilities grew in domestic currency because of the devaluation, raising the financial pressure of the debt service. Because of the global crisis, it became much harder to borrow in order to service old loans. The government was determined to avoid a domestic financial crisis or the bankruptcy of large SOEs, which would destabilise the economy and risk the collapse of strategic economic sectors. The administration decided, instead, to nationalise the external debt, by allowing the debtors (domestic, foreign or SOEs) to anticipate the payment of their foreign liabilities to the Central Bank, thus transferring the loans to the public sector. Nationalisation was successful: in the early 1970s, only 20 per cent of Brazil's foreign debt was owed by the state; by the late 1980s, this ratio had reached 95 per cent. No large firms went out of business, and a major economic collapse was avoided (in contrast with Argentina or Chile).

The nationalisation of the external debt transferred to the fiscal budget almost the entire cost of the debt crisis. Since the government was now the borrower, but it did not generate dollars, it had to purchase foreign currency from exporters and foreign investors through the banking system. In order to raise the necessary funds, the government tended to sell index-linked Treasury Bills in the domestic markets. Repeated use of this channel implied that the nationalisation of the external debt triggered the rapid expansion of the domestic public debt (DPD): it grew from 7 per cent of GDP in 1980 to 21 per cent in 1985.[69] By 1983, around 5 per cent of Brazilian GDP was being transferred abroad in this way; in common with other developing countries, Brazil had become a net exporter of goods *and* capital to the advanced economies. The only positive consequence of the debt crisis was that, by the mid-1980s, Brazil had become a significant exporter of manufactured goods, demonstrating the success of the industrialisation strategy that had been followed since the 1930s.

The fiscal budget was destabilised not only by the foreign debt service and the (closely-related) costs of the DPD but also by the subsidies and tax exemptions awarded to exporters, whose success was essential to generate hard currency. By the mid-1980s, the tax system and the market for public securities were showing signs of strain. Increasingly, the government had to print money to cover its regular expenditures.[70] The investment capacity of the public sector collapsed: it would not recover for three decades.[71] In other words, having chosen to fund the service of the external debt through the sale of Treasury Bills, the government found itself having to print money to cover current expenditures; at the same time, it had to cut public investment and social expenditures and starve the SOEs of funds. This would weaken the SOEs financially and, years later, it would help to justify their privatisation.[72] The growth slowdown and the deteriorating quality of public education, sanitation, health, roads and other infrastructure damaged the military government's reputation for economic 'competence'.

Creeping Hyperinflation

Brazilian inflation had shown a stubborn upward trend since the early 1970s. From under 20 per cent per year, inflation rose to 30 per cent after the first oil shock, 40 per cent in the late 1970s, and 100 per cent after the second oil shock, in 1979–80. It reached 200 per cent in 1983, after the international debt crisis, the currency devaluation and the recession. In early 1986, inflation was heading towards 400 per cent, when it was temporarily halted by the Cruzado inflation stabilisation plan (see below). The failure of that plan, after only a few months, created even greater turbulence. Several successive stabilisation plans were tried and failed. Inflation was spiralling out of control in mid-1994, when it was halted by the Real stabilisation plan (see Figure 1.1 and Chapter 3).

The pattern of stepwise rising inflation between 1973 and 1986 (see Figure 1.2) was due to the prevalence of price indexation in the economy, that is, the adjustment of prices, tariffs and wages by past inflation in order to restore their value in real terms. Indexation, originally introduced by the federal government in the late 1960s to expand the market for public securities, spread gradually.[73] It was extended to the exchange rate in 1968, replacing the fixed exchange rates typical of the Bretton Woods system with regular 'mini-devaluations' reflecting the difference between domestic and US price inflation (technically speaking, Brazil's new exchange rate system was a passive crawling peg driven by the difference in international inflation rates).[74]

Eventually, rents and all manner of prices and incomes were also index-linked. In this unstable environment, the financial institutions

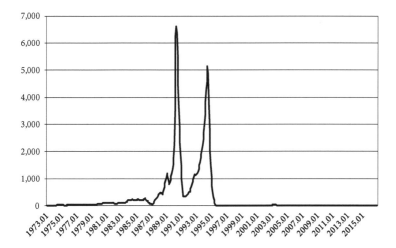

Figure 1.1   Inflation, annualised monthly rate, 1973–2016 (IGP-DI, per cent)
Source: Banco Central do Brasil, séries históricas.

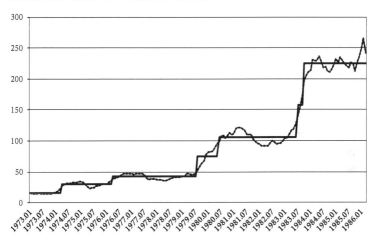

Figure 1.2   Inflation, annual rate and trend, January 1973 – March 1986
(IGP-DI, per cent)
Source: Banco Central do Brasil, séries históricas.

increasingly focused on trading short-term index-linked government securities, again privileging speculation at the expense of lending to support economic growth. Financial speculation was predicated on the government's provision of indexed papers that would be automatically corrected by past inflation plus a guaranteed real return. The secondary markets trading these papers expanded gradually and, by the early 1980s, they had consolidated into a large 'overnight' market where index-linked papers achieved almost complete liquidity.

Indexation was soon extended to wages, where it was meant to contain distributive conflicts by reassuring workers that their real incomes would be restored regularly. Although this wage rule was politically stabilising it meant that nominal wage growth would be rigidly determined by past inflation: as inflation reached increasingly high levels, wage growth was guaranteed to follow, making it *impossible* to reduce inflation gradually, because real wages would automatically shoot up. This would be both politically destabilising and contrary to the power relations at the core of the dictatorship.[75] The indexation of wages can be read in another way: the political crisis of the military government limited its capacity to devalue labour enough to accommodate the competing claims to national income, especially the external debt service.[76] Since definitive ('static') income losses had become impossible, the only alternative was a dynamic pattern of losses through escalating inflation.

Indexation made Brazilian inflation *inertial*, that is, prone to replicate past inflation. Inertial inflation is rigid downwards and tends to rise in steps, for three reasons. First, oligopolistic firms tended to set prices following simple mark-up-plus-inflation rules, while nominal wages were determined almost entirely by past wages plus inflation. For example, if last year's inflation rate had been 50 per cent, wages this year would automatically rise by that rate (plus a small productivity gain). The wage increase would push up production costs, tendentially leading past inflation to replicate itself.[77] Second, those rigid pricing rules were facilitated by government policy, import restrictions and the tendency of firms to adopt capital-intensive technologies to produce relatively sophisticated goods for small markets (given the concentration of income in Brazil). Third, production costs obviously included interest, and the orthodox adjustment strategies implemented in Brazil since 1979 invariably led to higher interest rates, increasing costs and inflation. It was similar with the transfers due to the external debt service, which compressed national income by up to 5 per cent per annum.[78]

These rigid rules for price- and wage-setting made relative prices impervious to shifts in demand or adverse fluctuations in the level of activity. Although price rigidity may have protected the capital stock and investment in key industries, it also made the economy vulnerable to sudden rises in inflation because of adverse supply shocks or distributional conflicts. They included the oil shocks and the currency devaluations in 1979 and 1983, and increasing worker militancy in the 1980s (see Chapter 2).[79] Each adverse shock raised costs and pushed inflation upwards, where it would stay because of indexation. The outcome was the stepwise increase in inflation since the early 1970s.

As inflation accelerated, the interval between price increases tended to shorten. This had regressive implications because some agents (banks, large firms, highly-skilled professionals) were better able than others (wage-earners, pensioners, small farmers) to raise their own prices and fees to protect their real revenues. Even worse, the shorter the interval between adjustments in prices and wages, the higher the inertial component of inflation, and the more sensitive inflation became to adverse supply shocks: inertial inflation *always* tends to slide upwards. By the mid-1980s, the Brazilian economy had become disorganised. Relative prices were inordinately rigid in the long run but highly variable on a day-to-day basis, depending on the date of adjustment and the chosen price index.

It became difficult to rank spending and investment priorities because of uncertainty about demand, relative prices and the country's accumulation strategy. Fiscal and monetary policy tended to become increasingly tight, in order to try to control a disintegrating macro-economy. Investment, savings and GDP growth rates fell. The government discovered that inertial inflation increased the cost of contractionary monetary and fiscal policies, because higher interest rates and lower government spending had a negligible impact on firms' pricing strategy. Conventional anti-inflation policies could even lead to *accelerating* inflation, if oligopolistic firms tried to maintain their gross profits despite declining sales and rising financial costs.

In order to stabilise the market for government securities and reduce the incentive to dollarise the economy (as in Argentina, Bolivia and other Latin American countries during the 1980s and 1990s, where prices were increasingly set in US dollars), the Central Bank started offering more and more attractive combinations of interest rates and liquidity. By the mid-1980s, the Central Bank allowed financial institutions to swap government securities for currency, and vice versa, on demand (*zeragem automática*), virtually eliminating the cost of reserves for the commercial banks.[80] This liquidity guarantee avoided dollarisation, secured the demand for public securities and stabilised the domestic financial system. However, it undermined the domestic currency: no one wanted to hold rapidly devaluing legal tender when they could have liquid index-linked public securities (that is, effectively, an asset fulfilling the role of the US dollar, but that was produced domestically and offered generous real returns). Unsurprisingly, the quantity of money in circulation fell precipitously, and the velocity of circulation of the currency increased.[81]

In sequence, the commercial banks started offering index-linked current accounts to their high-net-worth customers. The deposits would earn a share of the remuneration paid on the public securities, which could reach 40 per cent per month, depending on the rate of inflation. Those funds could be converted back into currency on demand, through the Central Bank liquidity guarantee. The index-linked accounts further increased the degree of indexation of the economy because, now, all manner of revenues could be swapped for index-linked interest-bearing securities and converted back into currency at the time of expenditure. Those accounts also intensified the concentrating dynamics of inflation, since distinct forms of income were index-linked in different ways – in particular, the rich could shelter their revenues almost completely, while low-paid workers remained unprotected.[82]

The erosion of the currency rewarded financial wealth and acumen at the expense of production, and helped to turn Brazilian banks into sophisticated service providers to *rentiers*, for whom they extracted speculative profits disguised as defensive indexation. At the same time, financial mechanisms became vitally important to industrial capital: this was not the provision of credit for investment, but it was more than speculation uncoupled from production. *Industrial capital was financialised through government policy, inflation and the DPD.*

These distortions fed the rejection of the currency and propped up alternative forms of money (government securities, US dollars, financial assets, real estate, automobiles, bags of rice, and so on); they also legitimised increasingly punitive stabilisation policies. While the Treasury collected seignorage as it printed money, the costs and risks of inflation to the financial institutions and the better-off were passed back to the state via the Central Bank that, consequently, lost control of the DPD and the money supply. Essentially, the Bank had to set interest rates at whatever level would guarantee that the outstanding stock of public securities, corrected daily for inflation, would find buyers *all the time*. This was essential to avoid a flight into goods or dollars and explosive hyperinflation. Monetary *and* fiscal policies were immobilised.

Distribution and Stabilisation

Brazil is one of the most unequal societies in the world, with enduring disparities of income, wealth and privilege. ISI reproduced these inequalities and, often, increased them. For example, in the absence of countervailing public policies, private investment tended to reflect the existing pattern of demand, and output growth was biased towards relatively expensive durable goods produced by TNCs with capital-intensive imported technologies.[83] The differential availability of consumer credit, trade and investment finance and, often, government incentives, reinforced these inequitable outcomes, further skewing the structure of demand and the distribution of income and wealth.

ISI also segmented the labour market. Skilled formal-sector workers employed in the leading (generally oligopolistic) industries, mainly based in São Paulo, were better organised and tended to have higher wages than workers in other regions, in service industries or agriculture. Those leading firms were also more inclined to accommodate wage demands, because their market power allowed them to add any additional wage costs to prices.[84]

The unequalising features of ISI were intensified by the acceleration of inflation and the differential indexation of prices and incomes between the late 1970s and the early 1990s. These processes contributed to the reduction in the wage share from 52 per cent of national income in 1970, to 45 per cent in 1990 (see Table 1.2; the real minimum wage declined, on average, by 1.6 per cent per annum between 1960 and 1980).[85] In the 1990s, the richest decile captured half the national income, and the top two deciles captured two-thirds; in contrast, the bottom two deciles earned only 2 per cent of total income.[86] The Gini coefficient increased from 0.56 to 0.64 between 1970 and 1989 (see Figure 1.3).[87] Widespread dissatisfaction with poverty and distribution, and with discrimination based on income, gender and skin colour, fostered increasingly bitter distributive conflicts. They were almost invariably repressed by the military government, but with decreasing success (see Chapter 2).

By the mid-1980s, it had become widely accepted that conventional fiscal and monetary policies were ineffective against inertial inflation, reduced growth and intensified social conflicts. It was also increasingly agreed that an effective disinflation strategy would require the coordinated deindexation of prices and wages.[88] In the mid-1980s, a group of economists based mainly at the Catholic University of Rio de Janeiro and

Table 1.2   Share of labour income in national income (average of two years)

1959–60	56.6
1969–70	52.0
1979–80	50.0
1989–90	45.0
1999–2000	40.0
2008–2009	43.6

Source: IPEA (2010, p. 4).

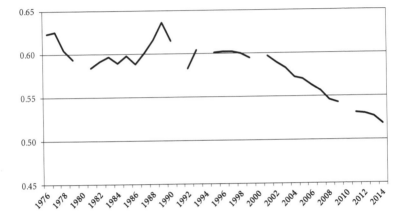

Figure 1.3   Gini coefficient of concentration of income, 1976–2014

Source: www.ipeadata.gov.br.

the Getúlio Vargas Foundation, in São Paulo, developed the 'heterodox shock' as a policy alternative to the orthodoxy. Their proposed strategy involved the simultaneous freezing of prices and wages at their average real level, the abolition of indexation (i.e. the prohibition of automatic rules of price and wage adjustment based on past inflation), drastic cuts in real interest rates and changes to contracts (including wages, rents, sales of goods and services, and so on), in order to incorporate the expected elimination of inflation. The currency would be changed simultaneously, in order to give legal and political legitimacy to the stabilisation programme and government interference in third-party contracts.[89]

Brazil's first experience with a heterodox shock was in February 1986.[90] The Cruzado plan (named after the currency introduced by the stabilisation programme) froze prices, wages and the exchange rate. The plan followed the template of Argentina's Austral plan, introduced a few months previously. Inflation rates fell from 15 per cent per month to almost zero for several months, but the Cruzado plan collapsed in November, as did similar stabilisation programmes.[91] When these plans failed, inflation tended to rise rapidly and to become increasingly volatile. The failure of the heterodox stabilisation programmes can be explained at two levels.

First, heterodox shocks tended to reduce real wages, because wages were always frozen at their average real level during the previous months while, for practical reasons, prices were frozen at their nominal peak. Since the previous *average* real wage becomes the new *peak* wage, if the stabilisation programme collapses and there is a new round of inflation followed by another shock, the 'new' average real wage will be *lower* than the 'old' average. With a sequence of heterodox stabilisation plans, real wages decline steadily, feeding social conflict and political crisis.[92]

Second, the price freezes transformed the short-term relative price imbalances routinely created by high inflation into permanent price differences. That is, the heterodox shock froze some prices at their peak real level (for example, if they had increased the day before the shock), while other prices were frozen at exceptionally low real levels (if, say, they were due to rise the day after the shock). These imbalances can trigger arbitrary shifts in profitability, bankruptcies and disruptions in supply chains. They can also foster scarcities, parallel markets and other forms of evading price controls, contributing to the disorganisation of the economy.

Several stabilisation programmes and policy shifts were attempted in rapid sequence:

> During the 1980s, there were eight different monetary stabilisation plans in Brazil, four different currencies, 11 different indexes for calculating inflation, five price and wage freezes, 14 wage policies, 18 changes in the exchange [rate] regulations, 54 modifications in the price control rules, 21 proposals for external debt negotiations, and 19 government decrees on fiscal austerity.[93]

These plans included both heterodox elements and conventional contractionary fiscal and monetary policies. Over time, the latter tended to become increasingly prominent, while the former lost relevance. This shift towards the orthodoxy was reinforced by the implementation of increasingly contractionary fiscal and monetary policies *between* stabilisation programmes.

The most heavy-handed stabilisation programme was the so-called Collor plan, imposed by Fernando Collor in 1990 when he became the first elected President in almost three decades (see Chapter 3).[94] Inflation appeared to be rising uncontrollably; by then, it was approaching 80 per cent per month. The Collor plan froze not only prices and wages, as in previous plans; it also froze all bank and savings accounts and holdings of Treasury Bills above a (very low) ceiling for 18 months. It was claimed that this would give the Central Bank the space to make monetary policy, instead of being compelled to set interest rates at whatever level was required to persuade the holders of government securities to keep their papers. The plan was accompanied by a substantial cut in federal spending, the closure of scores of ministries and state agencies, and the dismissal of tens of thousands of civil servants.[95] The Collor plan was followed by a drastic liberalisation of foreign trade, FDI and the exchange rate, extensive deregulation and a wave of privatisations. The institutional basis of ISI was disarticulated.

Yet the Collor plan failed comprehensively to eliminate inflation. In 1990, GDP declined by an unprecedented 4.4 per cent. Unemployment rose, and barter became widespread; with bank balances and financial investments frozen, automobiles were purchased with bags of rice and houses were exchanged for plots of land, but a low-inflation monetary economy never emerged. A demoralised Collor tried another shock in 1991 (the so-called Collor II plan), but failed again. The rate of inflation drifted upwards, and hyperinflation seemed inevitable.

Summary and Conclusion

A large manufacturing sector was built in Brazil under ISI, but this sector remained relatively inefficient, excessively diversified given the size of the markets and insufficiently integrated. These shortcomings were partly due to the global circumstances in which the manufacturing sector expanded, and partly the result of poorly articulated industrial policies, excessive reliance on foreign capital and technology, a weak tax system, and short-termist financial institutions that were unwilling or unable to fund large-scale investments in manufacturing and infrastructure.

These insufficiencies fostered monetary, fiscal and exchange-rate policies incompatible with balance of payments equilibrium.[96] The oil shocks of 1973 and 1979–80 worsened Brazil's terms of trade (see Chapter 5). They were followed by the contraction of advanced country markets, leading Brazil and other developing countries to depend heavily on external loans, but the Volcker shock made this debt-driven accumulation strategy unviable. A sequence of adverse external shocks culminated in the international debt crisis, in 1982; it also fuelled financial anarchy, including high inflation, capital flight and creeping stagnation.

The costs of the crisis of ISI in terms of output, profitability, coordination, financial coherence and monetary stability were magnified by distributive conflicts. These tended to intensify, especially as the legitimacy of the military government declined and, with it, the efficacy of its tools of coercion. Even though the dictatorship limped on until 1985, the SoA was increasingly disarticulated. These economic difficulties were not resolved by the transition to democracy: the inability of successive governments to implement consistent economic policies was symptomatic of the exhaustion of ISI and the limitations of the modes of political domination associated with it. Brazil was not confronting policy 'mistakes' defined technically; instead, the country was facing an historical impasse that would be resolved only by the transition to neoliberalism.

2

Building a Fragile Democracy

Overview

Brazil went through a political transition from military dictatorship to democracy between 1974 and 1988. This chapter reviews that transition, focusing on the limitations of the military regime, the mass movements that triggered its demise, and the elite pact that capped the transition. This chapter also examines the social, political and economic significance of the 1988 Constitution, which expressed the inclusive logic of democracy through the *expansion of citizenship*. Finally, this chapter offers an interpretation of the rise and political metamorphoses of the PT, as the party played an important role in the political transition, and would play an even more influential part later.

Brazil's military regime was institutionally strong, but it was vulnerable to charges of illegitimacy and brutality due to its undemocratic origins, routine human rights abuses and frequent recourse to state terrorism: that is, the military state embodied a strong but brittle form of domination. In order to consolidate its rule and legitimate repression, the regime needed to deliver macroeconomic stability and rapid income and employment growth.[1] Indeed, when growth faltered, the regime wilted and a nationwide democratic movement gained traction. This democratic movement was predicated on a socially and politically inclusive logic of citizenship, equality, distribution and creation of a universal welfare state. As the movement expanded, it triggered not only the implosion of the military regime, but also the formation of an elite pact aiming to contain any further expansion of democracy.

Detailed negotiations about the transfer of power to 'reliable' civilians virtually eliminated the risks of the transition for the bourgeoisie and the military: that is, political openness and stability were achieved but the demands for economic and social change that had animated the opposition were discarded. In this sense, the expansion of social security and public provision included in the 1988 Constitution were meant to *replace*, rather than realise, economic democracy. The Brazilian welfare state was also confronted by adverse financial circumstances due to the weakness of the economy, rising inflation and the economic transition to neoliberalism.

The democratic transition and the emerging welfare state were heavily influenced by the rise of the PT and they, in turn, shaped the party's trajectory. The PT was founded in the late 1970s as a genuinely working-class organisation aspiring to establish a never clearly specified 'democratic socialism'. The party grew rapidly, quickly becoming the most important organisation in the history of the Brazilian left. However, the pressures of functioning in a limited democracy gradually eroded the PT's radical edge. By 2002, the party had learned to compromise in order to exercise executive power 'responsibly'.

The Transition to Democracy

A nationwide mass movement for democracy emerged in the 1970s. It would grow slowly but steadily, confronting all manner of obstacles. Eventually, it would defeat the dictatorship. The movement emerged from several sources. One of the earliest was the realisation, in the 1970 census, that rapid economic growth had concentrated income and failed to deliver material improvements to the majority. The regime was embarrassed, but it stuck to the argument that 'the cake must grow before it can be divided'.

The accumulation strategy supporting the 'economic miracle' stalled in 1973, and the regime gradually ran out of excuses to explain away the country's deteriorating performance. Declining GDP growth rates and rising external debt and inflation were accompanied by the elimination of the final attempts at violent resistance against the dictatorship, through urban and rural guerrilla movements, which (perhaps paradoxically) severely weakened popular consent for the regime's harsh political repression.[2] Rejection of state terrorism was reinforced by the 'human rights' policies associated with US President Jimmy Carter (1977–81), which increased the pressure for the restoration of democracy while, at the same time, curbing Brazil's 'independent' foreign policy and disabling the symbolically and economically important nuclear agreement with West Germany (see Chapter 1). Finally, an endless sequence of corruption scandals came to light, helping to demoralise the dictatorship. As the foundations of military rule eroded, social discipline began to break down.

In 1974, the regime's political party, ARENA, suffered a crushing defeat in the legislative and local elections. Even though ARENA managed to hold a majority in the Chamber of Deputies, it lost the elections for the Senate in 16 out of 22 states, setting off alarm bells at the highest levels of government.[3] The growth of the opposition drew upon two key forces. First, a resurgent left, including the organised formal sector workers, trade unions, urban middle-class dissidents, illegal revolutionary parties and the Liberation Theology wing of the Catholic Church.[4] Their demands focused on the restoration of democracy and distributive economic policies. Second, and quite separately, a coalition of major domestic and foreign capital and financial interests *also* pressed the regime to open up the political system from what, later, would be recognised as an embryonic neoliberal perspective. This latter group coalesced in 1974, when prominent capitalists expressed their frustration with the government's technocratic interventionism and disinclination to 'listen to business'.[5]

The regime was increasingly divided internally, and aware of the erosion of its own legitimacy. It proved impossible to resolve this dilemma.[6] One wing of the armed forces and the technocracy opted for a slow process of liberalisation. Another wing of the armed forces and the intelligence services sought to continue to repress dissent, even though it undermined the regime's popularity in urban areas. Left-wing activists were imprisoned, tortured and killed, and well-known individuals were executed in prison or died in staged 'accidents' or 'suicides'.[7] In 1976, former Presidents Juscelino Kubitschek and João Goulart perished in quick succession, and in suspicious circumstances. Later that year, almost the entire leadership of the Communist Party of Brazil (*Partido Comunista do Brasil*, PCdoB) was massacred in São Paulo. . In 1977, Carlos Lacerda, a prominent supporter of the coup who later turned dissident also died unexpectedly. Finally, the 'deep state' launched a low-level campaign of urban terrorism culminating in the 1981 'Riocentro affair', when an intelligence officer was blown up inside his own car, holding a bomb meant for a large dissident music festival.[8] The regime's clumsy cover-up damaged its reputation even further. The terrorist campaign was suspended. Democratic resistance grew after each atrocity, while the regime's political coherence disintegrated.

Discontent with repressive outrages, corruption scandals and demonstrations of economic incompetence erupted in 1976 and 1977, when university students revolted across the nation. A new trade union movement burst onto the scene in 1978, with a major strike in the manufacturing belt around São Paulo.[9] Similar movements followed, engaging previously disorganised workers. Radicalised trade unions emerged across the country. At the same time, domestic capital withdrew its support for the regime's dash for growth through PND2, arguing instead for a contractionary strategy justified by liberal principles, global uncertainty and the deteriorating domestic situation. This policy shift marked the abandonment of developmentalism by Brazilian capitalists after half a century. Their views would evolve into a fully-fledged neoliberal project for the country.

Under increasing pressure, President Ernesto Geisel decided against an open-ended strategy of repression and opted, instead, for a gradual, limited and tightly-controlled political opening (*abertura lenta, gradual e segura*).[10] The goal was to broaden the regime's base of support to re-incorporate the middle classes and segments of the bourgeoisie that had been increasingly alienated by the country's economic difficulties and the government's strategy of repression. In other words, the idea was not to 'restore democracy'. Instead, the government aimed to build a stable constituency supporting the transfer of power to reliable civilians, as part of a constitutional arrangement securing the role of the armed forces as guardians of national security and protecting them from charges of any human rights abuses that had occurred during the dictatorship. This would require a sequence of reforms to the political system, the judiciary and the Constitution itself. Each of these self-serving initiatives angered the democratic opposition and increased the regime's isolation. In order to advance this agenda, the regime cancelled the 1980 legislative elections in which ARENA was expected to lose seats in the Chamber of Deputies and its majority in the Senate, hampering the government's ability to enact legislation.[11]

The regime's manoeuvres were challenged by a growing opposition that drew clear connections between authoritarianism, corruption, self-interested policy-making uninhibited by law and the unfolding economic crisis. Opposition to military rule included increasingly bold accusations of corruption, economic mismanagement and lack of democracy (insofar as was permitted by government control of the media), demands for political accountability, petitions, legislative initiatives, trade union activity and street demonstrations.[12] These campaigns achieved important successes. By the late 1970s, it had become impossible to justify the denial of civil liberties in order to secure economic growth, control of inflation, political stability, public safety or honest and competent public management.

Censorship was abolished at the end of the 1970s, starting with cinema and the printed media. Political amnesty was achieved in 1979, against the regime's bitter resistance.[13] All political prisoners were released, and most exiles returned. A sense of political awakening and vibrant creativity pervaded the country, its music, cinemas, theatres and literature; the universities, workplaces and streets were bubbling with political debate and new art forms. An emboldened left began to occupy spaces forcibly vacated by the military. Demands for democracy and a progressive shift in economic policy gained wide credence.[14] They were indirectly supported by business demands for the reduction of the 'size' of the state, which split the regime's base of support within the elite and helped to disarticulate government policies. By the early 1980s, political change had become inevitable. The precise form of that change, and the wider implications for the country's SoA, were yet to be determined.

In the meantime, a significant political shift took place among the country's elite: hesitantly, it, too, joined the emerging democratic consensus.[15] This was not driven by an about face on civil rights or the realisation of the importance of citizenship. Instead, it derived from the perception that attempts to contain the rise of the left by force could be severely destabilising. In contrast, a democratic regime would be politically legitimate, and it could secure the hegemony of capital and facilitate the reproduction of elite privileges more reliably than a crumbling dictatorship.

In the early 1980s, the bourgeoisie split into two: one group aligned with a renewal of ISI and the accommodation of mass demands, the other with global neoliberalism.[16] While the former engaged with a democratic movement that it could not control, the latter could not rely on the military to implement their programme (unlike Argentina, Chile and Uruguay, where the military used overwhelming force to impose transitions to neoliberalism in the 1970s).[17] Gradually, these capitalists realised that their best chance of securing an orderly transition to neoliberalism was through the restoration of democracy. Presumably, the new regime could provide a measure of social harmony, limit the 'size' of the state and curtail the autonomy of the bureaucracy from the short-term interests of 'business'.[18] It was hoped that democracy could also clear the way for a new economic policy to emerge, bypassing the confrontation between a decaying state-led ISI, and the left's democratic programme.[19]

The convergence of rival fractions of the elite around democracy was supported by changes in the composition of the bourgeoisie and the middle class since the 1970s (see Chapter 8). The new elite included a younger, professionally-trained and more outward-looking cohort of financiers and leaders of industry, and entrepreneurial landowners not wedded to traditional forms of privilege. They were able and willing to converse with the emerging urban movements, unlike the traditional elites.

The various strands of the democratic movement came together in the campaign for a constitutional amendment for direct presidential elections. The campaign started modestly at the end of 1983, but grew dramatically. In a matter of weeks, the country was taken over by the largest street demonstrations in its history. Here was a demand that was easy to understand, could not be sensibly opposed, and that promised equal citizenship, political freedom and the transformation of economic policy. Over 10 million people took to the streets in a matter of weeks, while the regime fell into a terminal state of disorganisation.[20] In the run-up to the congressional vote, a state of emergency was declared in several areas, including the capital city, Brasília.

Despite the strength of the campaign, the regime managed to defeat the constitutional amendment by a small margin. However, this titanic effort destroyed the regime's political base of support. ARENA split, with the dissident faction banding together with MDB. Early in 1985, the ultra-moderate MDB candidate, Tancredo Neves, was elected President by the dictatorship's own Electoral College. His Vice President was the leader of the breakaway faction of ARENA, Senator José Sarney, previously a key supporter of the military regime.

Serendipitously, Neves fell gravely ill hours before his inauguration, and died in hospital shortly thereafter.[21] On 15 March 1985, José Sarney was sworn in as President of Brazil. The dictatorship was over, and a 'New Republic' (*Nova República*) had begun, albeit in inauspicious circumstances. Sarney's administration convened a Constitutional Assembly in 1986, proclaimed the new Constitution two years later, and the country had its first direct presidential elections after three decades in 1989.

The substance of the political pact underpinning the New Republic was straightforward. Ample political freedoms would be secured. The citizenship of workers and the poor would be recognised and they would be granted marginal economic benefits, but there would be no substantive redistribution of economic power.[22] Within these limits, the democratic transition established the most open and stable political regime in Republican history. In the following three decades, there would be no political censorship, no parties or movements of any significance would be banned, and civil rights would be formally secured to a greater extent than in many 'traditional' democracies. For the first time since the late nineteenth century, the military rarely interfered in politics, and then only cautiously. The political influence of the Catholic Church was sharply curtailed.[23] Right-wing views were utterly discredited by association with the dictatorship. Until 2013, no mainstream politician or organisation would claim to be either 'conservative' or on the 'right', however right wing their policies and practices might have been.

Even though the democratic transition satisfied the immediate political demands of the left, it disconnected them from the economic demands of the democratic movement.[24] Civil rights, free elections and political pluralism were established, but the distribution of income and assets, the nationalisation of strategically important economic sectors and the repudiation of foreign debt were never seriously considered by the Sarney administration.[25]

Late Social Democracy, Late Welfare State

The first programmes of social insurance in Brazil were introduced by the populist dictatorship of Getúlio Vargas (1930–45). They focused on urban, male and relatively better-off workers with formal jobs in manufacturing, services and the public sector (see Chapter 8). These workers were granted minimum wages, employment stability, maximum working hours, paid holidays, trade union representation and pensions, provided by the state in association with (largely state-controlled) trade unions and business associations. Those benefits were not available to most women, rural or informal-sector workers.[26] In the meantime, the upper and middle classes purchased health, education, transport and other basic goods and services from a burgeoning private sector.

In doing this, the state subsidised the manufacturing sector through the socialisation of part of the costs of reproduction of its workforce. At the same time, the state secured political stability in a country where, until the mid-twentieth century, urban workers had been strongly influenced by anarchist, socialist and communist ideas brought in by European immigrants, mainly from Italy and Spain.[27] A similar pattern had prevailed under the dictatorship, which expanded social insurance at the margin, for example, through the provision of pensions and social security to some rural workers and funeral assistance to the destitute. In contrast, generous sums were awarded to the better off through free tertiary education and subsidies and tax rebates for the purchase of private healthcare and housing (see Chapter 1).

The 1988 Constitution embedded a fragile equilibrium, reflecting the balance of political forces at the end of the dictatorship. But it also created a dysfunctional political system, including a significant decentralisation of power, justified as a reaction against the centralising tendencies of the dictatorship. It transferred to state and municipal governments the duty to part-fund the provision of health, education and social programmes, but did not secure sufficient resources. The Constitution granted autonomy to the judiciary, but neglected its accountability (see Chapter 9). It created a powerful President, elected in two rounds, with great personal legitimacy but only limited powers, in parallel with a strong bicameral Congress elected by proportional representation. The new political system promoted fragmentation into a myriad of parties unmoored by ideology or principle, making it virtually impossible for the President to command a majority in Congress without unwieldy coalitions with many incoherent and squabbling parties and unruly politicians who were bound to bicker and jockey for position and to demand both attention and resources from the Executive, ceaselessly threatening the government with rebellion or political deadlock. Put all this together, and it becomes obvious that Brazilian democracy is *fragile by design*.[28]

The Constitution also had a hybrid economic content, due to left pressures for a national democratic project, and the division of the bourgeoisie between a fraction still tethered to the nationalist developmentalism associated with ISI, and those favouring the mounting tide of neoliberalism. As a result, the Constitution provided unprecedented advances for the left through social policy while, at the same time, strengthening the state monopoly of basic industries and protecting domestic firms and markets. It also left spaces open for the encroachment of neoliberalism (see below).[29]

Finally, one of the key demands of the democratic movement was for the creation of a universal and distributive welfare state. This demand drove the Constitution's social chapter, which founded a 'late welfare state' inspired by postwar Western European social democracy. Articles 194–203 of the Constitution recognised that everyone is entitled to a minimum standard of living guaranteed by the state, and mandated the universal state provision of essential public goods and services. The Constitution also created actionable rights based on principles of universality (rather than targeting), social security (as opposed to private insurance), and citizenship (instead of charity or conditional access). The state was legally and financially bound to provide social protection, pensions, housing and education to everyone, and mandated to create a National Health System (*Sistema Único de Saúde*, SUS) free at the point of use. Social rights and benefits were either introduced or enhanced. They included the limitation of the working week to 44 hours, employment security, protection against arbitrary dismissal, salary floors depending on skill and length of service, payments for overtime, minimum holidays, 120 days' maternity leave, 5 days' paternity leave, the right to strike and the independence of the trade unions.[30]

These social policies did not alter the exclusionary essence of the Brazilian state, but they opened the possibility of building a more equal society.[31] Because of the Constitution, Brazil was one of the few countries where social spending increased rapidly in the 1990s.[32] However, this was pushing against the momentum of the transition to neoliberalism around the world. In order to fund this emerging welfare state, the Constitution imposed a set of minimum expenditures, backed up by dedicated taxes and contributions.[33] They were intended to secure the provision of public health and education, unemployment benefits, old age and disability pensions (supporting *Benefício de Prestação Continuada*, BPC),[34] and social insurance (*Regime Geral da Previdência Social*). This ambitious programme of public provision would inevitably come into conflict with the political and budgetary limitations imposed by the transition to neoliberalism (see Chapter 6).

The social chapter was singled out for criticism as soon as the Constitution came into effect. Universal rights and public provision were described as being too expensive, with provision threatening fiscal and monetary stability.[35] Even if they were affordable, the constitutional rights were allegedly regressive because they would be appropriated by corrupt politicians, scroungers[36] and elite (i.e. middle-class, civilian, public-sector) workers, at the expense of the working poor. Presumably, those distortions could be addressed only by abandoning the idea of decommodified universal provision and focusing on means-tested cash benefits, aided by 'technical' criteria to channel social spending to those experiencing acute deprivation.[37]

This discourse would validate later initiatives to cut public investment in housing, sanitation and transport, postpone the provision of universal health, education and social security, prune workers' rights and pensions, dilute unemployment support and food assistance and curtail land reform; in the meantime, the government continued to service the foreign debt and subsidise private accumulation through the DPD.[38] For example, the federal government created a misnomered 'Social Emergency Fund' (*Fundo Social de Emergência*, FSE), in 1994, which cut social programmes by 20 per cent, reduced transfers to states and municipalities by 15 per cent, and raised federal taxes and contributions by 5 per cent. The Provisional Contribution on Financial Transactions (*Contribuição Provisória sobre Movimentações Financeiras*, CPMF), which should have funded SUS, the Contribution on Net Profits (*Contribuição sobre o Lucro Líquido*, CSLL) and the Contribution on Enterprise Revenue (*Contribuição sobre o Faturamento das Empresas*, Cofins), which should have funded the social security budget, were all also diverted to the DPD.[39]

Increasingly, in place of constitutionally mandated public services, the state would foster the individualisation of welfare provision backed up by private loans and insurance, supplemented by *ad hoc*, modest, targeted and ostensibly transitory relief, giving handouts to the desperately needy. As the Brazilian late welfare state morphed into a neoliberal 'minimal state' in the 1990s, pauperism crept into the core of social policy in Brazil.[40] A neoliberal state manages misery primarily through the conditional apportionment of tax-funded alms to the 'deserving' destitute. In doing so, the government assists the wretched while it subsidises the worst modalities of employment as it supplements 'conditionally' the lowest incomes.[41]

PT Rising

In the mid-1970s, small left-wing organisations banded together with progressive religious groups and a myriad of activists demanding democracy, human rights, amnesty and progressive economic policies (see above and Chapter 1).[42] They were followed by a new trade union movement, based around the most advanced industries under ISI: the metal, automobile and auto parts industries based in the manufacturing belt around the city of São Paulo. These industries were owned by trans-national and domestic capital, tightly integrated, and employing some of the best-paid blue-collar workers in the country.

In May 1978, 300,000 workers unexpectedly went on strike in 300 factories demanding a substantial pay increase.[43] Although the strike was illegal, the military regime was unable to defeat the movement. Eventually, the government had to sponsor negotiations with the employers, leading to an agreement that brought important gains for the workers. The success of the strike signalled to the country that resistance was both possible and potentially rewarding, and that the regime was vulnerable to mass action. The strike also propelled the metalworkers to the forefront of the Brazilian working class, and their leader, Luiz Inácio da Silva (Lula),[44] became the most important trade unionist in the country.

The emerging new left was based on the convergence of the 'political' and 'trade-unionist' wings of the opposition to the military regime, including Lula's metalworkers' union and, soon, other influential trade unions in manufacturing, services and the public sector. It also included the Liberation Theology wing of the Catholic Church, student organisa-tions, an assortment of activists, urban and rural movements and NGOs, prestigious intellectuals, clandestine left parties and a wide range of progressive organisations, from dissident newspapers to theatre groups. Long disappointed by the impotence of MDB and unwilling to join the traditional communist parties, these dissident groups embraced the idea of creating a new type of party. In late 1978, they started discussing the idea of a 'Workers' Party' untainted by the perceived vices of the Brazilian left: populism, corruption, clientelism and Stalinism. The PT was launched in 1980, with Lula as the undisputed leader.

In its early stages, the PT had three distinguishing features. First, it was an independent party of the working class, controlled and staffed by workers and intellectuals closely aligned with them. The PT shunned alliances with 'bourgeois' parties and even other left organisations and, in order to increase its own visibility, fielded candidates whenever possible, even if this fragmented the opposition or created friction with other opposition forces. Second, the PT was a mass democratic party that accommodated tendencies, groups and even entire political organ-isations. It was not overly centralised, like the old communist parties; instead, the PT was remarkably democratic internally, with a strong but not overpowering national executive deciding the political line but leaving space for dissent.[45] Third, the PT soon became the hub of a constellation of movements and organisations, especially the largest trade union confederation in Brazil (*Central Única dos Trabalhadores*, CUT, founded in 1983) and the landless peasants' movement (*Movimento dos Trabalhadores Rurais Sem Terra*, MST, founded in 1984).

The strategy and mode of organisation of the PT corresponded to the composition of the Brazilian working class and the opportunities offered by the crumbling dictatorship. The party grew rapidly, reaching 800,000 members in less than ten years. CUT represented up to 20 million workers, and the PT made significant inroads into the student movement (which, however, remained under the control of the PCdoB).[46]

The PT refused to vote for the 'bourgeois' candidate Tancredo Neves in the dictatorship's Electoral College and, when the military yielded power, the PT also refused to support the Sarney administration. For similar reasons, the party refused to sign the 1988 Constitution. In the meantime, the PT grew until it became hegemonic within the Brazilian left. Many influential left organisations were either affiliated to the PT or controlled by its militants, and most left parties became satellites of the PT, or had been expelled and defined themselves in opposition to the PT (especially two small Trotskyite organisations, the Unified Workers' Socialist Party, *Partido Socialista dos Trabalhadores Unificado*, PSTU, and the Party of the Workers' Platform, *Partido da Causa Operária*, PCO).[47] The PT's extraordinary success was reflected at the ballot box, with continuing growth at all levels eventually culminating in Lula's election to the presidency, in 2002, after three failed attempts in 1989, 1994 and 1998 (see Chapter 5).

The Workers' Party Grows – and Changes

The early growth of the PT was based on two drivers. First, political demands for radical democracy, that is, a democratic regime incorporating but not limited to the formal (procedural or 'bourgeois') democracy associated with Robert Dahl and Joseph Schumpeter. Formal democracy is typically defined by the protection of basic civil and political rights, clean competitive elections for the Legislature and the Executive, civilian government and civilian control of the armed forces. The PT demanded more: its tendencies advocated, in different ways, a 'socialist democracy', delivering power and economic betterment to the poor majority.

Second, the PT defended the corporatist interests of workers closely associated with the party, especially the auto, metal and bank workers, civil servants, teachers, health workers, other segments of the organised working class and a myriad of community organisations. The prestige of the party among these groups and with large segments of the middle class increased steadily, as the PT led successful mobilisations delivering gains to its supporters.

Unfortunately for the PT, both drivers of growth collapsed between the mid-1980s and the mid-1990s, under the combined pressures of the political transition to democracy and the economic transition to neo-liberalism (see Chapter 3). Political democracy radically changed the terrain in which the PT had emerged. It had been relatively easy for the PT to offer a progressive alternative to a decrepit dictatorship that was increasingly powerless to discipline the populace but remained wedded to a right-wing discourse that sounded anachronistic or even absurdist, especially to the young. The regime's incompetence, corruption, attachment to the tools of repression and abysmal track record on delivering income and welfare gains for the majority offered easy targets for the opposition.

The restoration of democracy changed everything. Pluralism diluted political power and removed many of the 'easy' targets previously available to the left. The institutions of the state were validated by their democratic veneer, compelling the PT to follow the electoral calendar and operate within the 'bourgeois' framework that the party had previously denounced. Political debates shifted away from intuitively appealing principles into matters of detail embedded within parliamentary politics. Mass demonstrations were normalised instead of being repressed. They also became less effective, as the new state officials could legitimately claim that, although they shared the concerns of the majority, changes were impossible because of financial limitations, judicial constraints or political deadlock.[48]

Implementation of PT policies now required a democratic mandate that, although feasible in principle, could be achieved only if the party submitted itself to the logic of campaign finance, coalition-building, piecemeal reforms, painstaking negotiations with conflicting interest groups and the imperatives of 'efficiency' and 'delivery' in local government. In this way, the democratic transition satisfied the essential political demands of the left, but it disconnected them from the economic demands of the majority. Those limitations tempered the PT's enthusiasm for direct action and head-to-head confrontation against the state, and increased the weight of the party cadres at the expense of the militants.

Increasingly, the PT showed signs of a split between 'moderates' pushing for the implementation of a social democratic programme by parliamentary means, and 'radicals' seeking to transcend conventional politics and, perhaps, capitalism itself. While the former found it difficult to garner mass enthusiasm for their strategy, the latter could never lead an electorally viable party. The radicals were increasingly marginalised within PT, especially after Lula ran for the presidency on a left platform, in 1989, and lost to Fernando Collor.[49]

Matters deteriorated in the late 1980s, as the Brazilian elite convinced itself that only neoliberalism would allow the preservation of democracy, the recovery of growth and the continuation of existing patterns of inequality. As the economic transition to neoliberalism took hold, the PT's sources of support were hit hard. The 'reforms' severely weakened the groups that had formed the backbone of PT, provided the bulk of its votes and were affiliated to the most active trade unions: the manufacturing working class, the middle- and lower-ranking civil servants and other formal sector workers (see Chapters 3 and 4).[50]

Privatisations removed from state ownership large unionised firms in strategic sectors, especially mining, steel, telecommunications, electricity generation and finance.[51] Many manufacturing and financial conglomerates were restructured and taken over by transnational corporations. Trade union laws were tightened up and the civil service mutilated by successive reforms justified by neoliberal ideology, the fiscal crisis and the 'restructuring' of the state. The trade union movement was seriously weakened. Radicals lost ground to pragmatic leaders within CUT, and the unions split between those unions (often the strongest) seeking immediate economic gains for their members, and other less powerful ones demanding radical changes in government policy. The student movement lost influence under the combined weight of the expansion of the private university sector, where mobilisations were more difficult, and the adverse economic circumstances facing young graduates. The social, economic and political conditions that had facilitated the growth of PT ceased to exist: even though the party could still win elections, its political achievements depended on coalitions; extra-parliamentary activity declined sharply. The parliamentary group and their advisers gradually came to dominate the PT.[52]

The PT had to rebuild its support base under these challenging cir-cumstances. The party's two-fold response helps to explain its later successes and the limitations of the federal administrations led by Lula and Dilma Rousseff.

First, after Lula's dramatic defeat, in 1989, the party leadership was persuaded that the PT must appeal to a more centrist constituency and downplay its commitment to social change. In doing this, the party continued to prosper, but its growth was no longer based on radical ambitions. Instead, the PT offered a discourse based on vaguely progressive ethics and efficiency in public administration. Increasingly, the PT presented itself non-politically, as the *only* party untainted by corruption; party cadres were now respected for their professionalism and managerial capacity. The narrowing of the PT's transformative ambitions and the party's shift towards administrative rather than radical priorities helped it to gain new constituencies, especially the moderate middle class, informal-sector workers and many domestic capitalists (see Chapter 8).[53]

Second, the leadership convinced itself that, in order to win elections and govern effectively, the PT must have allies, and this would require the dilution of the party's principles; it would also involve horse-trading and acceptance of the corrupt practices that had long dominated Brazilian politics. This was a slippery slope:[54] each election brought the PT more posts and greater responsibilities; it also pulled the party further towards the political centre ground. Each victory was due to alliances; successful administrations and future electoral gains depended on even broader coalitions. Every step on this road eroded the differences between PT and the other parties and diluted the aspirations that had brought the PT into being.[55]

'Early' PT administrations sometimes failed spectacularly because of the lack of administrative experience or wider support – for example, in Fortaleza and São Paulo, in the late 1980s. However, where those limitations were overcome, PT mayors achieved important successes, for example in Diadema, Ribeirão Preto, Santo André and Santos (in São Paulo state), Belo Horizonte and Governador Valadares (Minas Gerais), Vitória da Conquista (Bahia) and, most famously, in Porto Alegre (the state capital of Rio Grande do Sul). In these cities, PT mayors imposed new priorities aligned with the interests of the poor and introduced democratic and transparent policies, especially a (limited but valuable) participatory budget process that would become internationally recognised as an example of good practice and accountability.[56]

In 2000, the PT achieved further successes, re-electing the mayors of the state capitals of Belém and Porto Alegre, and the mayors of Aracaju, Belo Horizonte, Goiânia, Macapá, Recife and São Paulo. The party received almost 12 million votes (14 per cent of the total), and found itself running cities with a total population of almost 30 million, four times more than after the previous elections.[57] The PT also elected a growing number of local councillors, deputies and senators. The party's share of the vote in the first round of the presidential elections also grew, from 17 per cent in 1989 to 46 per cent in 2002.

The growth of the PT was overshadowed by the even more impressive growth of Lula's political stature. Eventually, Lula hovered above the PT as a semi-detached leader excelling at reconciling differences and building broad alliances in order to gain power.

In the early 1990s, in the wake of the collapse of the Soviet Bloc and the implosion of the mainstream left, Lula and party president José Dirceu drew up a multi-pronged strategy to neutralise the left wing of the PT.[58] Prominent leftists were removed from positions of influence, PT candidates refusing to establish alliances with mainstream forces were sidelined, increasingly moderate resolutions were passed at party conferences, militant supporters were expelled and left groups, trade unions, NGOs and social movements were excluded. The PT leadership engaged in a dialogue with business, especially the Industrial Federation of the State of São Paulo (*Federação das Indústrias do Estado de São Paulo,* FIESP), the country's most powerful manufacturing-sector organisation.[59] In 1999, the PT congress approved a 'Programme for the Brazilian Democratic Revolution', stating that social and democratic reforms could be achieved only by broad coalitions. The party congress also gave Lula *carte blanche* to establish any political alliances that might support his next bid for the presidency (see Chapter 5).[60] Finally, Lula set up the *Instituto Cidadania* (Citizenship Institute), in order to develop public policies independently of the PT. At the turn of the millennium, the PT leadership felt that it was, finally, ready to govern the country.

Summary and Conclusion

The Brazilian democratic transition was shaped by conflicting forces; on the one hand, mass demands for political freedom and economic equality and, on the other, elite pressures for the renewal of the structures of inequality and social domination. These forces created a shallow democracy. For example, while civil liberties, at a formal level, are at least as substantial as those in most 'old' Western democracies, in practice the legal and judicial systems are geared to the protection of privilege and the penalisation of the poor. The Constitution has been amended frequently (see below), and the law is often disregarded when it conflicts with the reproduction of power or the exclusionary foundations of the state.

The tensions between political and economic democracy help to explain the patterns of exclusion and social injustice in the New Republic, in parallel with its affirmation of democracy and commitment to a welfare state. These tensions also contributed to poor economic performance, as the Constitution consistently failed to address the shortcomings of ISI. Later, the Constitution would incorporate a neoliberal order inimical to growth and the emerging welfare state. As it included severe contradictions embodied in the opposition between democracy and neoliberalism, and since it created an unwieldy and barely workable political system, the political transition ended up creating a *democracy fragile by design.* Years later, the Constitution would be destroyed politically, as it was used to remove Brazil's first female President.

3

Inflation Stabilisation and the Transition to Neoliberalism

Overview

This chapter examines the economic transition to neoliberalism in Brazil. It starts from the analysis of neoliberalism as a system of accumulation; subsequently, it reviews the case of Brazil, focusing on the stages of the transition to the new SoA. The neoliberal reforms were justified by the presumed exhaustion of ISI and the developmental state and the imperatives to control inflation, improve economic efficiency and accelerate productivity growth. These tasks gained urgency because of the perception that the neoliberal world economy was undergoing a technological revolution in the fields of information and communication technology, immaterial labour, new materials and new sources of energy. It was widely accepted that ISI could not support catching-up under these circumstances because of the complexity of the new technologies, enhanced protection of intellectual property and reduction of policy space after the debt crisis and the creation of the WTO.

Gradual reforms to ISI eventually morphed into a fully-fledged transition to neoliberalism in 1990, under President Fernando Collor (1990–2). The new SoA was secured by the 1994 Real inflation sta-bilisation plan, implemented by Presidents Itamar Franco (1992–4) and Fernando Henrique Cardoso (1995–8, 1999–2002).[1] One of the key features of the Brazilian transition to neoliberalism is that it was both disguised *and* justified ideologically by an inflation stabilisa-tion programme.[2] This chapter reviews the Brazilian economy under the Real plan (1994–9), focusing on the achievements and limitations of government policy during this period, especially the elimination of high inflation, the internationalisation of the economy, and changes in the industrial structure, patterns of employment and the balance of payments.

The transition to neoliberalism brought not only significant economic changes, but also much slower GDP growth rates than in previous decades. The average rate of economic growth in the 1990s was only 1.8 per cent per annum, the lowest in the century. In contrast, between 1933 and 1980 the economy expanded, on average, 6.4 per cent per annum. GDP growth in the first decade of neoliberalism was even lower than in the so-called 'lost decade' of the 1980s (2.6 per cent per annum: see Chapter 4).[3]

The chapter concludes with a detailed examination of the crisis of the Real plan, in 1999, and the neoliberal macroeconomic 'policy tripod' introduced in the wake of the crisis.

Neoliberalism in Brazil

Neoliberalism is more than an ideology or a clearly defined set of policies, such as privatisation, the liberalisation of trade and finance or curbs on the welfare state. In what follows, neoliberalism is conceptualised as the dominant system of accumulation (stage, or mode of existence, of capitalism) today (see the Introduction).[4] This SoA has four distinguishing features: the financialisation of production, ideology and the state; the international integration of production ('globalisation'); a prominent role for foreign capital for globally-integrated production and the stabilisation of the balance of payments; and a macroeconomic policy mix based on contractionary fiscal and monetary policies and inflation targeting, with the manipulation of interest rates as the main policy tool. This combination of features has raised the rate of exploitation above that achieved under the previous SoAs, for example, Keynesianism in the advanced Western economies, different forms of developmentalism in the Global South or Soviet-style socialism in Eastern Europe.[5]

In most countries, the first (transition or shock) phase of neoliberalism normally foregrounds the narrow interests of transnationalised private capital, particularly finance, without regard to the consequences. This phase involves forceful state intervention to impose the new institutional framework and an accumulation strategy promoting the transnational integration of domestic capital at the microeconomic (firm) level, containing labour and disorganising the left. This is normally followed by a second (mature) phase, which aims to consolidate the expanded role of finance in economic and social reproduction, manage the new mode of international integration, stabilise the social relations imposed in the previous phase, nurture a neoliberal subjectivity and introduce neoliberal social policies to manage mass economic deprivation.

These phases and the ensuing accumulation strategies are, inevitably, framed more logically than chronologically. They can be sequenced, delayed, accelerated or even superimposed in specific ways depending on country, region and economic and political circumstances. However, both phases require extensive (re-)regulation of economic and social reproduction, with political implications, despite the rhetorical insistence of all manner of neoliberals on the need to 'roll back' the state, interpreted, in the first phase of neoliberalism, as 'hollowing out', followed by the 'rolling out' of new forms of intervention, typically in the second phase.

Across its phases, the neoliberal reforms transform the material foundations of the economy, society and social reproduction, with implications for class relations and the distributional balance between them. This includes policies to dismantle the previous SoA (which is invariably defined as being 'inefficient'), the reduction of the scope for state-led coordination of economic activity, the limitation of collective bargaining and wage growth and the creation of undesirable patterns of employment (see Chapter 4). These changes facilitate the concentration of income and wealth, preclude the use of industrial policy tools to achieve socially-determined priorities, and make the balance of payments structurally dependent on international flows of capital. Neoliberalism also influences social relations through the financialisation of social reproduction and the privatisation of the commons, that is, areas where property rights were either absent or vested in the state.

In Brazil, the political transition to democracy was followed by the economic transition from an increasingly dysfunctional ISI into a globalised and financialised neoliberalism. The Brazilian economic transition came relatively late and advanced slowly when compared with other countries in Latin America, Africa and Eastern Europe. This was due, in part, to the strong political left that emerged during the democratic transition, which drastically limited the scope for the neoliberal reforms. Brazil's unique path to neoliberalism was also shaped by the imperative of inflation stabilisation.[6]

During the 1980s, most analysts came to accept that ISI faced four insuperable challenges that, presumably, explained Brazil's disappointing economic performance, inflation and external vulnerability. First, the inefficiency of the financial sector, which was unwilling or unable to channel savings to long-term investment projects. Second, insufficient access to foreign savings, investment, technology and markets. Third, continuing industrial backwardness, because of the weakness of the national system of innovation, excessive diversification, lack of scale in manufacturing production and lack of foreign competition as a result of protectionism.[7] Fourth, the fiscal crisis and the tendency towards hyperinflation, caused by 'economic populism', distributive conflicts and widespread indexation of wages and prices.[8]

Supposedly, these obstacles could be overcome only by a strategy restoring rapid capital accumulation and 'modernising' the economy and society. This would require 'rolling back' the state through expenditure cuts, extensive privatisation, liberalisation of trade, finance and capital flows, and reforms of the fiscal, tax and social security systems. The fiscal reforms would reduce inflation, financial liberalisation would increase domestic savings and investment, and import liberalisation would cheapen inputs, increase the availability of quality consumer goods and reduce the monopoly power of inefficient producers and greedy trade unions. Finally, the liberalisation of capital movements would attract direct and portfolio inflows to fund economic restructuring. These policy reforms would increase productivity and improve the balance of payments. Economic liberalisation and the integration of Brazilian capital into transnational conglomerates would drive a virtuous circle of growth, transforming Brazil into a developed economy. This strategic shift was supported by the US government, the international financial institutions, the media and foreign and Brazilian capital, and validated by the apparent success of comparable countries, especially Argentina, Mexico and South Korea.[9]

These claims were misleading at three levels. First, ISI was intrinsically limited, structurally fragile and socially and distributionally regressive (see Chapter 1), but the crisis of the 1980s was only partly due to its shortcomings: it was also caused by external developments that countries like Brazil were powerless to address – for example, the international debt crisis.[10] Second, it would soon become clear that neoliberalism was unable to resolve the shortcomings of ISI, or match the country's growth performance under the previous SoA. Third, the examples of successful reforms were misleading.[11]

The Brazilian reforms had been implemented gradually but increasingly systematically since the late 1980s. In 1988, the Sarney administration relaxed controls on the exchange rate and international flows of capital, with further reforms following in 1992.[12] The domestic financial system was reformed, and the country began a unilateral process of liberalisation of imports that would be largely completed in 1994.[13] Average tariffs fell from 58 per cent in 1987, to 14 per cent in 1993, and 11 per cent in 2004,[14] while non-tariff barriers were slashed. Since this was not accompanied by a devaluation of the currency, temporary support for domestic producers or anti-dumping measures, the country's import bill increased sharply. Finally, Brazil concluded the renegotiation of its foreign debt through the Brady Plan in 1994.[15]

The shift towards neoliberalism was validated politically by the 1989 presidential election, when Fernando Collor's neoliberal platform narrowly defeated Lula's left-wing campaign (see Chapters 1 and 2).[16] However, Collor's stabilisation plan failed to tackle creeping hyper-inflation, his administration was paralysed by chaos and incompetence, and the President was forced out in 1992 because of a mind-boggling array of scandals involving thievery, drugs, sex and the misappropriation of public funds.[17] Collor's initiatives disarticulated ISI both institutionally and ideologically. They also disabled large parts of the machinery of state through the closure of scores of government agencies and a brutal staff cull. They were followed by two destructive waves of voluntary redundancies in the civil service, in 1998 and 2003.

The administrations led by Collor and his deputy, Itamar Franco, imposed increasingly contractionary monetary policies to control inflation, attract foreign capital and generate exportable surpluses.[18] They also supported amendments that started the long process of disfigurement of the constitutional text approved in 1988. Article 171 was revoked, erasing the distinction between Brazilian and foreign enterprises. Item IX of Article 170 was modified, allowing foreign companies to explore the subsoil. Article 178 was changed to remove the state monopoly of shipping on coastal routes. Item IX of Article 21 was altered to abolish the state monopoly of telecommunications. Article 177 was rewritten to relax the state monopoly of oil exploration, and Article 192 was modified to relax the regulations against the involvement of financial institutions in the social security system.[19] The constitutional reforms also advanced the privatisation programme introduced by the dictatorship in the wake of the international debt crisis, and supported reforms to increase labour market 'flexibility'.[20]

These policies were partly successful in the context of lower global interest rates, the devaluation of the US dollar and the worldwide expansion of capital flows. In 1992, despite domestic political instability and high inflation, capital inflows were restored for the first time since the 1970s, initially through the repatriation of Brazilian flight capital.[21] The incoming resources were invested in new financial markets or used to purchase SOEs or private firms ripe for restructuring. It seemed that everyone was gaining from financialisation. Finally, the Cardoso government implemented a fully neoliberal economic strategy drawing upon the Real inflation stabilisation plan, in place since early 1994, that provided ideological and political cover for the consolidation of neoliberalism.[22]

The Real Plan

Brazilian inflation increased gradually until mid-1994, when hyper-inflation loomed. By then, it had become essential to control inflation in order to make the new SoA economically viable, and politically to legitimise the transition to neoliberalism. The Real stabilisation plan addressed both problems simultaneously.

The Real plan was the outcome of years of research by some of the academics who had designed the heterodox shocks and who, later, had moved towards economic orthodoxy (see Chapter 1).[23] Their new predilections were aligned with global fashions and the tightening grip of mainstream economists on academia and most institutional positions in Brazil and elsewhere. The Real plan assumed that inflation was caused by fiscal deficits, and persisted because of indexation. This diagnosis synthesised monetarist views, in which the monetisation of fiscal deficits causes inflation, with a neostructuralist interpretation of inertia. It followed that contractionary policies were necessary but insufficient to reduce inflation; deindexation coordinated by the state was also essential, and should follow specific avenues, detailed below. By 1992–3, these views were largely uncontested. This emerging consensus was a reflection of the ideological convergence of the Brazilian economic and academic elites around neoliberalism, overcoming the divisions that had fuelled macroeconomic instability since the 1970s.

The Real stabilisation programme was based on seven key policies, detailed below, that would work *only* with the support of foreign capital inflows. The Real plan was innovative only in the way it deployed these policies and resources methodically, as part of an accumulation strategy aiming to eliminate two foes of the emerging neoliberal order at once: high inflation and the relics of a presumably exhausted ISI.[24] In this sense, the Real plan was *possible* only in the context of a globalising economy with highly liquid capital markets, and it *required* high interest rates, a stock of currency reserves and continuing resource inflows to secure the stabilisation of the currency. The key policies in the Real plan are described below.

First, import liberalisation. Imports would supply the Brazilian market with cheap foreign goods, limiting the prices that could be charged by domestic firms and constraining workers' wage demands because of the threat of unemployment due to foreign competition, especially in the heavily-industrialised and unionised state of São Paulo.[25]

Second, the overvaluation of the currency. Overvaluation would intensify the impact of trade liberalisation on inflation and support improvements in competitivity through the cheapening of imported capital goods. Initially, the government imposed an asymmetric float on the *real*; its minimum value was set at US$1, but the currency could appreciate under market pressure, further accelerating the elimination of inflation. High domestic real interest rates helped to attract an unprecedented US$47 billion to Brazil in the first six months of 1994, leading the currency to appreciate. In early 1995, the *real* reached R$0.83 per US dollar (see Figure 3.1). Government propaganda eagerly claimed that the *real* was 'stronger than the dollar', demonstrating the 'confidence' of foreign investors. This was economic nonsense, but it had a powerful impact in the country.[26] The implications of the appreciation of the *real* were boosted by the slow decline in the rate of inflation. Together, they led the real exchange rate to rise by 30 per cent in the first six months of the programme.[27] Brazil's trade balance shifted from a surplus of US$10 billion in 1994, to a deficit of US$3 billion in the following year.[28] Goods imports increased from US$21 billion to US$50 billion between 1992 and 1995, while imports of capital goods rose from US$9 billion to US$20 billion over the same period.[29] These were deliberate goals of the economic authorities. For example, Finance Minister Pedro Malan declared that:

> [T]he logic of the exchange rate policy is to reduce exports, raise imports and the current account deficit, and make the country import capital again. These [capital] imports and the domestic savings accumulated by the private sector will finance economic growth.[30]

Third, liberalisation of international flows of capital.[31] This was supposedly needed to attract foreign savings and modern technology and, more immediately, to finance the trade deficits created by the

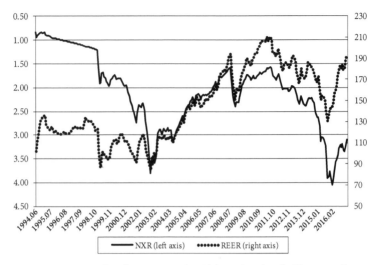

Figure 3.1   Nominal exchange rate R$/US$ (NXR) and real effective exchange rate (Jan 2003 = 100) (REER)

Source: www.ipeadata.gov.br.

policies outlined above. In this sense, the Real plan was viable *only* with large and continuing inflows of foreign capital. The vulnerability of the economy to shifts in foreign finance became evident after the Mexican, Asian and Russian crises, when Brazil was confronted by large and destabilising outflows of capital. In this sense, macroeconomic policy under the Real plan became synonymous with the consolidation of neoliberalism in conditions of permanent crisis management.

Fourth, domestic financial liberalisation. It was expected that this would raise the savings rate, attract foreign resources and increase the availability of funds for investment. In reality, the opposite happened: the investment rate fell from 22 per cent of GDP in the 1980s to under 18 per cent in the 1990s and 16 per cent in 2001–6.[32] In the meantime, domestic savings fell from 28 per cent of GDP in the mid-1980s to under 20 per cent in the mid-1990s and 15 per cent in the early 2000s. It is highly likely that the foreign capital inflows *replaced* rather than supplemented domestic savings, and financed consumption and speculation rather than investment.[33]

Fifth, high interest rates. They played a key role in the elimination of high inflation and the attraction of foreign capital. The average real (overnight) interest rate rose from 12 per cent per annum between June 1990 and December 1991 (when the degree of liberalisation was small), to 23 per cent between January 1992 and May 1994 (before the Real plan), and 24 per cent between July 1994 and December 1998 (after the plan). Consequently, the financial institutions could borrow abroad at, say, 12 per cent per annum, sell the hard currency to the Central Bank at a stable exchange rate guaranteed by the government, and purchase public securities paying vastly higher rates, thereby reaping massive profits at the taxpayers' expense. In contrast, the Central Bank received around 5 per cent interest on its foreign currency reserves. The difference between domestic and international interest rates drove the DPD to rise much faster than the country's stock of reserves.

It was difficult to lower interest rates under this policy mix, because it could trigger capital outflows (or, less dramatically, reduce inflows below the needs of the balance of payments), potentially leading the *real* to collapse. Alternatively, lower interest rates could reduce the demand for public securities, making it harder to refinance the DPD and, possibly, lead to its monetisation followed by an inflation bubble or catastrophic devaluation. In sum, the growth of the DPD under the Real plan was *not* due to the profligacy of the state.[34] Rather, it was due to the interest charges on the DPD, that is, subsidies paid to financial speculators, which led to the accumulation of foreign *and* domestic public debt simultaneously. This vicious circle would lead to the crisis of the *real*, in 1999.

Sixth, fiscal reforms to eliminate the public sector deficits that, allegedly, drove inflation. These reforms included a raft of privatisations, expenditure cuts and tax increases.[35] Yet, the DPD rose relentlessly, from under 30 per cent of GDP in 1995 to 60 per cent in 2002.[36] In other words, under neoliberalism the rapid growth of the DPD was *due* to the domestic interest rates and the need to sterilise foreign capital inflows, and it *caused* the fiscal crisis of the state.

Seventh, deindexation (see Chapter 1). The Real plan eliminated inertial inflation by introducing a price index, called Unit of Real Value (*Unidade Real de Valor*, URV), that was used to fix the real level of wages, the prices of government-controlled goods and services (electricity, telecommunications, oil, gas and so on), and the exchange rate. These key prices provided an anchor for the amalgamation of the units of account used across the economy (US dollars, Treasury Bills and a wide variety of price indices), which was essential for the emergence of a consistent system of relative prices.[37]

In summary, the Real plan offered a failsafe strategy to reduce inflation and lock in the neoliberal reforms. Imports were liberalised and made artificially cheap,[38] while high interest rates, foreign loans, privatisations and TNC takeovers of domestic firms brought the foreign currency to finance the spiralling external deficit. Inflation plummeted while consumers gorged on new automobiles, gadgets and cheap foreign holidays, paid on easy monthly instalments. Low inflation, rising demand, rapid GDP growth and falling unemployment brought substantial short-term gains for the poor.[39] Euphoria reigned supreme, and neoliberalism seduced many of those it had not previously managed to convince. The trade unions, the PT and the radical left were confounded by the success of the plan.[40] The country seemed poised for a long period of growth based on foreign investment and rising labour productivity.[41] The political consequence was the election to the presidency, in 1994, of Fernando Henrique Cardoso, the Minister of Finance who had steered the stabilisation plan.[42] Cardoso would be re-elected, in far less auspicious circumstances, in 1998.

Despite its achievements, the Real plan contained three vicious circles. First, it deliberately created a current account deficit. The country's manufacturing trade surplus, patiently built up since the late 1960s, was wiped out, making Brazil structurally dependent on fickle inflows of foreign capital to close the balance of payments. This required permanently high interest rates that, in turn, perpetuated the overvaluation of the currency, fed the current account deficit and fuelled deindustrialisation.[43]

Second, those capital inflows had to be sterilised in order to limit the expansion of the monetary base. However, this fuelled the growth of the DPD and created spiralling fiscal costs, partly due to the size of the DPD and partly because of the high interest rates required to attract those resources. The demand for public securities could be stabilised only with a permanently high interest rate policy, which locked the DPD into an unsustainable trajectory.

Third, high interest rates depressed investment and GDP growth, which limited tax revenues and, tendentially, pushed the fiscal balance into an escalating deficit. In order to finance the state budget under these circumstances, the government had repeatedly to raise taxes and cut non-financial expenditures.[44]

Since the Real plan included three mutually-reinforcing vicious circles undermining the sustainability of the country's accumulation strategy, it would have been impossible to sustain the plan indefinitely or to secure 'investor confidence' for long periods.

The Real Plan Unravels

International liquidity dried up in 1994. In the year from April, the US Federal Reserve raised the discount rate from 3.00 per cent to 5.25 per cent.[45] Higher interest rates sucked capital back to the advanced economies, making it harder for Brazil to finance its current-account deficit. The country's external reserves fell by almost US$10 billion during the year, 'threatening the stability of the Real plan'.[46]

Two emergency measures were imposed. First, temporary import controls were put in place, especially for durable goods, with tariffs rising from 20 per cent up to 70 per cent on selected lines. Second, the government abandoned the asymmetric float of the *real*; the currency was devalued by 5 per cent, and a new exchange-rate policy was introduced, devaluing the *real* slightly above domestic inflation each month. However, this gradualist policy forced the Central Bank to set interest rates high enough to defend an exchange rate that, the government itself recognised, was misaligned.[47] The contractionary bias of monetary policy led the economy to shrink by an annualised rate of 10 per cent in the second and third quarters of 1995. Unsurprisingly, the trade balance improved, and the resumption of capital inflows led to a renewed cycle of accumulation of currency reserves with falling inflation.

Since the Mexican crisis, at the end of 1994, Brazilian macroeconomic policy had become increasingly reliant on the manipulation of interest rates to control demand, regulate the value of the *real* and secure the desired currency reserves. This is obviously a complex exercise and, whenever these targets were incompatible, domestic activity became the adjustment variable. This arrangement intensified the vicious circles outlined above. Moreover, with high interest rates and a fast-growing DPD, the government needed a constantly rising primary fiscal surplus to service its debt (which is politically impossible), endless privatisations (which must be limited by the availability of assets) or, alternatively, lower interest rates (which could violate the balance of payments constraint).[48]

In 1997, in the wake of the East Asian crisis, the Central Bank raised interest rates to 43.5 per cent to discourage capital outflows; it was also forced to sell large quantities of forward exchange-rate contracts and securities indexed to the US dollar. That is, the government tried to stabilise the *real* through the nationalisation of the exchange-rate risk. Similar measures were applied in the wake of the Russian crisis, in 1998, but they were insufficient and the Brazilian balance of payments deteriorated drastically. The current account deficit rose from US$18.4 billion in 1995 (2.4 per cent of GDP) to US$33.4 billion in 1998 (4.0 per cent of GDP), because of the rising deficit in goods (from US$3.5 billion to US$6.6 billion), services (from US$7.5 billion to US$10.1 billion), and incomes (from US$11.0 billion to US$18.2 billion). The surplus in the capital and financial account, around US$30 billion per year, was largely due to privatisations, mergers and acquisitions (M&As) and portfolio investment, with only a small part of the inflows expanding productive capacity. This was also insufficient to cover the outflows of foreign currency, leading to a balance-of-payments deficit of US$16 billion in 1997–8.[49] Brazil's currency reserves tumbled from US$71 billion, in June 1998, to US$34 billion only nine months later. Under intense pressure, the Brazilian government negotiated a financial support package with the IMF and the G7, including loans of US$41 billion over three years, in exchange for large primary fiscal surpluses, the liberalisation of the exchange rate and the reduction of the current-account deficit.

In late 1998, the media was reporting daily on the decline in the country's currency reserves; government policies were criticised stridently, and lobbies for and against a large devaluation clashed in Congress and the media. Broadly speaking, finance and the monetary authorities defended the exchange-rate peg, arguing that it would facilitate industrial modernisation and preserve the value of assets owned by non-residents ('credibility'). In turn, the manufacturing elites and the trade unions argued for a devaluation to increase external competitivity, stimulate the economy and reduce unemployment.[50]

By December 1998, the macroeconomic imbalances had become unsustainable. Brazil's foreign reserves were falling by up to US$1 billion per day, regardless of the rise in interest rates to the destructive level of 49.8 per cent. Despite a fiscal surplus equivalent to US$11 billion, the DPD rose by US$41 billion during the year, while its average maturity shrank to only 3.3 months. Unable to hold on, the Central Bank devalued the *real* from R$1.21 to R$1.32 per dollar in the first days of 1999. The currency immediately collapsed, forcing the government to float the *real*. By the end of January, the exchange rate hit R$1.98 per dollar (the *real* fell 40 per cent in 17 days). The exchange-rate crisis destroyed the credibility of the Real plan and the reputation of recently re-elected President Cardoso.[51] His government would stagger on for another four years, increasingly unpopular and able to achieve very little.[52]

Mature Neoliberalism

The crisis of the *real* was remarkable in two ways. First, it marked the collapse of the Real plan as the macroeconomic strategy underpinning Brazil's transition to neoliberalism.[53] Second, the Brazilian crisis was different from the Mexican, Asian and Russian crises, which took most investors by surprise and led to substantial capital losses. The collapse of the *real* had been widely anticipated, and it brought substantial *gains* to the speculators. For example, the profits of several financial institutions in January 1999 were higher than their reported gains in the *entire* previous year.[54] The direct cost of the devaluation for the government was around 5.6 per cent of GDP, including an increase of R$44 billion in the net public sector debt,[55] and Central Bank losses of R$8 billion in the futures market.[56] The crisis showed that Brazilian neoliberalism had created a travesty of the welfare state, geared to the protection of financial capital regardless of cost, while the citizens' rights enshrined in the Constitution were implemented grudgingly, if at all.

Having completed the transition to neoliberalism, in March 1999 the government introduced a new macroeconomic policy framework as part of a *mature* neoliberal accumulation strategy.[57] The new policies aimed to secure low inflation, cut interest rates to stabilise the DPD and limit its fiscal cost, and reduce the current-account deficit.[58] The new policy framework included inflation targeting and the operational independence of the Central Bank, free capital flows with a floating currency and permanently contractionary fiscal policy, with interest rates as the adjustment variable. This became known as the *neoliberal policy tripod*. The tripod was supplemented, in 2000, by the Fiscal Responsibility Law (*Lei de Responsabilidade Fiscal*, LRF),[59] which imposed stringent limits on expenditures at all levels of government.[60]

The inflation targets were achieved in 1999 and 2000, but inflation rose subsequently because the devaluation of the *real* triggered an inflation bubble.[61] Interest rates could not be reduced significantly until that bubble had been eliminated, delaying the potential gains from the policy shift. Finally, the trade balance and the current account also improved more slowly than expected, with the former moving into surplus only in 2001, and the latter in the following year. Although export growth brought much-needed relief to the balance of payments, those gains were primarily due to the beginnings of the global commodity boom. There were no significant competitivity gains in Brazil.

In sum, the policy changes associated with mature neoliberalism were insufficient to support rapid or sustained growth. During the 1990s, the Brazilian economy remained locked in a low growth path; the productive and financial sectors were extensively denationalised, the DPD rose sharply and the concentration of income and wealth remained unchanged. Unsurprisingly, Brazil failed to converge with the 'core' advanced economies: Brazilian per capita income fell from 21.6 per cent of the developed country average in 1980, to 16.5 per cent in 1995, and 15.5 per cent in 2001.[62]

Summary and Conclusion

The liberalisation of trade and international capital flows and the over-valuation of the *real* helped to eliminate high inflation, but the Real plan failed to address the contradiction between monetary and fiscal policy created in the years of high inflation. Then, as under the Real plan, monetary policy tended to relax fiscal policy endogenously, with regressive implications for the distribution of income. Low inflation also did not reverse the tendency towards the deterioration of the public finances. Instead, after the neoliberal transition, the state lost the capacity to coordinate investment and production, and control of resource allocation was increasingly transferred to domestic and international finance.

The success of the neoliberal policies was contingent on substantial inflows of foreign goods, services and finance, but these inflows increased Brazil's vulnerability to balance-of-payments, exchange-rate and financial crises. The neoliberal reforms also created a new industrial structure based on the microeconomic (i.e. firm-level) integration of Brazilian production and finance into transnational circuits of accumulation. Although it was expected that new partnerships, M&As and the collapse of inefficient firms would raise average productivity and stimulate a new wave of modernisation, Brazilian firms tended to be tasked with the production of low-value-added goods, and the manufacturing sector was hollowed out.

The neoliberal response to these challenges was to embed the 'reforms' into the Constitution, through successive amendments limiting the social chapter and imposing rigid fiscal 'rules' allegedly to secure low inflation. In doing so, neoliberal governments sought to limit the expansion of citizenship and shackle the emerging welfare state.[63]

Unsurprisingly, shifts in international capital flows were the immediate cause of the crisis of the Real plan, but the ultimate cause of its collapse was the set of fragilities created by the neoliberal reforms. Those shortcomings were addressed, in part, by the neoliberal policy tripod introduced in 1999 and the Fiscal Responsibility Law imposed in its wake. They have structured Brazilian macroeconomic policy ever since.

4
Impacts of Neoliberalism

Overview

In spite of its poor growth performance, the Brazilian economy experienced greater changes in the 1990s than in any decade since World War II. The most important change was the replacement of ISI by a neoliberal system of accumulation based on financialisation, a new economic role for the state and the integration of Brazilian industry and finance with transnational capital. The neoliberal reforms secured a material basis for the reproduction of the new SoA, through the transformations that they wrought in the economy and society.

Previous chapters have shown that Brazilian economic policy between the late 1980s and the mid-1990s was dominated by attempts to address the limitations of ISI, especially the challenge of creeping hyperinflation. In the second half of the 1990s, the government was determined to put in place a consistent macroeconomic policy framework supporting a new cycle of growth under neoliberalism. This was impossible, and the vicious circles created by the Real plan undermined the government's strategy. In early 1999, a new set of policies was introduced through the neoliberal tripod.

The consolidation of neoliberalism transformed Brazil's industrial structure and patterns of employment. This chapter examines those changes, and explains the limitations of neoliberalism as a SoA. The chapter includes three substantive sections. The first examines the industrial structure emerging through the neoliberal reforms, stressing its distinctive form of integration with transnational capital, when compared to the pattern prevailing under ISI. The second focuses on the employment implications of the restructuring of production, explaining why neoliberalism was accompanied by much higher rates of unemployment and precarious employment. The third summarises the economic limitations of the neoliberal SoA.

The New Industrial Structure

Neoliberalism transformed the production structure established during ISI, which had been based on the sprawling diversification of manufacturing production and a specific pattern of ownership, technology and sectoral specialisation involving domestic capital, foreign capital and the state (see Chapter 1). This macroeconomic division of labour, and the corresponding pattern of employment, were replaced by a new structure of production and a new mode of competition based on the microeconomic integration of production and finance into transnational circuits. This included extensive denationalisation, the fusion of domestic and foreign capitals at firm level, and a pattern of specialisation determined by the global imperatives of each conglomerate rather than the needs of the domestic economy.

Extensive restructuring dismantled strategically important production chains established under ISI, while privatisations, 'downsizing' and agency closures destroyed the public institutions that had delivered planning, policy implementation and sectoral intervention under ISI, and that might have provided a platform for employment generation and the distribution of income in an alternative SoA.[1] The transition to neoliberalism embedded the interests of capital in general into policy-making through the transfer to the financial sector of state capacity to allocate resources and control the level and composition of output, employment, investment and consumption. Under neoliberalism, the financial institutions mediate the relationship between the country and the rest of the world, set the exchange rate, regulate the level and allocation of savings and investment and control the financing of the state, for example, through the pricing of government securities. Sectoral development policies were largely abandoned, and the state shepherded the 'liberalisation' and 'deregulation' of the economy. As part of this effort, BNDES, the Central Bank and the Treasury organised, promoted, financed and subsidised the restructuring and privatisation of several large SOEs.

It was expected that privatisations, trade liberalisation, the overvaluation of the exchange rate, the integration between domestic and foreign firms through partnerships and M&As, the foreign financing of investment and the 'flexibilisation' of labour law would weed out inefficient firms and production processes (see Chapter 3). They would facilitate the transfer of savings and technology, increase competition, facilitate access to foreign markets, assist macroeconomic stability and support productivity growth, ensuring that Brazil developed in harmony with the global economy.[2]

These outcomes were achieved to some extent, but mostly because firms tended to specialise in less complex products and adopted new organisational techniques, production methods and labour-saving technologies. These destructive changes were mostly responsible for the productivity growth that obtained in that period.[3] Many firms closed down or were taken over by foreign capital, and the Brazilian manufacturing base was severely disarticulated. The traditional manufacturing centres around São Paulo suffered extensive deindustrialisation, while new industries started up and many firms relocated to poorer, cheaper and less unionised areas in the Northeast and South of Brazil.[4]

Foreign firms participated in 49 per cent of the 3,276 M&As in Brazil between 1990 and 1999. Both the number of M&As and the degree of foreign involvement had increased continually since 1991. In that year, foreign companies participated in 47 out of 184 M&As (26 per cent). In 1999, they were involved in 341 out of 491 M&As (70 per cent).[5] The sectors most affected by the wave of transnational integration were electric and electronic goods, telecommunications equipment, auto parts and processed foods. New internationalised groups took over ports, steel, railways, energy and iron ore. Worldcom, Bell South, Telefónica, Portugal Telecom and Telecom Italia purchased parts of the former state telecoms monopoly Embratel; Enron, AES, El Paso, Duke Energy, Iberdrola, EDF and EDP bought sections of the electricity generation and distribution systems, and HSBC, ABN-Amro, BBV and Santander purchased state-owned banks. Large firms previously controlled by domestic capital were also taken over by TNCs, for example, Metal Leve, Lacta, Cofap, Freios Varga, Arno, Refripar, Renner, Agroceres, and the Nacional, Garantia, Bamerindus and Real banks.[6]

In search of efficiency gains, or in response to the global strategy of their new parent companies, many firms specialised in a narrower range of unsophisticated goods and shifted their product mix towards lower-value-added goods. In doing so, they reduced the domestic content of their outputs. Many supply chains were hollowed out through large-scale automation, the diffusion of lean production methods, just-in-time systems and total quality control. The economy became more dependent on foreign trade, investment and technology, and the import coefficient of manufacturing output rose dramatically (see Table 4.1).[7]

Table 4.1 Share of imports in manufacturing value added, 1993 and 1996 (per cent)

Sector	1993	1996
Standardised capital goods and electronic goods	29	65–75
Chemical inputs, fertilisers, resins	20–26	33–42
Auto parts, natural textiles, capital goods made to order, rubber	8–15	20–25
Pharmaceuticals, tractors, electric and electronic consumer goods, glass, chemical goods	7–11	13–16
Synthetic textiles, petrochemical inputs, cars, food, paper and cardboard	3–6	9–12
Beverages, shoes, plastics, dairy products, semi-processed foods	0.7–3	4–8
Non-tradable goods (cement, inputs and others)	0.5–2.5	1–4

Source: Coutinho, Baltar and Camargo (1999, p. 70).

For example:

> The participation of imported IC [intermediate consumption] in total IC increased almost 50 per cent between 1995 and 2008, from 7.5 per cent to 11.1 per cent, with this increase taking place entirely during the low-[GDP] growth period (1996–2002) … In the case of high-technology manufactured goods … the participation of imports in total IC rises from 17.9 per cent to 60.9 per cent between 1995 and 2008 … Brazilian intermediate consumption is increasingly satisfied by imports, but this process has not led to higher rates of growth of GDP.[8]

Those heavy blows against domestic manufacturing were softened by the transfer of some SOEs to Brazilian capital, especially steel and petrochemicals, and the growth of Mercosur, the common market of Argentina, Brazil, Paraguay and Uruguay (and, later, Venezuela), which opened new markets for 'old' manufacturing capital based in São Paulo.[9]

Manufacturing productivity growth accelerated to 7.6 per cent per annum in 1990–7.[10] These gains were concentrated on the durable goods industry (especially automobiles) and textiles, which benefitted from labour 'flexibility', technological modernisation and changes to the product mix. In summary:

> [T]he explosion of imports rapidly 'hollowed out' the productive chains, and led to a large reduction in intra-industry demand … which

curtailed the economy's capacity to create jobs ... [F]rantic attempts to cut costs led to successive rounds of innovation and rationalisation in production, that created tensions in the labour market ... [This is partly due to the] entry of new competitors and the redefinition of strategic alliances ... [that] destabilised the oligopolistic structures inherited from previous decades ... The 'modernisation' of ... [these] structures ... ruptured existing supply chains, led to the entry of new [foreign] suppliers, reduced the degree of verticalisation and increased import coefficients ... [The] higher coefficient of imported inputs and components (and, therefore, substantially lower value creation in the country) means that the success of efforts to stimulate domestic demand for intermediate goods and employment will tend ... to be very modest.[11]

This was not the 'efficient' outcome of a technically neutral process of rationalisation. Instead, those outcomes derived from a politically-driven shift in the SoA: the productive structure was adapted to service the short-term imperatives of *global* accumulation, including increased dependence on foreign suppliers, markets and technologies, and the subordination of strategic planning to the global interests of TNCs. In contrast, under ISI, production served the short-term requirements of *national* accumulation (see Chapter 1; the long-term interests of the poor majority were secondary in both cases). The dramatic impact of the transnationalisation of production was often assimilated to a 'reverse ISI' or 'production substitution' financed by foreign capital.[12]

The successive onslaught of the oil shocks, external debt crisis, rising inflation, high interest rates, currency overvaluation, trade liberalisation and the disarticulation of industrial policy created unprecedented economic stresses. During the 1990s, the share of manufacturing value added in GDP declined sharply, with mining and agribusiness expanding in tandem, leading the share of primary commodities in Brazilian exports to increase from 40 to 60 per cent.[13]

The reprimarisation of the economy was accompanied by declining aggregate competitiveness (even if the surviving firms were more efficient and highly profitable), sluggish GDP growth and a deteriorating pattern of employment. Export income became more dependent on global commodity prices, which is not easily compatible with the creation of quality employment and improvements in living standards in a large, urbanised economy. Given the high income-elasticity of Brazil's import demand, and the much lower world elasticity of demand for Brazilian exports, any economic expansion under neoliberalism tends to leak jobs abroad through the rapid increase in imports, straining the current account.[14] Even though deflation is destructive for development, it becomes the only remedy against these imbalances (see Chapter 7).

The need for inflows of foreign capital was perpetuated by low investment, the erosion of the industrial base, the simultaneous deterioration of the fiscal balance and the trade and current accounts, and the threat of recurrent demand compression in order to maintain macroeconomic stability. These factors also prevented the reduction of domestic interest rates. These core features of neoliberalism created the vicious circles that explain the declining trend of GDP growth rates since the late 1980s (see Chapter 3). Per capita income rose only 2.7 per cent per annum between 1981 and 2003, and Brazil fell from being the world's eighth largest economy in 1980, to the fourteenth in 2000; the country also declined from eighth to eleventh place in the world rankings of manufactured output.[15]

A New Pattern of Employment

The value of manufacturing output remained approximately constant between 1990 and 1997; in the meantime, manufacturing employment declined by 38 per cent, with the loss of between 1 million and 1.5 million jobs, especially in the auto parts, textile, toy, food, clothing and shoe industries.[16] For example:

> Firms achieved substantial output growth after 1994, without any corresponding increase in their productive capacity. The productivity gains became possible not only through new management and organisational methods, specialisation in less complex products and increased efficiency, but also because of the reduction in the local content of the output. Current investment projects reproduce these features, and they have low capital and employment coefficients.[17]

For the first time in Brazilian history, output and productivity growth coexisted with falling employment. In Greater São Paulo, 180,000 manufacturing jobs (7.7 per cent of the total) were lost in 1995;[18] another half a million workers lost their jobs in privatised industries in the rest of the country.[19] The number of stable and relatively well-paid blue-collar jobs fell, while unemployment, precarious employment and subcontracted work mounted. The labour market became increasingly fragmented (see Chapter 8).[20] Depending on the data source, the open unemployment rate increased from 4–8 per cent in 1990, to 8–15 per cent in 1999.[21] Unemployment in the six largest metropolitan areas[22] rose from 8.7 per cent in 1989, to 18.3 per cent in 1998, while the average length of unemployment increased from 15 to 36 weeks.[23]

While the manufacturing sector haemorrhaged posts, neoliberalism created a pattern of employment centred on low productivity, informal, precarious and low-paid female jobs in urban services.[24] During the 1990s, 11 million jobs were created; 54 per cent were either informal or unwaged.[25] The simplification of managerial structures and new information technologies sliced the number of middle managers, reducing the scope for middle-class employment and increasing precarity even for those in relatively well-paid jobs.[26]

This pattern of job creation neutralised the distributional gains achieved through the elimination of high inflation. The index of wages paid in the main place of employment increased from 96 in January 1993, to 145 in December 1996. It subsequently fell to 126 in April 1999.[27] Average real wages fell 8 per cent between 1994 and 2001,[28] and the wage share in national income declined from 50 per cent in 1980, to 40 per cent in 2000 (see Table 1.2).[29] Between the late 1980s and the late 1990s, the Gini coefficient remained stable at around 0.60 (see Figure 1.3).

The state played a key role in the transformation of these patterns of employment through the compression of demand, privatisations, changes in industrial and regulatory policy, widespread subcontracting and employment of precarious workers, shifts in labour law, lax implementation even of the new laws and outright repression, most clearly during the oil workers' strike in 1995.[30] It follows that high unemployment, precarious work and rising relative if not absolute poverty were *deliberate outcomes of public policy under neoliberalism.*

During the 1990s, Brazilian labour markets became more 'flexible' in three ways. First, the state curtailed the right of unions to represent individual workers in court. Second, a 1998 law introduced fixed-term employment contracts, facilitated dismissal, reduced holidays and other benefits and created 'overtime banks' that allowed firms to vary working hours almost at will. Finally, firms increasingly avoided labour law altogether, for example, by refusing to register their employees. This was condoned by the government and made possible as a result of the weakened bargaining power of workers and their unions. The number of registered (legally-protected) workers (*trabalhadores com carteira*) declined by 15 per cent in the 1990s; in the manufacturing sector, the decline reached 25 per cent.

Limitations of Neoliberalism

The Brazilian experience suggests that the neoliberal SoA is limited at four levels. First, neoliberalism is limited by creeping social conflict, although open dissent can normally be contained by unemployment, precarisation of labour, consumerism, ideological hegemony and the legal tools of repression.

Second, the balance of payments constraint. Under ISI, this constraint appeared through the scarcity of foreign exchange, payment arrears and regular scrambles for last-minute loans. Under neoliberalism, the balance of payments constraint appears either through high real interest rates (determined by the need to attract sufficient inflows of foreign currency), or exchange-rate volatility (if the required inflows do not materialise). However, it is known that capital flows tend to be more responsive to circumstances in advanced economies than to the policies of developing countries.[31] In addition, the remittances of profits and dividends tend to increase with the volume of inflows.[32] Even worse, the difference between the (high) rate of return of foreign investments, and the (much lower) rate of return of domestic investments abroad (especially the remuneration of the Central Bank's foreign currency reserves, see Chapter 3) tends to increase financial fragility. Consequently, the liberalisation of trade and capital flows did not eliminate the balance of payments constraint. However, it changed it, as it imposed higher domestic interest rates and created greater vulnerability to fluctuations in international liquidity and the cost of finance.

Third, interest rates tend to be relatively high under neoliberalism, overvaluing the currency and reducing employment, investment, output and income relative to what they would be in an alternative SoA in which growth and macroeconomic stability were pursued with a broader set of tools. High interest rates also trigger deficits in the current account, because demand leaks abroad and manufacturing is hollowed out even if productivity rises in the remaining firms. Structural unemployment rises because capacity tends to become fully utilised, and the balance of payments constraint becomes binding, long before the workforce has been fully absorbed. High interest rates also create incentives for external borrowing to finance consumption rather than investment, and they can foster the growth of speculative assets without any counterpart in production, e.g. predatory M&As, stock market booms or speculation in real estate. The ensuing fiscal, financial and balance of payments vulnerabilities require continuing inflows of foreign capital, again without any guarantee that productive capacity will rise.[33]

Fourth, under neoliberalism, finance acquires a much greater role in the determination of economic policy, the coordination of production and investment and the allocation of resources. In Brazil, this influence is not exercised primarily through the usual channels of industrial finance or the stock market, but through holdings of government securities. Given the size and liquidity of these assets, large financial institutions can control the sources and levels of output, employment, consumption, investment and growth, and impose monetary and exchange-rate policies that work to their own advantage.

These constraints created destabilising macroeconomic tendencies that drove the country into a *stabilisation-speculation trap*. Under neoliberalism, GDP growth rates were low and unstable, leading to two 'lost decades' (the 1980s and the 1990s) due to the debt crisis and the disintegration of ISI. In the meantime, the Brazilian economy was propped up by external booms and domestic bubbles. Yet the economy suffered from high interest rates, a competitivity deficit, the hollowing out of manufacturing, premature deindustrialisation, a persistent infrastructure gap and a shifting but permanently tight balance of payments constraint. For these reasons, the economy required large foreign capital inflows, which integrated Brazilian production and finance into global accumulation; however, when those inflows were insufficient, the exchange rate would slide and the balance-of-payments crisis would paralyse the economy.

Summary and Conclusion

Following the transition to neoliberalism, Brazil remained an unequal, dependent and poverty-creating economy but, in contrast with ISI, it became a *low-growth* economy, where performance was permanently limited by the threat of balance of payments and exchange-rate crises.

The new SoA failed to address the main shortcomings of ISI. It also imposed additional constraints on the economy, which entrenched stagnation and reduced the scope to accommodate social change without political upheaval.[34] Import liberalisation and closer international integration led the economy to specialise in a narrower range of relatively unsophisticated goods, hollowing out the manufacturing base, fostering reprimarisation and increasing the country's dependence on foreign trade, investment and technology. Manufacturing employment declined and productive capacity fell in important sectors, especially the capital goods industry. The economy lost dynamism and capacity to create jobs. The Brazilian state became even less capable than before of addressing the problems of coordination, restructuring, economic growth, employment creation and distribution of income.

Neoliberalism also relied on variables that Brazil could influence only marginally, especially the volume and cost of foreign capital flows. In sum, neoliberalism created severe fiscal, financial and balance-of-payments vulnerabilities as it shifted the engine of growth towards an unreliable combination of externally financed consumption and investment in non-traded goods. The poor performance of the Brazilian economy under neoliberalism was due to internal and external causes but, ultimately, it derived from the attempt to implement a SoA that could be stable only exceptionally.

Despite these disappointing outcomes, and regardless of the vulnerabilities of individual accumulation strategies, the neoliberal SoA is largely immune to endogenous 'economic' challenges. In particular, economic underperformance is insufficient to trigger a shift in the SoA, because unemployment and bankruptcies weaken the capacity of domestic constituencies to demand alternatives, especially the organised formal working class and the urban middle class. Underperformance also compels capital to move into new ventures that are, almost invariably, more closely connected with the interests of international capital and finance. These constraints suggest that the main driver of successful challenges to neoliberalism is likely to be *loss of political legitimacy*, rather than poor economic outcomes.[35]

5
Neoliberalism under the Workers' Party

Overview

Lula's election to the presidency, in October 2002, was the outcome of two mutually-reinforcing processes. First, there were the tensions between the inclusive logic of democracy and the exclusionary consequences of neoliberalism, especially through deindustrialisation, poverty, inequality and precarious employment. These tensions were intensified by the crisis of the *real*, which the Cardoso administration could never explain, much less respond to constructively. Second, the development of the PT as a political party born during the transition to democracy and, later, repositioning itself as a fresh and honest party led by an incorruptible leader sprung from the bosom of the working class. Lula was presented as a uniquely bright politician, larger than the PT, and perfectly suited to lead a new phase in the country's history.

In order to capture executive power, the PT demonstrated great political talent in building an 'alliance of losers'. These were social groups having in common only the experience of *losses* under neo-liberalism. The 'losers' were brought together by diffuse expectations of 'change', including demands for an efficient public administration, a more nationalist and growth-oriented industrial policy and income distribution at the margin. They shared little else. In order to keep their support, the PT committed itself to governing within the established rules, maintaining the neoliberal policy tripod and stabilising rather than reforming the neoliberal SoA.

During Lula's first administration, favourable external circumstances dislocated the balance-of-payments and fiscal constraints and lifted tax revenues and national insurance contributions. These favourable circumstances supported the virtuous dynamics of the labour market, including rising wages and employment, the formalisation of labour, higher transfers and improved social security provision while, at the same time, allowing the government to deliver low inflation and the fiscal surpluses demanded by the neoliberal elite.

This virtuous circle was hampered by the economy's sluggish growth during the first years of Lula's administration, the fragility of his parliamentary base and his growing isolation from the internationalised (neoliberal) bourgeoisie and the middle class. This political terrain favoured the eruption of real as well as imagined corruption scandals, which helped to destabilise the alliance of losers (see Chapter 9). Despite these challenges, Lula's political talent allowed him to replace the alliance of losers by a new 'alliance of winners' in 2005–6, which supported his bid for re-election.

Running to Win: The Alliance of Losers

Lula was elected President in 2002 with the support of an *alliance of losers*: a loose coalition of groups having in common only the experience of losses under neoliberalism.[1] This alliance was purely tactical, as those groups were essentially attempting to avoid or offset their losses during the transition to neoliberalism. There was no agreement about how to do this, or what alternative policies should be implemented.

The alliance of losers included four main groups (see Chapter 8). First, the unionised urban and rural working class, especially the skilled, manual and office workers, the lower ranks of the civil service and sections of the professional middle class. Historically, these groups were the backbone of the Brazilian left and the main source of support for the PT (see Chapter 2). They had also lost out heavily under neoliberalism through deindustrialisation, privatisations, job cuts, wage stagnation, dilution of employment rights and insufficient provision of public goods and services.

The second group comprised large segments of the informal working class who had previously been reluctant to engage with the PT, partly for ideological reasons, especially their attachment to clientelistic and populist practices and partly because of the absence of channels connecting them to the party. The most significant exception was the 'base communities' of the Liberation Theology wing of the Catholic Church, but those had declined steeply in the 1980s because of social and economic changes in Brazil and pressures from an increasingly conservative Vatican. In contrast, multiple channels linked the PT to the formal workers, for example, trade unions, community associations and social movements. In 2002, those large but unorganised groups tended to support Lula because of his perceived opposition to neoliberalism, promises of income transfers and social programmes, and because of the PT's pact with several evangelical churches.

Third, many prominent capitalists also supported Lula, especially among the internal bourgeoisie. This fraction had a contradictory relationship with neoliberalism and public policy. Although it remained wedded to neoliberal ideology and tended to support neoliberal fiscal, labour market and social policies, the internal bourgeoisie also recognised that government regulation, welfare policies and rising minimum wages could increase social cohesion, promote political stability and boost the domestic market. This group was also exhausted by the stagnation of the economy, the onslaught of transnational capital, high interest rates, the overvaluation of the currency and the pressure of cheap imports. Although segments of the internal bourgeoisie may be close to international capital by virtue of their involvement in particular sectors of the economy (e.g. finance and auto parts are especially close, while construction and processed meats are less integrated; see Chapter 8), this fraction as a whole needs a protective umbrella to shore up its control of domestic markets, defend it against global capital and support its expansion abroad.

Fourth, several notorious right-wing oligarchs, landowners and local politicians from the poorest regions also supported Lula. This was not driven by pressures from below or their fundamental disagreements with neoliberalism. Rather, it was due to a shrewd calculation. Since the early 1990s, these oligarchs and their *protégés* had been squeezed out of their influential positions in Brasília by a new cohort of upper- and middle-managers aligned with financial interests. Unlike the previous generation of lawyers, engineers and talentless political appointees from the poorest regions, the new state managers were economists, financiers and professional administrators, mainly from the rich Southeast, trained in the neoliberal arts in the best universities. The traditional oligarchy also resented the rationing of development funds imposed by fiscal austerity since 1990, which had eroded their political influence. By switching their support to the PT, the oligarchs anticipated that Lula would not seek to change the SoA, and would depend on their support in Congress and the states to pass legislation. They also calculated that the PT would be more sensitive than the neoliberals to the plight of poorer regions, which would help to maximise the oligarchs' own power.[2]

In his determination to consolidate the alliance of losers, Lula pushed the PT into a coalition with the right-wing Liberal Party (*Partido Liberal,* PL). The PL was a stalwart of neoliberalism, the political arm of evangelical churches and, later, a convenient parking spot for opportunist politicians who wished to be in government but were unwilling or unable to join the PT. The PL was also the home of José Alencar, a self-made businessman and one of the political leaders of the internal bourgeoisie. Alencar was Lula's personal choice for the vice presidency, and he helped to attract domestic capital and large donors to Lula's campaign. The coalition with the PL also helped to neutralise the reservations of the religious right about the PT.[3]

The memory of three failed bids for the presidency was always in the background. Lula's campaign was planned in minute detail. His beard was impeccably trimmed, he wore the best Armani suits, had far more resources than his opponents, and his TV advertisements were skilfully produced. Since it was impossible to incorporate the contra-dictory expectations of the alliance into a coherent programme, the PT simply removed any concrete commitments from Lula's campaign. His discourse was vague and appealed to pious sentiment, and his programme was a collection of unobjectionable but un-costed good intentions, with few commitments or targets. He gave his enemies little ammunition. This tactic worked brilliantly during the campaign, but it implied that Lula would receive a poorly specified mandate grounded on mixed expectations.

The alliance of losers won against a *neoliberal alliance* composed of three main groups. First, the internationalised bourgeoisie (see Chapter 8), which had been politically dominant during the administrations led by Collor and Cardoso. Their political project was anchored on the neoliberal policy tripod, further privatisations and 'deregulation', and the rejection of state-led distribution. Second, the urban middle class, with whom the internationalised bourgeoisie had established a robust alliance under Cardoso. Finally, the majority of informal workers that, in Brazil, traditionally voted with the right.[4]

Embracing Neoliberalism

In mid-2002, Lula was enjoying a comfortable lead in the opinion polls. However, his radical image worried international financiers and the internationalised bourgeoisie. They feared the loss of leverage in an administration led by the PT, and were concerned that Lula might default or reschedule the country's external debt or the DPD. Several financial institutions used these concerns to justify their refusal to buy government securities maturing after 31 December 2002, the last day of Cardoso's presidency.

The weekly open market auctions became fruitless, as the brokers demanded ever-higher interest rates to roll over the government debt. If higher rates were not forthcoming, the brokers liquidated their positions and shifted funds to the dollar market, devaluing the *real*. In 2002, US$9 billion passed through this channel, devaluing the *real* from R$2.32 to the dollar in March, to R$3.42 in July, and R$3.80 in October (inflation was only 4 per cent during the entire period). The country's net international reserves declined from US$29 billion in March, to US$16 billion in December. The devaluation of the currency and the financiers' complaints about 'lack of policy clarity' led to the downgrading of Brazilian bonds and foreign debt certificates that, in turn, triggered the recall of short-term loans and commercial credit lines by the foreign banks. Half of those lines were lost in a matter of weeks. The Brazilian balance of payments was on the verge of collapse.[5]

The proportion of the outstanding stock of public securities traded in the open market increased from 0.7 per cent in February, to 2.5 per cent in April, 5.3 per cent in July and 12.4 per cent in December. The Central Bank expanded its open market operations to prevent these funds from reaching the foreign exchange market. By September, the stock of liquid securities in the open market exceeded 5 per cent of GDP, far in excess of the monetary base and the Central Bank's international reserves.

There is no doubt that the Cardoso administration was complicit in the meltdown of the Brazilian balance of payments, the evaporation of the demand for long-term government securities, and the instability in the open market. The mainstream media howled with indignation, demanding that the presidential candidates (i.e. Lula) guarantee the continuity of Cardoso's economic policies in order to 'calm the markets'.[6] In doing so, the media fuelled frantic rounds of speculation. Eventually, the Minister of Finance and the President of the Central Bank theatrically demanded that 'all' candidates explain their economic programme to 'the markets'. Lula's poll leadership wobbled, but he was determined to win his fourth consecutive bid for the presidency. On 22 June, Lula issued a 'Letter to the Brazilian People' stating that his government would respect contracts (i.e. service the domestic and foreign debts on schedule) and continue the economic policies of the Cardoso administration.[7]

This bold move disarmed the media, contained the slide of the currency and secured Lula's lead in the opinion polls; however, it was insufficient to satisfy the neoliberal alliance. Realising that Lula was poised to win, the neoliberals demanded *institutional* guarantees for neoliberalism, including an independent Central Bank committed to a 'responsible' monetary policy, and a new IMF agreement extending well into the new administration. Lula acquiesced, and the wheels turned rapidly in Brasília and Washington. A new IMF agreement was signed on 4 September 2002. It stated that:

> a combination of a worsening external environment and increased uncertainty among investors about the future course of economic policies has led to a deterioration in financial market variables in recent months. The ... new Stand-By Arrangement with the Fund ... [is] designed to safeguard economic stability, *and provide a framework for the continuity of core macroeconomic policies next year* [under the new administration].[8]

The agreement involved a loan of US$30 billion, of which only US$6 billion would be available immediately. The rest would be released to the new government *if* its policies were approved by the Fund. Lula's consent opened the doors of financial institutions and conservative governments around the world to the PT, and virtually ensured his election. Lula received 40 million votes (46 per cent) in the first round of the elections, and 53 million (61 per cent) in the second round. His nearest rival, José Serra, a former minister in F.H. Cardoso's administration, was beaten by 20 million votes in both rounds.[9]

The looseness of the PT alliance, and Lula's concessions to neoliberalism, imposed strict limits to his administration, implying that his government would maintain the institutional architecture of mature neoliberalism and follow Cardoso's economic policies, but with greater competence, honesty, creativity and sensitivity to the need for compensatory social policies.

Enforcing Neoliberalism

Lula's administration was shaped, in three ways, by the economic and social changes imposed by neoliberalism, the unstable alliances underpinning his election and the PT's reaction to the 2002 exchange-rate crisis, as we have noted.[10]

First, Lula was elected by a coalition of social and political forces attempting to shed the stagnationist bias of neoliberalism. Beyond this, the 'losers' had very few goals in common, and the coalition was in no position to offer consistent support to the government. Second, the capitulation of the PT leadership to the interests of domestic and international finance signalled the party's defeat in the struggle for some form of 'socialism' (however bland or vacuous), for which the PT had been fighting for two decades. Third, the alliance of losers and the forces supporting the new administration never even tried to shift government policy away from neoliberalism.

The PT reached the presidency when the social forces that had originally sustained the party had already been degraded by the transition to neoliberalism. The party's left-wing ideology had lost legitimacy and political traction, and the legal and administrative tools that could have effected economic and social change had been blunted by successive waves of state 'reform'. These limitations would have made it almost impossible for the organised working class to exercise hegemony through its political party.

The disparity between Lula's impressive victory, the party's position in Congress, where the PT and the allies it could depend upon held fewer than one-third of the seats,[11] and the left's negligible influence on the judiciary, showed that radical changes were not uniformly popular, and might have been unenforceable. Therefore, even though Lula's election created the expectation of change, especially among his leftist supporters, he never had a mandate for radical change, was not committed to specific outcomes or even processes of change, and would probably have been unable to drive significant change even if he had wanted to. Given its earlier political choices, the PT was limited to managing neoliberalism, with marginal tweaks at best.

Lula took office on 1 January 2003. His government enforced a thoroughly neoliberal accumulation strategy earning the admiration of backers of former president Cardoso and warm praise from the IMF.[12] The first significant economic policy decision of the new administration was to raise the primary fiscal surplus target to 4.25 per cent of GDP, in contrast with the 3.75 per cent agreed with the IMF. The government eventually delivered a primary surplus of 4.3 per cent of GDP in 2003; then it raised the 2004 target to 4.5 per cent. This initiative served two purposes: it signalled the government's commitment to neoliberalism, and reduced the need for politically damaging interest rate rises in order to contain inflation. Despite the supportive fiscal policy imposed by Finance Minister Antonio Palocci, Central Bank chairman Henrique Meirelles (former World President of BankBoston, and a member of Cardoso's (misnamed) PSDB, *Partido da Social Democracia Brasileira*, Brazilian Social Democratic Party), felt the need to demonstrate his independence.[13] The Central Bank raised base rates from 25.0 to 26.5 per cent in the first three months of the new administration, and cut them only after the inflationary bubble created by the devaluation of the *real*, in 2002, had been completely eliminated.

The new administration implemented another four key policies. First, it pushed through Congress a reform of public sector pensions that Cardoso had been unable to implement, largely because of the PT's staunch opposition. The PT's *volte face* divided the left and the trade unions. Second, the government passed a tax reform inspired by another of Cardoso's failed initiatives, raising indirect taxes and offering rebates for financial transactions. Third, it forced a constitutional amendment separating the regulation of the Central Bank from the regulation of the financial system as a whole, in order to simplify the process of granting operational independence to the Bank.[14] Fourth, in early 2004 the government sent to Congress a bill including only a very small increase in the minimum wage. The opposition sensed an opportunity to embarrass the administration, and tabled an alternative bill raising the minimum wage more than the PT had proposed. The government found itself in the unenviable position of having to explain its own very small increase in the minimum wage, *and* having to vote down a bill that offered the poorest people in Brazil another US$5 per month. To win the vote, the government had to offer substantial incentives to wavering Deputies and Senators, in an unseemly display of pork-barrel politics that tainted the PT.[15] The neoliberal credentials of Lula's policies were tempered only by a significant expansion of the federal programmes of social assistance, starting with the new food distribution programme, *Fome Zero* (Zero Hunger; see Chapter 6).

The Central Bank's high interest rate policies eventually choked inflation, but real interest rates hovered around 10 per cent, easily among the highest in the world. Manufacturing output fell 1 per cent in 2003, and GDP declined 0.2 per cent; this was the first contraction since the Collor administration. The recession was mitigated by the expansion of export agriculture, which was starting to profit from the global commodity boom.

The employment results in 2003 were also disappointing.[16] Open unemployment in the largest metropolitan areas increased from 11.7 per cent in December 2002, to 12.3 per cent one year later. Total unemployment (including open and hidden unemployment and discouraged workers) reached 20 per cent in São Paulo. Labour income in the six major metropolitan areas fell 10 per cent in 2003 (18 per cent since 2001), while wage income fell 5 per cent (14 per cent since 2001). The economy performed better in 2004, when GDP expanded by 5.2 per cent, pulled by commodity exports.

By then, the global boom was starting to pull the Brazilian economy (see Figure 5.1). The country's terms of trade (the unit price of exports divided by the unit price of imports) rose. Export earnings increased 50 per cent between 1999 and 2003, to US$73 billion, while imports remained stable, around US$50 billion. Brazil had its first trade surplus in seven years in 2001 and, in 2003, the first current-account surplus in eleven years. Exports continued to grow in the following years; they reached US$138 billion in 2006, and US$256 billion in 2011. The inflows of portfolio capital increased sharply, from *minus* US$4.7 billion in 2002, to *plus* US$5.1 billion in 2003. These gains supported a limited recovery of the foreign currency reserves (up US$8.7 billion since 2002, to US$25.0.0 billion in mid-2004). The tax intake increased sharply

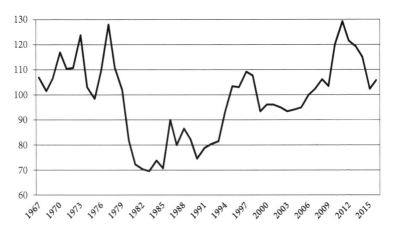

Figure 5.1   Terms of trade, 1967–2016 (annual average, 2006 = 100)

Source: Ipeadata.

between 2005 and 2007, and the Bovespa index of the São Paulo stock exchange gained 127 per cent in 2003. J.P. Morgan's EMBI+ Brazilian risk index declined from more than 2000 points to only 480 points during 2003. The growth spurt in 2004 was presented as 'proof' that the PT's neoliberal strategy was sound. In 2005, Brazil repaid ahead of time the US$23.3 billion outstanding IMF loan that had signalled Lula's commitment to neoliberalism.[17] The conditions for policy change were falling into place.

Lula Hits the Buffers

The new administration appointed a large number of progressive political, trade union and NGO cadres to the federal administration: the President, a former metalworker, appointed five working-class ministers; over 100 trade unionists took high-level posts in the administration and the SOEs, and they appointed hundreds of lower-level colleagues.[18] Their elevation opened the floodgates to the election of an unprecedented number of lower-income candidates by parties across the political spectrum.

The social composition of the Brazilian state changed. For the first time in the country's history, millions of poor citizens could recognise themselves in the bureaucracy and relate to close friends and comrades who had become 'important' in Brasília. This shift in social composition enhanced the legitimacy of the state enormously, secured the support of the bureaucracy for the PT's distributive ambitions, and promoted the claims of the poor for improved services within the public sector. These changes were called a 'democratic revolution' by some analysts.[19] This is an exaggeration, but it illustrates the changes in the relationship between citizens and the state under Lula.[20] At the same time, the personnel changes aligned the material interests of the leaders of the most combative social movements and NGOs with the government's neoliberal policies and the interests of the state bureaucracy: effectively, *the PT government nationalised the organised left*.[21] These personnel changes also distanced Lula's government from the bourgeoisie, financial interests and large swathes of the middle class that traditionally had dominated the state sector. They resented the loss of political space to the newcomers, for ideological as well as employment reasons.

Within two years, Lula's administration found itself in a cul-de-sac. The government's neoliberal policies failed to catalyse private investment; GDP growth was patchy; and the social and employment indicators had either stagnated or were improving very slowly. These outcomes frustrated everyone, especially the PT's traditional supporters. They felt that their concerns were being ignored and their support was taken for granted, while government officials schmoozed with bankers and rich industrialists, parroted their neoliberal discourse and delivered very little. Even this apparent sell-out was insufficient to remove the resistance of the elite against Lula. His administration was widely criticised both for what it did ('packing the state with acolytes' and 'taxing producers to fund sloth'), and for what it did not do (deliver rapid growth and social improvements). The disarticulation of the left and their disappointment with Lula's attachment to neoliberalism forced the government to rely on the internal bourgeoisie, the regional oligarchies and the disorganised workers. However, these groups had never been committed wholeheartedly to the PT. Their support was conditional on Brazil's economic performance, which was essential to satisfy the demand of the rich for markets and profits, and to generate resources for transfers to the poor.

The administration soon had to face another challenge. Realising Lula's vulnerability and aware of his inevitable bid for re-election, the neoliberal alliance launched a vicious attack in 2005, focusing on allegations that the PT was buying votes in Congress with monthly cash payments (the grotesque *mensalão* scandal).[22] The media pursued this story relentlessly.[23] The scandal claimed the scalps of Lula's likely successor, Finance Minister Antonio Palocci, Lula's Chief of Staff, PT strategist José Dirceu, president and treasurer of the PT, and other high-ranking cadres of the administration. Years later, some of them would be imprisoned after a contentious trial at the Supreme Court. The attack almost brought down the government, and it triggered a catastrophic loss of support for the PT. After a quarter-century of steady growth, the PT had reached 25 per cent of voter preferences in early 2005; after the *mensalão*, these rates fell by half.[24]

Lula discovered that he could not count on the support of the radical left or the formal-sector workers, nor could he rely on the oligarchs for his political survival. He retreated to the urban peripheries and the poor Northeastern region, where his government's social programmes made him popular. He also renewed his commitment to the internal bourgeoisie that, by and large, continued to support his administration.[25]

Summary and Conclusion

By 2002, Lula had grown tired of losing and was determined to be elected President. By then, Lula's electoral agenda dominated the PT, and the party complied with enthusiasm. The party built a broad coalition including important fractions of capital, the country's largest trade unions and social movements, evangelical churches, assorted oligarchs and opportunistic political parties. A nationalist businessman became Lula's running mate; Lula committed his administration to harsh neoliberal policies, and subjected government initiatives to the veto of the IMF. Yet it would be misguided to say the PT sold its left-wing soul for power in 2002: the party's soul had been sacrificed long before, when it genuflected before the altar of neoliberal democracy.

Once in power, the PT unwittingly drove a transformation in the social composition of the state, which reinforced the party's social democratic agenda both inside and outside the bureaucracy. In doing this, the PT inadvertently irritated finance and the middle class. Once neoliberal economic policies proved, once again, unable to deliver fast or even sustainable economic growth, Lula's administration became vulnerable to attack by the mainstream media and the middle class. The PT also discovered that it had run out of committed supporters on the left and among the organised working class and the social movements. They had been demobilised years before, in order to secure the PT's electoral viability. Subsequently, many left leaders were taken into service as high-level public administrators. When the PT found itself under attack, disorganised and with its social base fractured and demotivated, it had to rely on the internal bourgeoisie and the disorganised informal workers. Lula marched to re-election in 2006 in very different circumstances to those surrounding his triumph four years earlier. Once again, his success would transform the country.

6

Developmental Neoliberalism and the PT

Overview

This chapter reviews the second administration of Luís Inácio Lula da Silva (2007–10). It focuses on the neodevelopmental economic policies implemented in this period, which were superimposed onto the neoliberal tripod. Implementation of this hybrid variant of the neoliberal SoA had significant implications for growth, distribution and social welfare, not only in Lula's administration, but also in the administration led by his successor, Dilma Rousseff.

The inflection in Lula's second administration, when compared to the policies implemented in his first term in office, was associated with the transformation in the sources of support for the government led by the PT. Instead of the alliance of losers that had originally elected Lula, his re-election was supported by a new 'alliance of winners', which brought together the groups that had *won* the most under the PT.

The successful coexistence of the neoliberal policy tripod with neodevelopmental policies (inspired by Latin American structuralism, new Keynesian and post-Keynesian economics, evolutionary political economy and other heterodox schools of thought) can be explained by the favourable external environment during Lula's second administration. In these circumstances, the interaction between *prima facie* incompatible policies proved to be conducive to significant successes. They included the acceleration of GDP growth, Brazil's dramatic recovery after the global crisis, and a sustained improvement in employment, wage, welfare and distributional indicators.

The Hour of Neodevelopmentalism

Neodevelopmentalism emerged in Latin America in the 2000s, as a heterodox alternative to neoliberalism. Although neodevelopmentalism has been understood in very different ways,[1] all of its versions claim that the old Latin American developmentalism, associated with ISI, failed because it was not conducive to the internalisation of the sources of innovation and productivity growth, and it tended to concentrate income and wealth.

Neodevelopmental writers suggest that government policies should aim beyond the mainstream goal of monetary stability. Instead, they should build a strong interaction between the state and the private sector to support distributive and growth-promoting policies across the fiscal, financial, monetary, exchange-rate, labour and social domains.[2] In this policy framework, the state does not need to own productive assets or control private enterprises. Instead, the state should secure macroeconomic stability, including inflation control, an appropriate exchange rate and balance-of-payments sustainability. This should be supported by controls on international flows of capital, intertemporal fiscal balance, low interest rates and the reduction of uncertainty about future demand, all of which are essential to support private investment. In some versions of neodevelopmentalism, the state should also promote competition, secure distributive outcomes and nurture selected local firms ('national champions', inspired by the South Korean *chaebol*).

The main theses of neodevelopmentalism can be summarised as follows:

(1) there is no strong market without a strong state; (2) there will be no sustained growth ... without the strengthening of the market and the implementation of adequate macroeconomic policies; (3) strong markets and states will only be built by a national development project that reconciles growth ... and social equity; and (4) it is not possible to [reduce] inequality without consistently high growth rates.[3]

In the early 2000s, economists aligned with neodevelopmentalism insisted that there was significant underutilised potential in Brazil, given the output, productivity, employment and export gains that could be realised through state support for private investment. This did not suggest that miraculous outcomes were possible. It was merely suggested that more activist fiscal and credit policies might nudge GDP growth 'one or two percentage points above the rates expected by the supporters of the neoliberal view'.[4] These modest hopes implied that the neodevelopmentalists were willing to compromise with neoliberalism in order to deliver slightly faster growth alongside political stability.

In principle, neodevelopmentalism could support a systemic alternative to neoliberalism. A hypothetical neodevelopmental SoA could be grounded on a macroeconomic policy regime including low interest rates, a relatively undervalued exchange rate and strong industrial policy, in order to rebuild the production chains hollowed out under neoliberalism and strengthen Brazil's capacity to export manufactured goods. Those outcomes could be supported by income distribution, through higher wages, employment and transfers (the distribution of assets was to be avoided, since it would be politically destabilising), and more credit for consumption and investment. Those outcomes, in turn, would lead the expansion of domestic markets and drive a self-sustaining growth based on domestic demand.

Neodevelopmentalist ideas gained traction in academic, NGO and policy circles during Lula's first administration, driven by the perception of severe economic underperformance under neoliberalism. This view was substantiated by the strong heterodox traditions within Brazilian social sciences, which supported the argument that there was significant scope for success, at low cost, under a different policy compact.

The Alliance of Winners

Despite the damage wrought by the *mensalão* scandal, Lula fought a vigorous re-election campaign in 2006, and trounced his main rival, PSDB candidate Geraldo Alckmin, by 61–39 per cent of the vote in the second round of the elections.[5]

Lula's achievement was based on a very different base of support when compared to his previous election. After the *mensalão*, Lula lost most of the middle class;[6] however, during his first administration Lula gained the solid support of the internal bourgeoisie, which led his defence and prevented the *mensalão* from culminating in his impeachment.[7] Lula also won heavily among first-time voters, low-wage workers (who had benefitted from the increases in the minimum wage since 2005), poor women (the main recipients of *Bolsa Família*, see below), and beneficiaries of social and transfer programmes (university admissions quotas, mass connections to the electricity grid and federal transfers and pensions, most of which were linked to the minimum wage). Although Lula lost in most of the affluent states, he won more than three-quarters of the vote in several of the less affluent states. In contrast, the PT elected only 83 federal deputies in 2006 (down from 91 in 2002), showing that the support of the poor was tightly focused on the President himself, rather than his party.[8]

The transformation in Lula's support base can be captured through the notion of an *alliance of winners*, that is, a coalition of groups that had 'won' economically during Lula's first administration, and that supported a shift towards a neodevelopmentalist variety of neoliberalism.[9] Symptomatically, for the first time, support for the PT was inversely correlated with income.[10] In households earning more than ten times the minimum wage (roughly, the upper middle class), PT support fell from 32 per cent in 2002, to 17 per cent in 2006. Lula's rejection by voters with university education jumped from 24 per cent to 40 per cent between August and October 2005; 65 per cent of those voters supported the opposition candidate in 2006. In 1997, the PT had 5.5 million 'high-income' and 3.1 million 'low-income' supporters, and only 17 per cent of PT supporters earned less than twice the minimum wage. In 2006, the PT had only 3.3 million 'high-income' supporters but 17.6 million 'low-income' ones, while 47 per cent of its supporters earned less than twice the minimum wage.[11]

In his second administration, Lula disbanded the original (neoliberal) economic team, and appointed heterodox economists and nationalist diplomats to the Ministry of Finance, the Office of Strategic Affairs, the Institute of Applied Economic Research and BNDES.[12] However, the Central Bank, still under Henrique Meirelles, remained untouched. This was either because it was politically impossible to limit its independence or change the inflation-targeting regime, or because Lula believed that this would help stabilise his government.

The new administration did not radically change the macroeconomic policy framework that had been in place since 1999. Instead, the government introduced a range of neodevelopmentalist initiatives in parallel with the neoliberal tripod. Their juxtaposition introduced a variant of the SoA (and a new accumulation strategy) that can be called *developmental neoliberalism*.[13] This shift expressed the frustrations of Lula and the PT with the inability of orthodox policies to deliver growth, and the realisation that sluggish economic performance was incompatible with political stability for an administration led by the PT. The policy shift also responded to the imperative to reconstruct the administration's base of support in the wake of the *mensalão*.

Given the favourable global economic environment in the mid-2000s, developmental neoliberalism supported a marked uplift in macroeconomic performance and employment creation, and an unprecedented reduction in poverty and inequality (see below). Lula's popularity reached spectacular heights. He balanced the demands of *prima facie* rival groups through his legendary shrewdness and the allocation of public resources through wages, benefits, state investment and development funds, as well as regulation. Brazil was anointed as one of the BRICS, and Lula became a global statesman. By the end of his second administration, Lula's approval rates touched on 90 per cent, and only 4 per cent of voters considered his administration 'bad' or 'very bad'. Despite these strengths, Lula's popularity was heavily skewed towards the poor, and his government remained isolated from the middle classes and the neoliberal bourgeoisie.[14]

Developmental Neoliberalism in Practice

In the early 2000s, most low- and middle-income countries benefitted from prosperity in the OECD, rapid growth in China, abundant capital flows, and the so-called 'commodity supercycle'. Brazil and other developing countries experienced a relaxation of their balance of payments constraint and a period of global convergence followed (the so-called 'Rise of the South').[15] Domestically, developmental neoliberalism was associated with strongly positive outcomes in terms of GDP growth, investment, SOE and private enterprise growth, poverty reduction and income distribution. The government also promoted the expansion and transnationalisation of selected 'national champions', especially in the Global South. Those firms included Odebrecht (construction), Inbev (beverages), Gerdau (steel), Itaú and Bradesco (banking), Embraer (aviation), Vale (mining) and JBS Friboi (processed foods).[16] Their growth was buttressed by regulatory incentives, preferential contracts and share purchases by state-owned banks and pension funds, diplomatic support and subsidised loans from BNDES, which became the largest development bank in the world, its portfolio far exceeding even the World Bank's.

In 2007, the government launched a Growth Acceleration Programme (*Programa de Aceleração do Crescimento,* PAC), focusing on energy, transport and infrastructure, which had been suffering from underinvestment since the international debt crisis.[17] PAC coordinated public sector outlays with investments by SOEs and private enterprises. It was supplemented by a substantial expansion of credit on the part of state-owned financial institutions, especially BNDES, and tax rebates to selected industries.[18] Regulatory changes allowed public investment to be financed either through taxes or new debt, and the primary fiscal surplus target was redefined to exclude investments by the public sector and the state-owned oil and electricity conglomerates, Petrobras and Eletrobrás.

PAC was followed by a major housing programme ('My Home My Life', or *Minha Casa Minha Vida*, MCMV),[19] increased funding for education, health and other public services, and the expansion of the civil service, together with significant pay increases, in order to recover policy-making capacity and reduce the number of subcontracted workers in the state sector.[20] Several poor countries were offered BNDES loans for infrastructure projects led by Brazilian companies. In doing this, the PT administrations brought the internal bourgeoisie in to the core of the country's foreign policy.[21]

Finally, Brazil pursued an independent diplomacy that would have been unthinkable in the previous decade. Brazil sought to counterbalance US influence in South America and led the effort to derail the US-sponsored Free Trade Area of the Americas, which was supported by the internationalised bourgeoisie and the PSDB. Brazil also shored up the 'Pink Tide' administrations in Argentina, Bolivia, Ecuador, Paraguay and Venezuela, in addition to supporting the governments of Cuba and Nicaragua.[22] In line with this strategy of global projection and support for domestic capital, the country opened 40 new embassies and deftly exploited US difficulties in maintaining hegemony in the wake of the invasion of Iraq and the global crisis starting in 2007. This strategy was aided by Brazil's growing economic power and the country's peaceful image: Brazil has a large and diversified economy, but its armed forces are relatively weak; it has no conflicts with its neighbours; and the Constitution prohibits the assembly or storage of nuclear weapons.

Developmental neoliberalism and the favourable global environment led to a marked uplift in macroeconomic performance. The country's investment rate rose from 15.9 per cent of GDP in 2005 (17.1 per cent in the new data series), to 19.1 (19.4) per cent in 2008, and 19.5 (20.5) per cent in 2010. The expansion of global liquidity and demand supported Brazil's export growth and an increase of inward as well as outward investment flows helped to avoid the threat of a balance-of-payments crisis. In turn, consumption rose because of the rapid increase in the minimum wage[23] and the rise in federal transfers to pensioners, the unemployed and the disabled from R$135 billion (US$50 billion) to R$305 billion (US$113 billion) between 2002 and 2009. Personal credit quadrupled, rising from 24 per cent of GDP to 45 per cent, while mortgage lending expanded from R$26 billion (US$10 billion) in 2004 to R$80 billion (US$30 billion) in 2009.[24]

The strengths of developmental neoliberalism were further demonstrated in the wake of the global economic crisis. Despite the pressure from finance, the mainstream media, neoliberal economists and the opposition parties for a contractionary policy response, the government implemented aggressive countercyclical policies alongside other developing countries, especially China. The Brazilian response included higher expenditures (public sector and Petrobras investment peaked at 2.6 per cent of GDP in 2009, and MCMV reached 1.2 per cent of GDP), and tax rebates worth 0.3 per cent of GDP. The state-owned banks expanded credit to offset the contraction of loans by private institutions (BNDES lending alone expanded by 3.3 per cent of GDP in 2009), while the Central Bank cut interest rates, deployed US$72 billion to provide export credit and stabilise the exchange rate, and injected another 3.3 per cent of GDP into the financial institutions.[25]

Despite these aggressive initiatives, the fiscal deficit remained stable, as the expansion of public sector activity was almost entirely funded by the additional tax revenues and social security contributions resulting from faster GDP growth and the formalisation of the labour market. The primary fiscal surplus fell by only 0.2 per cent of GDP to 2.3 per cent between 2003–5 and 2006–8, and the domestic public debt declined from 55 per cent of GDP in mid-2002 to 40 per cent in 2010. The average rate of growth of real per capita GDP rose from 0.75 per cent per annum in 1995–2002, in the Cardoso administration, to 2.4 per cent in 2003–6, and 3.5 per cent in 2007–10, despite the global crisis. It seemed that the more heterodox the government's policy choices were, the more successful they would be (this correlation would not last; see Chapter 7).

Developmental neoliberalism also contributed to the internalisation of the drivers of growth. Exports had driven growth in 2003–5, but they contributed only 6 per cent of GDP growth between 2006 and 2011 (an average of 0.2 points per year). Their role was dwarfed by private consumption (59 per cent of growth, or 2.6 points per year), private investment (23 per cent, or 1.0 points), and government consumption (12 per cent, or 0.5 points).[26] Even though exports and capital inflows did not influence growth significantly, they helped to alleviate the balance-of-payments constraint. The ratio of Brazil's foreign debt service to exports fell from 127 per cent in 1999 to 73 per cent in 2003 and 19 per cent in 2008. The country's foreign currency reserves rose from US$53 billion in 2003, to US$373 billion in 2011 (see Table 7.1).[27] For the first time in its history, Brazil became a net external creditor.

Distributional Gains

Fiscal activism, booming exports, higher minimum wages and transfers and the expansion of credit and social provision helped to sustain a virtuous circle of growth and distribution supported by domestic investment and mass consumption. Together, they drove an unprecedented reduction in income inequality and an equally unprecedented improvement in the living conditions of the poor.[28]

The PT administrations extended social provision in three ways.[29] First, the minimum wage rose in real terms by 72 per cent between 2005 and 2012, while real GDP per capita increased by 30 per cent. Rising minimum wages lifted the floor of the labour market and triggered simultaneous increases in federal transfers and pensions.

Second, social security coverage increased from 45 per cent of the workforce in 2002, to 51 per cent in 2010, and federal social spending increased 172 per cent in real terms (125 per cent per capita) between 1995 and 2010, rising from 11.0 per cent of GDP to 15.5 per cent (16.2 per cent in 2011).[30] Higher expenditures permitted the expansion of existing programmes, the creation of new ones, such as *Bolsa Família*, which reached 14 million households (50 million people) in 2011, and higher payments (two-thirds of which were fixed at one minimum wage). The number of individual beneficiaries increased from 14.5 million to 24.4 million (by 2012, 77 per cent of citizens above the age of 60 received benefits). However, the informal workers remained largely excluded from social security coverage, including maternity pay, illness cover and pensions in case of retirement, illness or death.[31]

Employment growth in the metropolitan areas alone increased from 150,000 jobs per year under Cardoso to 500,000 per year under Lula. In the 2000s, 21 million jobs were created, in contrast with 11 million during the 1990s. Around 80 per cent of these new jobs were in the formal sector.[32] Significantly, around 90 per cent paid less than 1.5 times the minimum wage (in contrast with 51 per cent in the 1990s) (see Tables 6.1, 6.2 and 6.3).[33] Unemployment fell steadily, especially in the lower segments of the labour market.

Table 6.1 Distribution of the workforce (1940, 1980 and 2000), per cent

	1940	1980	Annual growth rate 1940–80	2000	Annual growth rate 1980–2000
Workforce (%)	100.0	100.0	2.6	100.0	2.9
With paid occupation	93.7	97.2	2.6	85.0	2.2
Of which:					
1. Employer	2.3	3.1	3.3	2.4	1.6
2. Waged	42.0	62.8	3.6	57.2	2.4
(a) Formal	12.1	49.2	6.2	36.3	1.3
(b) Informal	29.9	13.6	0.6	20.9	5.1
3. Own account	29.8	22.1	1.8	19.1	2.1
4. Unpaid	19.6	9.2	0.6	6.3	0.9
5. Unemployed	6.3	2.8	0.5	15.0	11.9
Precarious work*	55.7	34.1	1.1	40.4	3.7

*: Own account + unpaid + unemployed.
Source: Pochmann (2006, p. 126).

Table 6.2 Net new employment creation (thousands)

	1970s	1980s	1990s	2000s
> 5 minimum wages	2,856	5,980	953	−4,279
3–5 minimum wages	3,100	3,377	482	311
1.5–3 minimum wages	5,437	4,084	4,002	6,122
< 1.5 minimum wages	5,892	4,586	−295	19,941
Unwaged	−62	126	5,905	−1,080
Total	17,223	18,153	11,047	21,015

Source: Pochmann (2012, p. 27).

Table 6.3 Distribution of wages, per cent

	1970	1980	1990	2000	2009
> 5 minimum wages	4.7	9.6	14.5	16.7	7.5
3–5 minimum wages	4.3	10.0	11.4	12.0	8.9
1.5–3 minimum wages	13.8	21.1	21.3	25.5	24.9
< 1.5 minimum wages	64.3	51.9	45.3	34.3	47.8
Unwaged	12.8	7.4	7.5	11.5	10.9

Source: Pochmann (2012, p. 28).

After a decade-long period of stagnation, average real wages grew 4.2 per cent per year between 2003 and 2012, and real per capita household incomes grew 4.6 per cent per year. The incomes of the bottom decile rose by 91 per cent between 2001 and 2009, while the incomes of the top decile increased by a more modest 16 per cent.[34] Incomes rose by 42 per cent in the poorer Northeast against 16 per cent in the Southeast; more in the periphery than in the centre of São Paulo, and more in rural than in urban areas. Female income rose by 38 per cent against 16 per cent for men (60 per cent of the jobs created in the 2000s employed women), and the income of blacks rose 43 per cent against 20 per cent for whites.[35]

The country had 60 million poor people in 1993 (41 per cent of the population) and the same number again in 2003 (35 per cent).[36] Poverty fell rapidly, to under 30 million (15 per cent of the population) in 2012.[37] The number of extremely poor individuals touched 29 million in 1993 (19 per cent of the population), and 26 million in 2003 (15 per cent), but fell to under 10 million in 2012 (5 per cent). The proportion of poor households fell from 35 per cent in 1993 to 28 per cent in 2003, and 12 per cent in 2012.[38]

The Gini coefficient of household per capita income fell from around 0.60, between the mid-1970s and 2001, to 0.52 in 2014 (see Figure 1.3), while the income ratio between the top 10 per cent and the bottom 40 per cent fell from 23 to 15.[39] Those improvements were driven primarily by the labour markets: higher labour income (due to labour-market shifts, greater demand for labour and rising minimum wages) was responsible for 65 per cent of the decline of the Gini coefficient between 2001 and 2008, while transfers were responsible for 34 per cent.[40]

Higher wages, social programmes and consumer credit benefitted tens of millions of people. For the first time, many poor people could visit shopping centres, fly across the country and buy a small car. Some of these aspirations deserve critical scrutiny, because they were socially undesirable, environmentally unsustainable, or were not supported by adequate infrastructure.[41] These policies were also often deployed primarily to support large capital rather than to improve the lives of the citizens.[42] However, they reflected the demands and aspirations of tens of millions of people. The result was that Brazilian roads and airports became crowded, and their previous (elite) users, the middle and upper classes, complained about the congestion caused by the influx of 'poorer' groups, who had no business using these facilities.

Despite these important improvements, tax returns data indicate higher levels of inequality than the household surveys, smaller distributional improvements and stability in the top incomes. The combination of tax returns with household surveys suggests that the Gini coefficient of household income per capita remained stable around 0.69 between 2006 and 2012, largely because of the contribution of capital-related income sources (mainly profits and interest) which, in Brazil, are not taxed.[43] In addition, subcontracting continued to increase in the service sector, large private companies and SOEs. Those workers earned 40–60 per cent less than their peers in formal employment, which may help to explain the number of low-paid jobs created in the 2000s, and the slow recovery of the wage share of national income, which rose from only 40 per cent in 2000 to less than 44 per cent in 2009 (below its level under the dictatorship; see Table 1.2).[44]

During the PT administrations, there was redistribution of income through expanded access to public pensions, cash transfers, consumer credit and higher earnings in the labour market, but – in sharp contrast with postwar European social democracy – mass consumption coexisted with the preservation of wealth inequality and a deteriorating pattern of employment. That is, as the incomes of the poorest rose, poverty declined and wages became less unequal; in the meantime, the rich preserved their incomes, and jobs remained precarious and badly paid.

It follows that the social and employment policies under the PT administrations were not transformative: they reduced poverty, but did not support significant improvements in the living conditions of the working class. This is unsurprising, since attempts to distribute income through transfers and poorly-paid precarious jobs, leaving wealth and capital gains untouched, would inevitably be limited. In addition, the middle class was squeezed by the ability of the rich to maintain their position, the improvement in the lot of the poor, and the scarcity of well-paid jobs. This pattern of growth would also inevitably raise costs in the urban services sector, which is labour intensive and where most low-wage employment is concentrated. The ensuing inflationary pressures would inevitably affect the middle class disproportionately, as a net buyer of those services.[45]

This suggests that the drivers of poverty reduction, job creation and income distribution under the PT were intrinsically limited and, in part, perverse. These limitations emerged as the economic boom of the 2000s evaporated because of fiscal, financial, inflation, balance-of-payments and exchange-rate constraints (see Chapters 7–9). As these constraints reduced the government's ability to create jobs and expand social provision, they also undermined its legitimacy.

The Bolsa Família Programme

In April 2003, the Ministry of Finance announced that the new administration would focus on the expansion of targeted rather than universal social programmes. This was a significant policy shift, since the PT had previously rejected targeting. The party used to argue that public services should be available to all, rather than only those whom the state deemed unable to purchase them as commodities; that is, they should be available to 'citizens' rather than 'the poor'.[46]

The most important outcome of the new orientation of social policy was the Family Grant Programme (*Programa Bolsa Família*, PBF), which would become recognised as one of the most successful conditional cash transfer programmes (CCTs) in the world.[47] CCTs are conditional safety nets, comprising small transfers to households that are either extremely poor or highly vulnerable to deprivation, especially those with children. The benefits are often paid to mothers, both to empower women and because their behaviours are, presumably, more closely aligned with the intended use of the funds.

The introduction of conditionalities into social policy derives logically from their application in country-level structural adjustment programmes. At the household level, conditionalities were meant to weed out the 'undeserving poor' and reward behaviours that built 'human capital', promoted economic growth, blocked the inter-generational transmission of poverty and secured taxpayers' support through the reassurance that no one is given too much, for free, or indefinitely. Lack of compliance with the conditionalities would lead to the suspension of benefits, fines and exclusion from the CCT. Within these parameters, CCTs are flexible. Assistance can be provided in the form of cash, food, housing, subsidies, fee waivers, scholarships or employment, and the conditionalities can include school attendance, preventative health care (especially participation in health workshops, vaccinations and regular check-ups for pregnant women and children), and community work, typically cleaning or rubbish clearance.[48]

Despite its low cost, which never exceeded 0.5 per cent of GDP (0.8 per cent of total household income), it has been claimed that PBF accounts for one-third of the decline in extreme poverty, 16 per cent of the decline in poverty, and 16 per cent of the reduction of income inequality between 1999 and 2009.[49] Government studies estimate that PBF raised school attendance by 4.4 percentage points and improved progression by 6.0 percentage points, supported child nutrition and vaccination, and that PBF mothers had more prenatal appointments than non-recipient mothers.[50] Importantly, these transfers did not displace paid work or encourage 'idleness'. Three-quarters of the recipients of income transfers in Brazil are economically active, an almost identical proportion to the wider population. However, unemployment and informal employment are higher than average amongst PBF recipients.[51] They are, literally, the *working poor*.

PBF gained significant support among the poorest, and the votes received by Lula and Rousseff in 2006 and 2010 were strongly correlated with the number of PBF beneficiaries in each municipality (however, this pattern was not reflected in municipal or state elections).[52]

Notwithstanding its positive impact for the destitute, PBF is limited. First, it contravenes the universal principles in the Constitution. Second, despite near-universal agreement that 'trickle down' and targeted social programmes benefit the poor, marginal compensatory policies can be overwhelmed by the contractionary and poverty-generating impact of neoliberal macroeconomic policies. Third, PBF does not address the causes of poverty, which derive from the lack of assets and income opportunities for the poor, because of their concentration elsewhere. The poor also suffer disproportionately from vulnerability due to low pay, precarious employment, lack of land and dependence on fragile ecosystems. Hence, since it bypasses the causes of poverty, social policy under neoliberalism remains a palliative addressing only the most glaring symptoms of poverty; moreover, since it supplements the lowest incomes, PBF ends up subsidising the worst modalities of employment in the country. In this sense, PBF and other CCTs are fundamentally *conservative*.

Regardless of these limitations, PBF implicitly recognises that everyone is entitled to a minimum standard of living guaranteed by the state. This offers an avenue for the improvement of social provision through an increase in the value of benefits, their universalisation and the removal of conditionalities.[53]

Summary and Conclusion

Economic growth during the PT administration was initially driven by exports. The drivers of growth were gradually internalised, as the global commodity boom faltered and the balance of forces shifted towards neodevelopmentalism. During the second Lula administration, the government implemented a developmental variant of neoliberalism driven by public loans, SOE investment, transfers and improvements at the lower end of the labour market, and personal credit. Faster growth raised the demand for low-skilled labour, further lifting incomes through the creation of labour scarcities and the formalisation of labour, and reinforcing the synergies between growth and distribution.[54] High commodity prices and abundant liquidity alleviated the balance of payments constraint, while the appreciation of the *real* reduced inflation. However, private investment failed to pick up, no significant transformations took place in the productive structure, public investment was insufficient to modernise the country's infrastructure, and there was no attempt to tax the highest incomes or address asset inequality.

The chapter also reviewed the social policies implemented by the PT. Neoliberal economic policies created a tendency towards deindustrialisation, high unemployment, the creation of precarious jobs and concentration of income, which eroded the tax base, created needs and imposed tighter budgetary limits on the emerging Brazilian welfare state. The PT discovered that successful transfer programmes require a strong economy, which neoliberalism never delivered. Despite their limitations, Brazil's late welfare state and late social democracy were validated in four consecutive presidential elections. Their advance was blocked by the timidity of the PT, economic mismanagement and, eventually, the coup against President Dilma Rousseff, as is shown in the following chapters.

7

From Glory to Disaster

Overview

Dilma Rousseff became Brazil's first female President in January 2011. There was great optimism in the country after the achievements of Lula's administrations and Brazil's impressive recovery from the first wave of the global economic crisis. The PT was politically strong, and Rousseff's coalition had a commanding position in Congress.

The Rousseff administration was committed to faster growth and income redistribution through the strengthening of neodevelopmentalism; however, there was no suggestion that the neoliberal tripod would be abandoned. Instead, the government introduced a 'new economic matrix' (*Nova Matriz Econômica,* NEM) aiming to support private investment through monetary, exchange-rate and industrial policies. In particular, there was an understanding that the *real* had long been overvalued, with adverse implications for economic growth in general, and manufacturing industry in particular.

In order to address these structural problems, the government aimed to introduce a new set of development policies focusing on infrastructure and basic goods. The goal was to boost productivity, reduce production costs and develop strategic production chains, especially around oil (in the wake of the discovery of vast 'pre-salt' oilfields in the South Atlantic),[1] electricity, transport and housing. The government also wanted interest rates to fall, in order to support production at the expense of financial interests. The outcome was to be a reversal of the country's current-account deficit.[2] None of these ambitious initiatives would be successful, and these policy failures would set the tone for the President's impeachment, in 2016.

Developmental Neoliberalism under Dilma Rousseff

Dilma Rousseff was a revolutionary activist in her youth. She was tortured and imprisoned for three years during the dictatorship.[3] Much later, she rose through the ranks of the state administration in Rio Grande do Sul, initially in the left-leaning Democratic Labour Party (*Partido Democrático Trabalhista*, PDT) and, later, the PT. Rousseff was appointed Lula's Minister of Energy in 2003. Her ministry introduced the 'light for all' programme of connections to the electricity grid, and developed a new regulatory regime for the sector, in order to address the consequences of the reckless privatisations and systematic under-investment under Cardoso, which had forced the country to ration electricity in 2001.

Rousseff was promoted to Chief of Staff when Lula's administration was crippled by the *mensalão* (see Chapter 5). She had a leading role articulating the government's industrial policy and designing the exploration contracts for the newly discovered pre-salt oilfields. These contracts were severely criticised by the media and the political right on several grounds. Allegedly, they unnecessarily vested ownership of the reserves in the state, unduly restricted the operations of the oil majors, needlessly demanded a leading role for Petrobras in all prospecting areas, imposed unmanageable investment commitments on the firm, anachronistically required it to purchase most of its equipment from Brazilian companies, and unreasonably barred exports of crude oil in order to privilege the export of refined products with greater value added.[4]

Rousseff had never been elected to public office until she was chosen by Lula to be his successor.[5] Once anointed by him, she inherited both Lula's voters and his detractors. Unsurprisingly, the voting pattern in 2010 closely mirrored that of the 2006 elections: Rousseff obtained 56 per cent of the vote in the second round, against 44 per cent for José Serra, the PSDB candidate. She won in the poorer states of the North and Northeast and in most of the Southeast, except in São Paulo state. In each state, her vote was concentrated in the poorer areas and among the least educated voters. Her rival won in São Paulo and in the richer states in the 'arch of agribusiness' across the South and Centre-West and, nationally, among higher-income voters and those with more years of formal education.

Rousseff's coalition also won 22 out of 27 state governments, 74 per cent of the Senate and 68 per cent of the Chamber of Deputies. However, these numbers were largely notional, because only one-third of the seats was held by the left parties in the coalition.[6] With 22 ill-tempered and poorly-disciplined parties in Congress, painstaking negotiations were necessary at every juncture.[7]

There is no doubt that Rousseff was the most left-wing President of Brazil since João Goulart. She maintained Lula's core economic team, but replaced the long-standing President of the Central Bank, Henrique Meirelles, with Alexandre Tombini, a career civil servant more closely aligned with Rousseff's priorities. Her government expanded further the federal programmes of social assistance, and identified lagging competitivity as the most important challenge to sustained economic growth in the short term and, at least implicitly, to a future break with neoliberalism.[8]

For the government, three sets of measures were necessary to reduce production costs, raise productivity and promote private investment and credit-based consumption: lower interest rates; the devaluation of the *real*; and the reduction of energy and transport costs. The policies to address these challenges were called a 'new economic matrix'. NEM was so closely aligned with the demands of the internal bourgeoisie that it became known as the 'FIESP agenda', after the economic programme of the country's most powerful business organisation.[9]

Monetary Policy

The Central Bank shifted monetary policy in August 2011, when it started reducing base (SELIC) rates gradually, from 12.4 per cent to 7.16 per cent, in early 2013. At that point, real interest rates touched on 2 per cent, their lowest level since the early 1990s. The monetary policy shift aimed to reduce the inflow of speculative foreign capital, devalue the currency and lower the cost of credit, in order to promote private investment and consumption instead of rewarding speculation. These policies were assisted by the capitalisation of BNDES through the sale of Treasury bills, allowing the bank to expand significantly the supply of subsidised credit to domestic firms.

Simultaneously with the interest rate cuts, the administration and the large SOEs restricted their spending plans and the government imposed limits on loans by the state-owned banks, especially *Banco do Brasil* and *Caixa Econômica Federal*. This was perceived to be important to limit the inflationary impact of the devaluation of the *real*, and to accommodate the anticipated growth in consumption and investment. It was also clear that large capital expected inflation to shoot up because of the devaluation, rapid GDP growth in the previous period and the expansion of BNDES loans. The fiscal and credit restrictions were signals that the government was aware of these inflationary pressures, and that its policies were meant to support private investment, rather than seeking to 'expand' the state or use monetary policy for 'populist' ends.

The monetary policy shift was initially successful. The *real* had been chronically overvalued for several years (see Chapters 3 and 4, and Figure 3.1).[10] That overvaluation had continued during the PT governments, as an inevitable consequence of the neoliberal policy tripod. The average nominal exchange rate rose from R$3.08 per dollar in 2003, to an annual peak of R$1.67 in 2011, even though the rate of inflation in Brazil was much higher than in the USA (which suggests that the *real* should have *fallen* rather than risen relative to the dollar). The rise of the *real* created irresolvable tensions in the Brazilian current account.

The relaxation of monetary policy drove the *real* from R$1.67 per dollar to R$2.25 in 2013.[11] However, it soon became clear that lower interest rates and the devaluation of the currency would not induce a growth cycle driven by private investment, as the government had intended. Instead, GDP growth rates plummeted from 7.5 per cent in 2010, to 2.7 per cent in 2011 (revised data lifted the outturn to 3.8 per cent, but the political damage caused by the slowdown was irreversible).

The government attempted to stimulate private-led growth through more aggressive credit policies. In 2012, the state-owned banks expanded their loans by 20 per cent; BNDES loans grew by 16 per cent in 2012 and 15 per cent in 2013. In order to push for private-sector-driven growth and control the impact of the extra credit on inflation, the government tightened up fiscal policy further, cutting and postponing state expenditures.[12]

Unfortunately for the administration, the net impact of these policies was contractionary; in addition, the devaluation of the *real* was undermined by foreign capital inflows. These inflows were due, first, to FDI attracted by high commodity prices and the continuing prosperity of the Brazilian economy relative to the (stagnant) 'core' OECD countries and, second, to the second round of quantitative easing (QE2) in the USA, UK, Eurozone and Japan, following the Eurozone crisis.[13] As capital poured into the country, the Brazilian balance of payments achieved surpluses of US$49 billion in 2010 and US$59 billion in 2011. These outcomes were largely due to the financial account, which reached surpluses of US$99 billion in 2010 and US$111 billion in 2011. The government responded with marginal controls on capital inflows, but they were too little and came far too late.

The pass-through of the depreciation of the *real* raised the rate of inflation slightly above the Central Bank's target range.[14] In the meantime, and paradoxically, the government's mildly contractionary fiscal policy and the stagnation of private investment reduced GDP growth further, to only 1.9 per cent in 2012 and 3.0 per cent in 2013.[15]

In early 2013, the country was gripped by a finance- and media-driven panic because of the alleged (but wholly unrealistic) threat of runaway inflation because of poor food crops, excess aggregate demand (due to falling interest rates and rising employment and wages, see Chapter 8), and the pass-through from the devaluation.[16] Under intense pressure from finance, the media and the opposition, the Central Bank abandoned its dalliance with heterodoxy. The Central Bank imposed credit restrictions in March, then started jacking up interest rates. This was meant to contain inflation and, more significantly, signal to 'the markets' the enduring primacy of the neoliberal policy tripod.[17] This policy shift was successful in terms of holding back inflation. The rate of inflation between 2011 and 2014 was within the Central Bank's target band; however, in 2015, inflation edged above 10 per cent, driven by the devaluation of the currency. Another bout of monetary policy tightening followed, and the economy contracted further.[18]

The administration reacted badly to the Central Bank policy reversal. It reiterated the government's developmental and social policy goals, expressed concern with the falling rates of GDP growth, and increased fiscal spending across current expenditures, public sector investment and credit provision by the state-owned banks. The disconnect between the Ministry of Finance and the Central Bank triggered a further deterioration of expectations, on top of the existing worry that the global economy was going into a long-term stagnation that would require a contractionary policy response in Brazil. The government disagreed, but capital did not trust President Rousseff's 'interventionism' or Finance Minister Guido Mantega's unreasonable optimism. Moreover, while the government wished to deploy fiscal policy as a counterweight to monetary policy, 'the markets' saw this policy difference as an unpardonable trespass upon the hallowed grounds of monetary policy, and a frightening rupture with the principles of neoliberal policy-making.

The government's economic strategy reached an impasse. It was not just that fiscal and monetary policy were working at cross-purposes. On the one hand, continuing attempts to control inflation through high interest rates and an overvalued exchange rate would worsen the current account deficit and intensify the economic slowdown. On the other hand, trying to control inflation by containing wages, transfers and public investment would stall the improvements in distribution and compromise GDP growth and the sought-after competitivity gains. The government opted, instead, to impose price controls and distribute subsidies, despite their limited effectiveness and high fiscal costs.

Transport, Energy, Tax

Having failed to improve competitivity through fiscal spending or the relaxation of monetary policy, the government shifted its focus to improvements in infrastructure, especially the costs of energy and transport. The initial step was to change the regulatory framework of road transport. Several road concessions would expire in 2012, and new roads were added to the package, but with demanding conditions in terms of payments for the concessions, investments, cheaper tolls and maximum rates of return, to be partly covered by subsidised BNDES loans.

The most important obstacle was the imposition of a maximum rate of return on the concessions. Potential investors challenged the government's attempt to limit profitability, but the administration refused to budge, arguing that this was the only way to ensure that tolls and haulage costs would fall. While the government was convinced of the technical merit of its case, investors refused to comply, for ideological reasons, claiming that the attempt to regulate profits infringed capital's property rights. There were no bids for the roads, and every auction scheduled for 2012 failed.

The government's heavy-handed approach to the road concessions triggered a political rupture with capital, and changed the political mood in the country. The impasse also delayed the improvement of the transport infrastructure, and postponed indefinitely the reduction of road haulage costs. The process would resume only with the Plan of Investment in Logistics (*Plano de Investimento em Logística*, PIL). PIL was launched in 2015, but by then the government was already paralysed and the economy was in freefall; it led nowhere. Regulatory changes to rail and ports also failed to take off. The only policy achievement during this period was the privatisation of several airports through the emergency measures allowed by FIFA football World Cup regulations. Those privatisations had flexible rules, with guaranteed returns for the investors, and no cap on profits.

The third line of attack centred on the electricity sector. In late 2012, the administration claimed that electricity tariffs were unjustifiably high because the government-owned Eletrobrás system, and several state-level electricity generating companies, were charging huge sums for the amortisation of even their oldest dams. These charges kept tariffs high, and served only to beef up the dividends distributed to the firms' minority shareholders, especially large domestic and transnational investment funds.

In order to cut tariffs, support industry, please the voters and score a goal against speculation, the government decided to eliminate those artificial charges. Since it lacked the power to change existing contracts, the administration offered to anticipate the renewal of the concessions to the generating companies, most of which would expire between 2015 and 2017, if they signed new contracts with lower depreciation charges.

The new contracts were submitted to Congress. There, the government had to confront the investment funds lobby, and even a disguised lobby of the (majority state-owned but, in practice, autonomous) electricity companies, seeking smaller tariff cuts. The administration was, again, intransigent. They pushed through a sharp reduction in the amortisations, and extracted from the generating companies an immediate reduction in electricity prices. The tariffs charged by the oldest hydro-electric dams fell from R$80/MWh to R$13/MWh. Residential electricity costs fell 20 per cent, while business costs fell 29 per cent.

After the failure of the monetary policy shift and the fiasco of the road concessions, the reduction in electricity prices was an important achievement for the government. However, this was also Rousseff's final victory in Congress, and the last time the government implemented bold policies with the support of the internal bourgeoisie. The administration's image was permanently tarnished in the eyes of domestic and foreign investors and pension funds because of its 'arbitrariness' and its penchant for 'violating contracts'.[19]

The political cost to the government was both high and irreversible. Capital became convinced that the Rousseff administration was interventionist, 'populist', uncompromising and had an adversarial relationship with business.[20] To make matters worse, the competitivity gain due to the reduction in electricity prices was marginal, especially given the failure of the other government initiatives. These gains were also transitory, because the country suffered one of the worst droughts in recorded history between 2013 and 2015. The reservoirs dwindled and hydroelectric generating capacity fell, often by half, especially in the Southeast. The media brayed that government incompetence was leading the country to a catastrophic blackout.

This was untrue. The deficit in hydroelectric generating capacity was easily covered by gas-fired and nuclear power plants that are normally kept in reserve. However, they operate at much higher costs, forcing the electricity companies to borrow heavily in order to fulfil their contracts. Eventually, the entire sector fell into a deep financial crisis. Rescuing the generating companies required large subsidies and extensive debt guarantees, precisely during the electoral year of 2014. In the meantime, the adverse publicity and the unavoidable electricity price increases after the elections neutralised the government's political gains and increased further the hostility of capital and urban households towards the administration.

As its last option to raise competitivity, the government proposed a tax reform. Politically, this was the most complex initiative the administration could have considered and, by 2013, it far exceeded the government's capacity to deliver. Eventually, the tax reform boiled down to a programme of tax rebates for the export industry. However, the rebates gradually spread into many other industries and even services, as the weakness of the administration reduced its capacity to withhold concessions. Yet, many businesses gaining tax rebates would soon forget the government's generosity and join the effort to overthrow Rousseff (see Chapters 8 and 9).

The tax rebates brought no economic gains.[21] Privileges were granted to all manner of businesses with no conditions governing terms of exports, investment, output or employment. Lack of control made it impossible to evaluate the programme, and the tax rebates were merely incorporated into profits. The economic slowdown and the waste of tax revenues were the main reasons for the fiscal deterioration during Rousseff's administration.[22] The cost of federal subsidies rose from 0.2 per cent of GDP in 2012 to 0.5 per cent in 2015; during the same period, public sector investment fell by 0.5 per cent of GDP. Since the multiplier effect of public investment is much higher than the expansionary impact of the subsidies (that is, GDP responds much more strongly to government investment than to subsidies to private capital), the net effect of the government's policies was – once again – contractionary.[23]

In summary, the Rousseff administration tried to catalyse a new cycle of growth driven by private investment that never materialised.

Instead, rising interest rates, the revaluation of the *real* and the economic contraction generated heavy losses for manufacturing industry, and pushed almost the entire business sector into supporting the opposition.

The External Sector

The policy failures described in the previous section compounded the adverse implications of deindustrialisation, ongoing since the 1980s (see Chapter 4).[24] Deindustrialisation was both caused *and* intensified by the transition to neoliberalism, the restructuring of the manufacturing sector, the policy tripod and the overvaluation of the *real*, all of which had severe consequences for competitivity and the balance of payments (see Figure 3.1). The process of deindustrialisation intensified during the global commodity boom, both because it shifted Brazil's competitive advantages strongly towards unprocessed commodities, and because the ensuing inflows of foreign exchange held the *real* at a level wholly incompatible with the prosperity of the manufacturing sector.[25]

The global environment turned strongly against Brazil in 2008, even if the consequences would be felt only much later. In contrast with the contractionary bias of the policies implemented in 'austerity-driven' advanced economies, many middle-income countries confronted the global crisis with expansionary policies; in many cases, they were successful.[26] However, the persistent growth slowdown in Brazil's largest markets (China, the USA and the EU) had negative implications for the country's exports. Even worse, several large economies engaged in export-led recovery strategies backed up by aggressive devaluations (Germany and Japan in particular).

Brazil and China were among the few countries where the consumption of manufactured goods increased after the global crisis. However, in contrast with China, Brazil was not competitive in manufactures, and its industry was unable to stem the flood of imports that followed the country's attempt to grow faster than the world average. Instead of developing new competitive advantages under neoliberalism, Brazilian manufacturing industry became, effectively, a *maquiladora* for the domestic market, importing machines, inputs, parts and components (especially the electric, electronic, auto, pharmaceutical and chemical industries) to produce for the home markets.[27]

It has already been noted that Brazil's imports have much higher income elasticity than its exports. The consequence is that, given the economic structure built under neoliberalism, Brazil *must choose* between permanently slow growth rates, *or* finding ways to finance a spiralling deficit in manufactured goods imports. In either case, domestic industry is damaged; with neoliberalism, the Brazilian manufacturing base is always under pressure, *and* the economy is unable to grow rapidly enough to generate jobs and income for the country's population.

Brazil's trade and current account balances peaked in 2005–6, with commodity-boom-induced surpluses around US$45 billion and US$14 billion, respectively (see Table 7.1). Then they started to deteriorate. The balance of trade in goods remained in surplus until 2013, but exports started declining in 2011, while imports rose from US$48 billion in 2003, to US$91 billion in 2006, US$226 billion in 2011 and US$239 billion in 2013. The trade deficit in manufactured goods rose uncontrollably as Brazilian growth and the overvaluation of the *real* sucked in foreign consumer goods, machines, services and inputs.

Brazil's current account turned negative in 2008. The deficit reached 2.1 per cent of GDP in 2011, and 4.3 per cent of GDP in 2014.[28] Despite this gaping hole, the country was not threatened by a currency crisis, because large inflows of foreign currency (see Table 7.1) supported the balance of payments – but they also kept the *real* misaligned. As a result, Brazil's currency reserves kept climbing even when the economy was performing poorly and the manufacturing sector was in decline.[29] Private capital was fully aware of these dangerous developments; as expectations worsened, the calls for a contractionary policy response intensified.[30]

The Wheels Fall Off

Dilma Rousseff was re-elected in 2014 with a reduced but convincing majority of 52 per cent against 48 per cent for the PSDB candidate, Senator Aécio Neves (a difference of 3.5 million votes). Rousseff's triumph was fragile for two reasons. First, it coincided with a rapid deterioration of the economy. GDP growth rates had been falling since 2010, turned negative in 2014, and continued to fall as the Brazilian economy plunged into its worst-ever crisis (see Figure 7.1). The distributional improvements that had legitimised the PT administrations stagnated. Repeated policy failures, the media onslaught, the persecution of the PT through the *lava jato* corruption scandal (see Chapter 9), and the decomposition of the government's political base in the most right-wing Congress in decades triggered a generalised dissatisfaction focusing

Table 7.1 Balance of payments, 1999–2016 (US$ million)

	1999	2000	2001	2002	2003	2004	2005	2006	2007
CURRENT ACCOUNT	-25,335	-24,225	-23,215	-7,637	4,177	11,679	13,985	13,643	1,551
Trade Balance (Goods)	-1,199	-698	2,650	13,121	24,794	33,641	44,703	46,457	40,032
Exports	48,011	55,086	58,223	60,362	73,084	96,475	118,308	137,807	160,649
Imports	-49,210	-55,783	-55,572	-47,240	-48,290	-62,835	-73,606	-91,351	-120,617
Services and Income	-25,825	-25,048	-27,503	-23,148	-23,483	-25,198	-34,276	-37,120	-42,510
Services	-6,977	-7,162	-7,759	-4,957	-4,931	-4,678	-8,309	-9,640	-13,219
Income	-18,848	-17,886	-19,743	-18,191	-18,552	-20,520	-25,967	-27,480	-29,291
Profits and dividends	-2,832	-2,173	-3,438	-4,034	-4,076	-4,937	-9,142	-11,445	-16,745
Portfolio investment income	-7,710	-8,545	-9,621	-8,384	-8,743	-8,743	-8,743	-8,743	-8,743
FINANCIAL ACCOUNT	16,981	19,053	27,088	7,571	4,613	-7,895	-10,127	16,152	88,330
Foreign investment	32,121	41,430	23,329	11,793	15,272	14,150	21,722	27,898	82,689
Portfolio	3,542	8,651	872	-4,797	5,129	-3,996	6,655	9,076	48,104
FDI	28,578	32,779	22,457	16,590	10,144	18,146	15,066	18,822	34,585
RESULT	-7,822	-2,262	3,307	302	8,496	2,244	4,319	30,569	87,484
Memo: International Reserves	33,011	35,866	37,823	49,296	52,935	53,799	85,839	180,334	193,783

	2008	2009	2010	2011	2012	2013	2014	2015	2016
CURRENT ACCOUNT	-28,192	-24,302	-47,273	-52,473	-54,249	-81,227	-91,288	-58,882	-23,530
Trade Balance (Goods)	24,836	25,290	20,147	29,793	19,395	2,286	-3,959	17,670	45,037
Exports	197,942	152,995	201,915	256,040	242,578	242,034	225,101	190,092	184,453
Imports	-173,107	-127,705	-181,768	-226,247	-223,183	-239,748	-229,060	-172,422	139,416
Services and Income	-57,252	-52,930	-70,322	-85,251	-76,489	-86,879	-89,251	-89,251	-71,527
Services	-16,690	-19,245	-30,835	-37,932	-41,042	-47,101	-48,928	-36,919	-30,447
Income	-40,562	-33,684	-39,486	-47,319	-35,448	-39,778	-40,323	-21,941	-41,080
Profits and dividends	-25,348	-17,765	-23,591	-27,379	-17,183	-19,251	-19,840	-20,799	-19,433
Portfolio investment income	-8,743	-8,743	-8,743	-8,743	-8,743	-8,743	-11,102	-1,142	30,257
FINANCIAL ACCOUNT	28,302	70,172	98,793	110,808	71,886	73,159	97,809	-54,734	-16,394
Foreign investment	44,291	72,107	116,301	85,113	81,806	98,660	96,026	79,500	58,367
Portfolio	-767	46,159	67,795	18,453	16,534	34,664	33,531	67,900	-19,815
FDI	45,058	25,949	48,506	66,660	65,272	63,996	62,495	11,600	78,182
RESULT	2,969	46,651	49,101	58,637	18,900	-5,926	10,833	3,600	-32,788
Memo: International Reserves	238,520	288,575	352,012	373,147	358,808	363,551	356,464	356,464	365,016

Source: Ipeadata.

largely on the state.[31] This was followed by escalating demands from all sides of the political spectrum, symbolised by the transport crisis, in 2013, and the scarcity of water and electricity in the Centre-South, in 2014–15. The fulcrum of both crises was in São Paulo, the country's economic powerhouse, bedrock of the right wing, and birthplace of the PT (see Chapter 2).

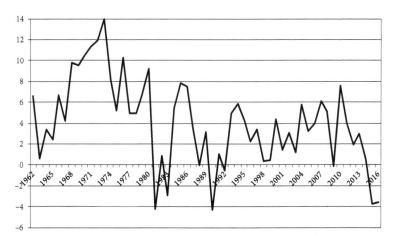

Figure 7.1   Real GDP growth rate, 1962–2015 (per cent per annum)

Source: Ipeadata.

Second, Rousseff's campaign in 2014 had an unprecedented left-wing flavour. While she had been elected originally by the alliance of winners built by Lula, Rousseff was re-elected by a much narrower *progressive alliance*, including organised workers, the unorganised poor and left parties, movements and NGOs. During the campaign, the PT claimed that the PSDB would impose harsh neoliberal economic policies, overturn labour rights and reverse the social and economic achievements of the PT administrations. In contrast, Rousseff promised faster growth and continuing improvements in wages, benefits, employment and social rights. The radical tone of her campaign alienated the bourgeoisie and the middle class almost entirely. The campaign also created misplaced expectations among Rousseff's supporters, since it suggested that the election posed a clear choice between right and left, and her government was firmly committed to the workers and the poor. Confusingly, immediately after her victory, she appointed banker Joaquim Levy to the

Ministry of Finance. Levy was overtly chosen by the CEO of Bradesco, one of Brazil's largest financial conglomerates. This choice shows that Rousseff recognised the need to find an accommodation with finance and the neoliberal camp; however, her supporters were stunned by this policy U-turn (see Chapter 9).[32]

The PSDB sensed an opportunity. The party was bitterly disappointed by its fourth consecutive defeat in the presidential elections, and the losing candidate immediately appealed to the Supreme Electoral Court. Even if Aécio's howls of protest were groundless,[33] they raised the political temperature another notch.

In the first weeks of her second administration, Rousseff faced converging crises that would lead to the collapse of both axes of the rule of the PT: the developmental variant of neoliberalism, and the political alliances supporting the administration. Joaquim Levy was given the impossible task of stabilising the economy and building bridges with capital through the implementation of an orthodox adjustment policy. He was also ordered to protect social rights, entitlements and programmes, even if they could no longer be funded, given the falling fiscal revenues because of the economic downturn and the government's expansive tax rebates. As the mainstream media stepped up their attacks, the government found itself unable to garner the support of any major constituency.

The political crisis escalated. Every government initiative was blocked in Congress. Each concession was met with passive resistance from a disgruntled left and intensifying opposition from an agitated right. The media ratcheted up the pressure, and started speculating about an economic disaster. By mid-2014, political pragmatism and attempts to do 'deals' with the opposition had become counter-productive. The government lost allies with each round of cuts and with every short-termist concession to either side.[34] The country was confronted by a perfect storm. The accumulation strategy was paralysed, the economy was imploding, national politics faced an impasse and seemingly Biblical plagues arrived with the Zika virus, chikungunya, dengue fever and H1N1. Then the judiciary and the Federal Police tightened the screws on the PT. Another massive corruption scandal, long lurking in the background, captured the headlines and provided a focus for the opposition. The progressive alliance crumbled and, with it, the political hegemony of the PT. Dilma Rousseff was doomed (see Chapter 9).[35]

Developmental Neoliberalism: A Reckoning

Global conditions were exceptionally supportive of economic development in the early 2000s, because of the combined effect of the 'great moderation' in the USA, relative prosperity in the EU and rapid growth in China. Most low- and middle-income economies benefitted from high export prices due to the so-called 'commodity supercycle' and abundant inflows of capital.[36] During that period, Brazil experienced a growth surge that can be divided into two phases (see Chapter 9). The initial uptick was driven by the devaluation of the *real*, in 1999, the global economic boom in the early 2000s and the expansion of Chinese demand for primary commodities. These factors contributed to a significant increase in Brazil's trade earnings, as the volume of exports increased by 64 per cent and prices by 24 per cent between 2001 and 2005. Export growth explains 44 per cent of the expansion of aggregate demand between 2003 and 2005. This was the main reason why GDP growth rose from 1.1 per cent in 2003 to 5.8 per cent in 2004.[37]

The tax revenues due to export-led growth allowed the Lula administration to expand its transfer programmes and start raising the minimum wage, setting off a cycle of inclusive growth. In the meantime, the global boom also brought to Brazil steeply rising FDI and portfolio capital flows: they reached US$15 billion in 2003 and 2004, and climbed to US$116 billion in 2010. They remained around US$80 billion per year until 2015, falling under US$60 billion in 2016 (see Table 7.1). These favourable conditions facilitated the implementation of selected neodevelopmentalist policies in Lula's second administration and in Rousseff's first years in office.

The expansion of exports faltered after the global crisis. Brazilian GDP growth became increasingly dependent on personal and BNDES credit, and on public policies lifting the lowest incomes (the growth impact of private investment was always secondary).[38] In the meantime, faster GDP growth increased the demand for low-skilled labour, further lifting incomes because of the creation of labour scarcities; this outcome was reinforced by the government's push to formalise employment. The links between growth and distribution strengthened at every step. In turn, high commodity prices and abundant international liquidity alleviated the balance-of-payments constraint, while the appreciation of the *real* kept a lid on inflation.

In summary, the Lula administration delivered growth and distribution through a limited set of non-confrontational policies that could be sustained by market processes, as long as they were supported by public policy, favourable external conditions and Lula's legendary ability to bridge differences and find points of agreement between conflicting agendas.[39] Those hybrid neoliberal-neodevelopmental policies supported an unprecedented virtuous cycle of growth, including high profits, large-scale job creation, income distribution, social inclusion and political stability, with significant gains at both ends of the income distribution chain.[40] Yet, there were few changes in the productive structure, and no internalisation of sustainable drivers of growth (see Chapter 6). Developmental neoliberalism was also limited by the PT's commitment to the 'rules of the game', that is, the preservation of the (highly unequal) distribution of assets, the country's inordinately regressive tax structure and the macroeconomic policy tripod. The PT governments also avoided extra-institutional mobilisations, ideological confrontation or appeals to class-based politics. These political decisions helped to secure the government's credibility with capital, but they reduced the scope for developmental initiatives and left just enough space to redistribute income flows at the margin – as long as the other permissive conditions remained in place.

The PT's strategy of flexibilisation of neoliberalism in order to build a neodevelopmentalist SoA incrementally was unsustainable, for six reasons.

First, the contractionary impact of the neoliberal tripod, high fiscal surpluses and the overvaluation of the *real* locked the country into a vicious circle of deindustrialisation, reprimarisation and financialisation, and made macroeconomic performance overly dependent on exports of primary products. Neoliberalism created undesirable patterns of employment, rendered intractable the productivity gap with the OECD and limited state capacity to improve infrastructure, especially in urban areas, where transformative projects have high costs, long lags, complex environmental implications and uncertain political rewards. In the meantime, faster economic growth with low public investment overwhelmed the electricity, water and sanitation systems, leading to power cuts and disasters in the rainy season. Marginal income distribution, consumer credit and poor public transport triggered an explosive growth in automobile sales,[41] but insufficient investment in infrastructure led to traffic gridlock. Public health and education expanded, but they were widely perceived to offer poor-quality services. There was no progress on land reform, condemning millions to a life of marginality while agribusiness boomed under the umbrella of the Workers' Party.

Second, the hybrid SoA since the late 2000s would inevitably lead to a rising current-account imbalance and mounting pressure on the fiscal budget, because of the combined costs of the DPD, the sterilisation of currency inflows,[42] public investment, subsidised BNDES loans and income transfers. Any economic slowdown would make it impossible for the PT to sustain its signature policies, reconcile conflicting interests through public expenditure and maintain distribution through the creation of low-paid jobs and transfers.[43]

Third, the Brazilian experience shows that marginal changes in the neoliberal SoA *can* be driven by technocratic means, supported by negotiations with unreliable partners. However, these incremental reforms tend to stall. Further progress transcending neoliberalism would require the transformation of the field of politics, including reforms of the electoral system, party-political funding, land tenure, the media, justice and the tax system and the abandonment of the neoliberal policy tripod. These transformative shifts in the system of accumulation were unachievable without mass pressure.

Fourth, and perhaps surprisingly, the PT became the best-funded political party in the country as it managed to run neoliberalism efficiently, according to the interests of the internal bourgeoisie (see Chapter 8).[44] However, this was a short-lived privilege, as it would inevitably corrupt the party and turn its most influential members into retainers of powerful interests (see Chapter 9). Instead of striving to transcend conventional politics in order to deliver its original programme, the PT chose to play by the rules of a dysfunctional political system. Since the interests of the groups that the PT decided to please converged only conditionally, political stability required the party to deliver gains to almost everyone while, at the same time, keeping an extra-parliamentary base strong enough to amplify its influence in Congress. The PT could fulfil these conditions only in times of economic prosperity.

Fifth, the model of growth and distribution under the PT implied that the middle class would be squeezed by the preservation of the privileges of the rich, the improvement of the conditions of the poor, and the deteriorating quality and rising costs of urban services. The erosion in the relative position of the middle class could be compensated only temporarily, through the accumulation of personal debt and the appreciation of the currency (see Chapter 8).

Sixth, economic prosperity and the greater legitimacy of the state that accompanied Lula's election disarmed the political right, disconnected the radical left from the working class, and secured unprecedented political stability in the country. Since the PT avoided challenging the hegemony of neoliberalism, the party could become politically dominant without great turbulence.[45] However, the prominence of the PT and the viability of its administrations remained dependent on unstable alliances with right-wing parties and shady individuals. These 'allies' would, inevitably, seek to protect reactionary interests, limit the scope for reforms, undermine the PT's claim to the moral high ground and split the party from its mass base. To the organised workers and the youth, the PT seemed to have political hegemony without the substance of power, and to engage in the same dirty political games as everyone else. Yet, the PT would never be able to rely on its opportunistic political allies in times of trouble. The widening gulf between the party leadership, its militants, workers and the youth left the PT unable to withstand the onslaught.

In power, the PT was also riven by contradictions.[46] The party defended economic stability and structural reforms, supported large capital while postulating a socialist future and propounded a new political culture, while at the same it forged alliances with unsavoury characters. Beyond its inability to choose a programme that it could actually defend, the PT neglected its most committed supporters and shied away from reforming the mainstream media even though that media overtly sought to destroy the PT, jail its leaders and cripple its administrations.[47]

This was not simply motivated by a rejection of the left; it was also personal. Despite his party's moderation, commitment to neoliberalism and achievements in office, Lula was never fully accepted by the internationalised bourgeoisie, and he became anathema to most of the middle class. His humble origins, lack of formal education, ungrammatical Portuguese, missing finger (lost in a workplace accident) and militant trajectory were mocked and vilified. The bile was driven not just by narrow economic concerns, but also by bourgeois prejudice (and, in the case of the middle class, the perception of relative as well as absolute losses; see Chapter 8). Lula insisted, probably rightly, that:

[the elite] never made so much money in their whole lives as they did in my government. Not the TV networks, that were all bankrupt;

the newspapers [were] almost all broke when I became President. The firms and banks also never made so much money, but the workers also gained.[48]

It was worse for Dilma Rousseff. She was attacked for being an unmarried woman with a radical past, and accused of being shrill, authoritarian, unable to listen and a lesbian. The media measured the Lula and Rousseff administrations against very different standards to those applied to mainstream politicians, and highlighted any shortcomings without regard to proportion or consequence. When their personal or political limitations were insufficient, convenient faults were invented. These tensions exploded in 2013, and the ensuing catastrophe led to the collapse of Rousseff's government three years later (see Chapters 8 and 9).

Summary and Conclusion

This chapter followed the rise and fall of the administration led by Dilma Rousseff. Her government sought an incremental break with neoliberalism in order to address a key challenge to development and one of the most damaging consequences of the neoliberal transition: the loss of competitivity in manufacturing and services. The government's goal was to reform neoliberalism gradually and, perhaps, introduce a new SoA inspired by neodevelopmentalism and driven by domestic investment. This would start with the adoption of a new economic matrix (the 'FIESP agenda').

Even though this accumulation strategy expressed the demands of important fractions of capital and the expectations of large sections of the working class, it did not support consistent economic policies, especially as the Brazilian economy was battered by the adverse winds of the global economic slowdown. Private capital systematically failed to respond to a plethora of incentives and subsidies provided without conditions in terms of investment, exports, employment or performance. At the same time, the contractionary impact of the government's fiscal and monetary policies contributed to a slowdown that reduced the tax intake and social security revenues, and created a fiscal crisis.

Rousseff's difficulties were compounded by the government's limitations in Congress, where the left never controlled more than one-third of the seats. This made it impossible for the PT to govern without alliances with undisciplined right-wing parties and questionable individuals, who had to be managed under the gaze of a hostile press and the aggressive scrutiny of a judicial system openly aligned with the political right. The administration's stubbornness and inability to find points of agreement with capital and the moderate opposition (while it existed) contributed to the fragmentation of its political base. These difficulties coincided with the growing incoherence of the government's policies, starting with the widening gulf between monetary and fiscal policy, followed by incongruous fiscal, tax, public investment, labour-market and transfer policies.

As the economy slowed down, capital joined an investment strike, and the government shifted frantically towards neoliberal orthodoxy, trying to accommodate an increasingly hostile bourgeoisie. However, neoliberal contractionary policies stalled demand, employment and distribution, plunging the economy into a depression and eroding the PT's support among the workers and the poor. *The win-win 'class conciliation' scenario of the 2000s turned into its opposite.* Under adverse economic and political circumstances, pragmatism fed economic decline and left the government fatally isolated. Policy incoherence and the deterioration of the macroeconomic indicators reinforced capital's conviction that the government was both unreliable and untrustworthy, feeding their drift into the opposition. In turn, the opposition became increasingly bold as it profited from the aggressive corruption investigations of a runaway judicial system. This avalanche culminated in the President's impeachment on a flimsy pretext.

8

Class and Class Politics in Brazilian Neoliberalism

Overview

The economic, political and distributional shifts associated with the transitions to democracy and to neoliberalism have realigned Brazil's class structure.[1] In broad strokes, the country's class structure includes the élite (the bourgeoisie and the traditional middle class) and the broad working class (the formal and informal proletariat, which, in turn, comprises the semi-proletariat and the lumpen-proletariat, not detailed in what follows).[2] As a rough approximation, the 2010 Census suggests that less than 1 per cent of a population of 200 million are part of the bourgeoisie; 16 per cent are in the middle class; a little over 70 per cent are formal and informal workers; and 11 per cent are in the semi- and lumpen-proletariat.[3]

This chapter describes the Brazilian class structure and examines how it has changed in recent decades. These insights inform a class interpretation of the protests against the Rousseff administration, in 2013, and the disintegration of her administration. These were the largest mass demonstrations in Brazil since the campaign for democracy and the downfall of President Collor. The demonstrations had a shifting class character and strong political implications: for example, they broke the alliance of winners that had re-elected Lula and elected Dilma Rousseff.

The protests against the PT are significant for another reason: they are symptomatic of the forms of political contestation under neoliberalism. Class analysis can offer a rich vantage point for the examination of the relations between social structure, the expression of class interests and political protest in neoliberal societies. The concept of 'lumpenisation of politics' is introduced, in order to underpin the interpretation of the emerging forms of contestation in Brazil and elsewhere.

The Bourgeoisie

The bourgeoisie, or class of capitalists, owns the means of production, including productive and interest-bearing capital, the bulk of the titles of ownership to fictitious capital, large-scale commercial capital and large landed property. This class directly or indirectly employs the wage-workers, controls the allocation and performance of labour and the level and composition of output and investment, and claims the surplus value produced. The Brazilian bourgeoisie includes two fractions, distinguished by their relationship with the process of accumulation and, specifically, with neoliberalism, international capital and financialisation.

The internationalised bourgeoisie includes the owners of financial capital (banks, insurance companies, large consultancy and accountancy firms), transnational and internationally-integrated manufacturing and the mainstream media (which, legally, must be controlled by domestic capital). Ideologically, the internationalised bourgeoisie is closely aligned with transnational capital and globalised finance. They reject 'national' accumulation strategies and support, instead, the financialisation and international integration of the economy.[4] This project is anchored by the neoliberal policy tripod, privatisations and market liberalisation, the minimisation of state capacity to allocate resources and steer development, and the rejection of state-led distribution. This fraction tends to support the PSDB and its allies,[5] and it was politically dominant during the administrations of Fernando Collor and Fernando Henrique Cardoso (and, after Rousseff's impeachment, Michel Temer's).

The internal bourgeoisie includes the leading capitalists in construction, agribusiness, food-processing and other domestically-owned conglomerates, and some banks. This fraction has a contradictory relationship with neoliberalism and state policy. For ideological reasons, it demands 'fiscal rectitude', a large role for the private sector and neoliberal labour-market and social policies; for similar reasons, it was sceptical about the expansion of the civil service during the Lula administration. Yet, the internal bourgeoisie recognises that government intervention, skeletal social protection and rising minimum wages can enlarge the domestic market and support social cohesion and political stability (see Chapter 6). At the policy level, the internal bourgeoisie rejects the wholesale liberalisation of trade and capital flows because they threaten its competitive position. This fraction wishes to compete globally, especially in the South, which can only be done with state support.

Consequently, it pleads for low real interest rates, state investment in infrastructure and research and development, diplomatic assistance, subsidised BNDES loans, preferential rules for state procurement and restrictions against foreign capital. The internal bourgeoisie supported the neoliberal reforms introduced by Fernando Collor only reluctantly, and joined the mobilisation for his removal in 1992 (see Chapter 1). It opposed the neoliberal programme of the Cardoso administration and, mostly, supported Lula in 2002. It led his defence during the *mensalão*, and was committed to developmental neoliberalism until around 2013 (see Chapters 7 and 9).[6]

There is no neat or *a priori* separation between the two main fractions of the bourgeoisie and between them and the small and medium-sized capitalists, who may belong to production chains dominated by either fraction. For example, the automobile dealerships are dominated by medium-sized domestic capital that is obviously dependent on the transnational automakers; while the latter have a surprising degree of autonomy vis-à-vis their head offices, the dealers are also closely connected to parts manufacturers, banks and insurance companies dominated by Brazilian capital. In turn, the domestic banks generally concur with their foreign counterparts on the need for inflation targeting and Central Bank independence, but they have an economic interest in neodevelopmentalist policies supporting investment and consumption. The transnational manufacturers dominating the consumer durables sector are also close to the Brazilian producers of capital goods, despite tensions concerning the role of the domestic market, fiscal, monetary exchange-rate policy, capital controls and so on.

The tensions between the two fractions of the bourgeoisie during the Real plan expanded the political space for the PT enormously, just as its traditional base in the industrial working class, the civil service and formal service-sector workers had been eroded by neoliberalism.[7] In this sense, the PT's developmental neoliberalism brought together the interests of the broad working class with those of the internal bourgeoisie, under the hegemony of the latter.

The Formal Working Class

The formal working class does not own the main productive and financial assets, and does not control the process of labour or the conditions of work. This class reproduces itself primarily through the regular sale of labour power for a wage, whatever the structure of the labour markets, the content of the labour performed and the use value of the product, and whether or not their work is directly productive of surplus value.[8] Wage employment is the main source of household income for the working class, the typical form of provision of labour to firms and governments, and the most important structure of exploitation and reproduction of inequality.

The transition to neoliberalism increased significantly the heterogeneity of the Brazilian working class. While the working class created under ISI was based around a fast-expanding manufacturing sector, today's workers have a much more diversified employment pattern centred in urban services. The contemporary working class also includes a large proportion of young, low-paid, poorly-educated, badly-trained subcontracted workers, who have difficulty accessing stable and well-paid jobs, because there are fewer jobs available, and because these workers are ill-prepared to apply for the posts available.[9] Even when they are employed in the formal sector, today's workers have less job security than their predecessors did in the 1970s,[10] but they can draw state benefits that were unavailable to the 'old' working class during ISI.

In the absence of any prospect of socialist transformation (see Chapter 2), the formal and informal (broad) working class share an interest in policies supporting the reduction of poverty and inequality. They also share with the internal bourgeoisie an interest in expansionary macroeconomic policies and domestically-centred capital accumulation. Given the economic interests of the broad working class, these policies should be supported, first, by the expansion of employment, wage growth, the formalisation and regulation of the labour markets, improvements in working conditions and the limitation of working hours. Second, the implementation of the social rights in the Constitution, especially the public provision of health, education, transport, housing, sanitation and security, and the expansion of income transfer programmes. Evidently, these goals are incompatible with the project of the internationalised bourgeoisie, for whom 'social cohesion' and the construction of a diversified, integrated and technologically advanced economy with a strong manufacturing sector would be either superfluous or undesirable.

There is, however, a significant divide concerning the sources of funding for a distributive economic strategy. The broad working class would benefit from a more progressive tax system, including a wealth tax, steep capital gains taxes and higher property taxes, while the élite objects to any additional taxation. This contradiction can be bypassed, at least in part, if Brazil's natural resource rents are used to fund infrastructure provision and the expansion of the domestic market. At a further remove, since the formal working class is not limited by the contradictions in the internal bourgeoisie and the middle class, or the dispersion of the informal proletariat, it could become the most dependable source of support for a more democratic SoA. This would be very different from the experience during the Lula and Rousseff administrations, whose neodevelopmentalist ambitions were led by the internal bourgeoisie.

The political project of the working class can be limited internally at two levels. First, although the working class as a whole would benefit from a distributive strategy of development, its most organised and relatively better-off segments (São Paulo metalworkers, employees in the oil and bank sectors, middle-level civil servants) can always bet that 'market-led' industrial relations might benefit them at the expense of weaker categories and the informal proletariat (see Chapter 2).[11]

Second, difficulties of a different order concern the inexperience of the 'new' working class in social struggles, given the long interval since the previous peak in mobilisations, between the mid-1970s and the late 1980s. Trade union activity declined sharply under neoliberalism, measured by the number of strikes, the fragmentation of collective bargaining and the decline in trade union-led agreements.[12] There were around 2,200 strikes per year in Brazil in the second half of the 1980s, falling to fewer than 1,000 between 1991 and 1997 and declining still further to 300 between 2004 and 2007. Then numbers started climbing again, to reach 900 in 2012, and over 2,000 in 2013. In this latest period, the number of strikers fluctuated between 1.2 million and 2 million per year, with a rising trend. Strikes under developmental neoliberalism tended to take an 'offensive' character, leading to gains in real wages and working conditions. They also tended to involve a growing proportion of private-sector workers, and were centred on 'traditional' sectors (metal-mechanic, oil, construction, banks, education, health and the civil service), where pay and working conditions were already better, the workers more experienced and the trade unions stronger.[13]

Despite the recovery of some traditions of struggle, this is a very different working class from that which led the previous cycle of mobilisations. This class is more atomised and relatively inexperienced in collective action, and most young workers have grown up under a heavily anti-state, anti-political and anti-collective action discourse propagated by the neoliberal media. Consequently, their aspirations are more strongly influenced by individualism and consumerism than was the case in the past.

There is also no evidence that the 'new' working class has found either the interest or the strength to organise through radical left parties, or identified alternative forms of representation and channels of mobilisation supporting social transformation.[14] The task of finding mechanisms of representation supporting a radical project is further complicated by these workers' attachment to digital communication. Hence, the 'new' working class is, largely, paralysed by the social, technical and cultural divisions imposed by neoliberal capitalism.

The Informal Working Class

The informal proletariat is highly heterogeneous. They are not routinely hired in structured labour markets, and may own or control unsophisticated tools, small plots of land or a few animals used to produce non-standardised commodities. They can be informal (irregular and unskilled) workers, domestic servants, unregistered street sellers, prostitutes, vagrants and criminals. Their survival strategies are normally based on occasional wage work (either irregular productive labour or work paid out of revenue rather than variable capital), informal exchanges, opportunistic engagement with the surrounding economy and reliance on transfers, which may be legal (state benefits or remittances from relatives or friends), voluntary (charity) or involuntary (crime).

The dividing line between the informal proletariat and the formal working class has become increasingly permeable in 'liberalised' labour markets. One or two generations ago, the informal proletariat was, generally, the provider of ancillary goods and services for capital, the condition of a relatively stable lumpen-proletariat, or a holding station for aspiring formal-sector workers arriving from the countryside or going through hard times.[15] The pattern of accumulation under neoliberalism has fused the informal proletariat with the margins of the formal working class.[16] Millions of semi- and lumpen-proletarians offer capital a readily available reserve of labour, which may be mobilised either directly, through the payment of wages or, in disguised form, as 'independent' micro-entrepreneurs (handymen, hairdressers, drivers, door-to-door retailers, home-based food-producers, street-sellers and so on). The strong performance of the Brazilian economy in the 2000s led to the absorption of many informal workers into the formal labour market, but this has not changed their marginal position, where they would be deposited again when accumulation slowed down.

The historical ambition of the informal proletariat is its own extinction, either through absorption into the working class via formal employment, or into the middle class through entrepreneurship. Their heterogeneity, precarious economic position and self-destructive aspirations suggest that the informal proletariat cannot normally articulate an alternative mode of social organisation, and will rarely develop stable political alliances.[17]

The informal proletariat has strong reasons to support the distribution of income and assets (especially land), the social provision of basic goods and services and government income transfer programmes, making it a natural ally of the working class around a democratic strategy of development.[18] In turn, the working class has a vital interest in the improvement of the lot of the informal proletariat. This is not only out of solidarity but, also, to prevent employers from undercutting everyone's pay and conditions.

Given its economic and social vulnerabilities and inability to develop strong bonds of work-based solidarity, the informal proletariat tends to abhor political uncertainty and social 'chaos'.[19] This can lead it to project its political intervention onto Napoleonic figures who may deliver this group's aspirations autonomously.[20] This helps to explain the attachment of informal workers to authoritarian leaders including, most recently, President Fernando Collor, who promised to protect the 'shirtless' while implementing a neoliberal programme that fleeced the entire working class.

The early attachment of the informal proletariat to neoliberal reforms was not due to their powerlessness or 'idiocy'. Informal workers can benefit from the overvaluation of the currency and the success of orthodox macroeconomic policies, since they reduce the cost of living. They can also gain from the expansion of credit and the demand boost associated with financial liberalisation and foreign capital inflows, regardless of their adverse implications for (a remote prospect of) stable employment. The support of the informal proletariat for neoliberalism may also include a rejection of state intervention which, allegedly, benefits the 'insiders' – corrupt politicians, oligopolistic entrepreneurs, formal-sector workers and civil servants – against such 'outsiders' as themselves. This is, evidently, a self-defeating strategy in the long term, since neoliberal policies to control inflation and reduce state capacity to intervene in the economy benefit primarily the *rentiers*, whose financial gains are secured, and the large capitalists, who can easily move to new sectors. In turn, cuts in public services divide the broad working class and remove an important platform for welfare provision and democratic economic change. Finally, the neoliberal reforms dismantle two of the best-organised segments of the working class, who can support the informal workers: the civil servants and employees of SOEs.

The contradictions enmeshing the informal proletariat create difficulties for their organisation and mobilisation. This can also lead to volatile political attachments and infrequent but explosive mobilisations. For example, these groups have been associated with the destruction of buses and train stations following tariff increases since the 1940s.[21] Nevertheless, the lasting success of the landless peasants' movement, MST, demonstrates that fractions of the informal proletariat can be organised, disciplined and radicalised.

The Middle Class

The petty bourgeoisie ('middle class') provides services supporting the extraction, accumulation, investment and consumption of surplus value, but it does not itself own or control significant productive or financial assets. This class includes the managers of most large and medium-sized private firms, cadres of the state bureaucracy (judges, prosecutors, senior administrators, high-ranking military and police officers), skilled professionals offering non-reproducible services (lawyers, doctors, engineers, academics, artists, chefs and so on),[22] independent merchants, small-scale *rentiers* and commercial landowners, and capitalists hiring a small number of workers, often family members (however, own-account or subcontracted workers producing standardised commodities or providing undifferentiated services, and dependent on a disguised wage, belong to the working class).

The central political tension within the middle class is between notions of social justice binding them to the underprivileged and the pull of joining the bourgeoisie individually. The former can be inspired by religious ideas, democratic values or ideological commitment to a 'level playing field' against capitalist power. Historically, this has included instances of voluntarism and ultra-leftism, especially among students, civil servants, intellectuals and religious leaders.[23]

However, more often than not, the middle class incorporates a capitalist ethic of competitiveness, accumulation and social exclusion, typically among managers, small business-owners and landowners. This is reinforced by the potential gains offered by neoliberalism, including overvalued exchange rates (which cheapen imported goods and foreign holidays), liberalised finance and capital flows (easier credit), and foreign direct investment (skilled jobs and easier access to fashionable goods). A similar logic can lead the middle class to support authoritarianism, in order to secure their own property rights and social privileges by political, bureaucratic or symbolic means. These groups can join right-wing parties, demand protection for specific professions (in Brazil, economics, journalism and psychology, in addition to the usual examples of medicine, engineering, architecture and law), or purchase expensive homes, cars, clothes and personal services in order to emulate the bourgeoisie and differentiate themselves from the working class (which may itself be influenced by these values, and seek to emulate the middle class).

These tensions are important because the middle class plays an essential role in securing bourgeois hegemony through its privileged access to the political system, the media, NGOs, lobbies and the justice system, and its management of schools, universities, churches and the media. Consequently, the middle class can express its economic interests and ideological prejudices in powerful ways, however diverse, reactionary, inconsistent or strategically untenable they may be.[24]

The attachment of the Brazilian middle class to its privileges, and its rejection of encroachment by the broad working class, created a growing antipathy to the expansion of social rights and the distributional improvements during the PT administrations.[25] This was understandable. While large capital generally prospered under neoliberalism and under the PT, the middle class did not share these gains. They were squeezed by the exhaustion of ISI and the subsequent economic slowdown, the retreat of traditional occupations with the neoliberal transition, the low-wage intensity of the recovery in the mid-2000s, and the downturn since 2011. So-called 'good jobs' in the private and public sectors have become scarce, higher education no longer guarantees sufficient income or status, and the young find it hard to do better economically than their parents. For example, 4.3 million jobs paying more than 5 times the minimum wage were lost in the 2000s, in contrast with the net creation of 950,000 such jobs in the 1990s (see Chapter 6).

The relative position of the middle class was also eroded by the prosperity of the bourgeoisie and the gains of the broad working class under the PT. The working class benefitted from the new pattern of employment, higher minimum wages (which are a cost for the middle class, as a net buyer of low-end personal services), means-tested transfer programmes funded by general taxation (which the middle class helps to fund but cannot claim), the formalisation of labour and diffusion of higher education and, under Rousseff, the expansion of employment rights to domestic workers, including cleaners, nannies, cooks, drivers, gardeners and security guards, who are commonly employed in middle-class households. This policy raised costs to the employers and threatened the paternalistic relationships within their households: the top became increasingly distant, the bottom seemed to be catching up fast, and the privileges of the middle class were evaporating.[26]

Many in the middle class blamed the universalisation of rights and rising incomes under the PT for the deterioration of urban infrastructure and public services since they, presumably, allowed too many people to access airports, universities and health facilities and to own automobiles.[27] These dissatisfactions provide material reasons for the middle class to prefer commodified public services, rather than universal provision.[28] Social media has bubbled for several years with intense discomfort over the social and racial mix seeping into previously exclusive spaces. The middle class seems to consider that its privileges are due to hard work and personal merit, while low-income workers are presumably lazy, their work is less meritorious and they can advance only through taxpayer-funded support. Their abject living conditions are the 'inevitable' outcome of their preference for leisure and poor professional choices, and their social and economic progress is, almost by definition, unmerited.

Middle-class groups desperately want economic growth but they also want exclusivity. They also remain ideologically attached both to a neoliberal-globalist project that slows growth, and to clientelistic politics, landowner interests and a neoliberal ideology that gives them advantages over the poor. This is a recipe for political instability. These pressures led the middle class to abandon the PT *en masse* and shift their support to the PSDB and other right-wing parties in the mid-2000s; on rare occasions, some individuals shifted to far-left parties, movements and NGOs.[29] Neither alternative offered a cogent response. The far-left parties remain small; the neoliberal mainstream has repeatedly demonstrated its dysfunctionality; the centrist parties are vacuous; and the NGOs and social movements can be politically limiting. What remains is a set of vague but deeply-felt demands, expressed through slogans against corruption and for the rule of law and better public management. They do not provide a realistic political programme, but they *can* turn the middle class into the mass base of the far right (see Chapter 9).

Breakdown

On 6 June 2013, the radical left Free Fare Movement (*Movimento Passe Livre*, MPL), an autonomist organisation founded in the early 2000s, led a demonstration of around 2,000 people along Avenida Paulista, São Paulo's main thoroughfare. They demanded the reversal of a recent increase in public transport fares from R$3 to R$3.20 (a similar fare increase had also been introduced in Rio de Janeiro).[30]

This demonstration was attacked by the police and criticised by the mainstream media for making unrealistic demands, disrupting the traffic and vandalism.[31] The MPL returned in larger numbers in the following days, and the police responded with increasing brutality, beating up demonstrators, passers-by and journalists indiscriminately, and firing rubber bullets into the crowd. Police savagery brought the protests to the attention of the country. The movement spread. Then strange things began to happen. Suddenly, the right-wing TV channels and most newspapers stopped criticising the demonstrations, and started supporting them. The protesters were no longer hoodlums, but bearers of the energy of youth who were expressing the country's justified rejection of its dysfunctional political system. The mainstream media tried to lead the mobilisations, offering blanket coverage even at the expense of Brazil's beloved *telenovelas* (soap operas).[32]

The demonstrations exploded in size, leading to the largest protests since the campaign for democracy, in the early 1980s, and the demonstrations against Fernando Collor, in 1992. The federal government, disconnected from the organised workers and shunned by the middle class, was bewildered. In less than two weeks more than one million people took to the streets in hundreds of cities, mostly students, left-wing activists, trade unionists, young workers, categories with corporative demands (bus drivers, lorry drivers, health-sector workers, and so on), neighbourhood associations seeking local improvements and, increasingly, the middle class. As the demonstrations spread, they tended to become increasingly white and economically privileged.[33]

In common with contemporaneous mass movements in Egypt, Iran, Spain and Turkey, the Brazilian demonstrations were heterogeneous, including multiple groups and movements with unrelated demands organised primarily via social media and, in Brazil, through the mainstream media. Most demonstrations had no clear leaders and included several independent marches, which would meet only casually. Generally, there were no speeches. Anyone could come up with their own demand or call their own demonstration. Random groups would organise themselves on Facebook and Twitter, meet somewhere, and march in directions determined by unknown persons on the spot.

As it sought to take over the movements, the media sponsored the multiplication and de-radicalisation of demands, focusing on public-service provision, especially transport, health and education, and issues of governance covering corruption, taxation, privatisation and the administration of justice. The demonstrations became displays of individual creativity, including hundreds of home-made placards with original slogans. If they were anti-political and humorous this increased the chance of appearing on TV. For example, the demonstrations included banners about public services (for); FIFA, the 2013 Confederations Cup and the 2014 World Cup (against); compulsory voting (mostly against); gay rights and the legalisation of drugs (mainly for, but most churches were against); abortion and religious issues (contradictory); public spending, privatisation and the state monopolies (unclear); Dilma Rousseff and the PT (against); and, strongly highlighted by the media, corruption (against which everyone could march together; see Chapter 9).[34] Many middle-class protesters seized the opportunity to criticise the provision of public services that they rarely if ever used (although, if the services were better, people higher up the income scale might be willing to use them). Popular approval for the government tumbled from over 70 per cent to 40 per cent in a matter of days.[35] Then the movement took a sinister turn.

At the margins of large gatherings, small groups of people would go on the rampage. The police sometimes attacked the demonstrators, sometimes the hooligans and, frequently, disappeared entirely. Since 'all politicians are corrupt' (a message subliminally repeated by the media since the *mensalão*), some marches were, somehow, proclaimed to be 'party-free', and left-wing militants, trade unionists or anyone wearing the colour red would be harassed and beaten up. Muscular men with cropped hair, wrapped in the national flag, roamed around screaming 'my party is my country'. There were calls for the impeachment of President Rousseff, and for a military coup.

When the federal government finally pushed São Paulo and Rio de Janeiro to reverse the fare increases, the movement had already been hijacked by a revived political right. In late June, the government, after considerable hesitation, sought left support for the first and (as it would turn out) only time. President Rousseff met with left organisations and, in a separate conference with state governors and mayors of the largest cities, proposed a 'national pact' against corruption and for political reforms and improved public services, to be funded by the oil revenues accumulating in Brazil's brand-new sovereign wealth fund.

Rousseff wanted to call a plebiscite to reform the electoral system and the political parties, but this was vetoed by the media, the right-wing opposition and her own Vice President, Michel Temer, from the centrist PMDB (Party of the Brazilian Democratic Movement, *Partido do Movimento Democrático Brasileiro*).[36] Rousseff dropped the idea. The government also announced plans to bring thousands of foreign (mainly Cuban) doctors to municipalities with no health facilities. Despite the popularity of this initiative, it was bitterly resisted by the media and several medical associations that, invariably, are dominated by middle-class professionals. Their rejection was transparently due to elitism, racism and opposition to the Cuban regime.[37]

In the meantime, eight trade union confederations, including CUT, joined the MST and other mass organisations on a 'day of action' on 11 July, attempting to shift the focus of the protests back to the working class.[38] They demanded the reduction of the working week from 44 to 40 hours, higher state pensions and restrictions on subcontracting. The demonstrations and strikes included hundreds of thousands of workers, but media coverage was modest. The demonstrations had dwindled by the end of June. Nothing came of the workers' day of action, and the government never recovered its popularity.

The 2013 protests were the outcome of a confluence of dissatisfactions expressing a deep and, until then, unrecognised malaise in the country. They also highlighted three vulnerabilities of the PT and the federal administration.

First, the expectations of the workers, the poor and the young had risen faster than their incomes, and they demanded both full social inclusion and higher levels of consumption, *immediately*. In contrast, the middle class was hostile to the government, the PT and the poor; they also demanded public services, but refused to pay higher taxes to fund them. They claimed that they already paid too much, that corruption spirited away government revenues and that 'their' taxes were supporting a parasitic mass of undeserving poor through the transfer programmes. The outcome was that, while the middle class was angry and confused, the workers were unhappy for very different reasons, marginalised and disorganised. Those contradictory demands could be managed if the Brazilian economy was growing, but the slowdown, government ineptness and media hostility made every grievance more urgent, and every constraint tighter (see Chapters 7 and 9).[39]

Second, the PT and the country's progressive organisations were shown to be politically isolated and unable to channel the demonstrations towards progressive ends. Their impotence illustrated the chasm between the government, the mass organisations and the working class that was supposedly represented by them. The government's reputation was further dented by the PT's evident exhaustion and its depressing acrobatics in Congress, where it struggled to maintain a working majority through fickle alliances and incoherent deals with unprincipled politicians.

Third, the frustrations of the neoliberal alliance were packaged aggressively by the mainstream media. Given the weakness of the political parties of the right since the early 2000s, the media took up the mantle of the opposition,[40] and pursued the PT and its allies systematically, under the flimsiest of pretexts.[41]

The Lumpenisation of Politics

The analysis sketched above can help to contextualise the wave of protests in 2013, and their consequences for the PT and for Dilma Rousseff. Those protests were closely associated with the worldwide tendency towards the evacuation of democracy under neoliberalism, and its counter-tendencies in Brazil under the PT governments.

Political democracy expanded dramatically in Brazil since the mid-1970s. Mass movements gained sufficient strength to secure political freedom and competitive elections. The 1988 Constitution extended citizenship and social provision. Four centre-left federal administrations were elected since 2002 and, between 2006 and 2013, inclusive policies inspired by neodevelopmentalism supported economic growth, employment creation, the formalisation of labour and income distribution.

These advances were limited by, first, the insulation of the economy from democratic processes through a raft of norms and institutions designed to shield neoliberalism from majority pressure. These are common to most neoliberal countries; they include privatisations, 'market-friendly' regulatory agencies, inflation targeting, Central Bank independence, the LRF, the independence of the judiciary, and so on.[42] Second, the fragmentation of public provision through the dilution of universal programmes into conditional and means-tested social policies.[43] Third, the change in the patterns of production, work and social life under neoliberalism. They have fragmented the working class and eroded its cultures and its sense of collectivity based on shared material circumstances. The political capacities of the workers and their structures of representation, across political parties, trade unions and social movements, have been similarly impaired.[44]

The 'new' working class under neoliberalism tends to be atomised, structurally disorganised, inexperienced in collective action and distrustful of structures of representation that, from its point of view, have been rendered ineffective. There is also a narrowing of political ambition and rejection of collective aspirations to change society: working-class goals tend to be limited by the frame of reference imposed by neoliberalism. Correspondingly, the mass base of the left is in disarray; collective action has become harder; and most mass organisations have been tainted by association with PT administrations that never welcomed them into national politics. Similar changes have affected the 'progressive' middle class.

These developments have narrowed the economic debate and reduced the scope for policy reform. Even though a reformist agenda gained ground in the mid-2000s, the base of support for the expansion of economic and political democracy had already been degraded, weakening reformism even as it achieved noteworthy successes. These paradoxes make it difficult to articulate working-class demands and campaign effectively, both because the targets have become more diffuse, and because the working class has been decomposed and the workers are less able and willing to engage in collective action. In the meantime, cultural identifiers and social interaction have been transformed by digital communications. Everyone can communicate directly, creating the impression that structures of representation have become superfluous. Presumably, now, aspirations and desires can be expressed in an unmediated form.

The protests in 2013 thrived as a result of the disconnect between classes and their traditional structures of representation. The demonstrations were mostly against politics *as a whole*, rather than focusing on specific administrations or political leaders. Many demonstrated against Rousseff and the PT, but no one demonstrated for neoliberalism, the return of Cardoso's policies or the PSDB. It was also sobering to realise that there were no mass demands for socialism: discontent was rife, but revolution was not on the agenda.

When groups organised in this way appear in the 'real world' they tend to perform a spectacle that can be relayed to their 'friends' in the ether, creating incentives for the individualisation of demands and the personalisation of delivery through humour, colourful disguises and so on. Facebook and YouTube become the world, and the world becomes a larger-than-life internet. Unsurprisingly, the Brazilian demonstrations were media-friendly, and many demonstrators were more intent on taking selfies than anything else.[45] In addition, the structural inability to express common demands cogently, or to find channels of representation, has led social protest under neoliberalism to become subsumed by political forms of representation akin to that of the lumpen-proletariat. Disorganised and cut-off from their bonds of class, often disenfranchised yet dependent on the state, the expression of needs remains a-political: needs are decoupled from strategic goals and transformative projects. *Under neoliberalism, politics and protest tend to be lumpenised.*

Lumpenised protests are infrequent and unfocused. When they emerge, they do not tend to coalesce around organisations and movements that can accumulate experiences and achieve long-term successes; instead, they become destructive. Just as the demands of the lumpen-proletariat are vulnerable to capture by the bourgeoisie,[46] social movements under neoliberalism tend to become individualistic and vulnerable to capture by the political right. Since the social structures and technologies of neoliberalism feed the unmediated expression of demands, they tend to drive a universalist ethics supported by a 'common-sense' philosophy bypassing notions of social exploitation; there are only individual virtues or tribulations, which can be captured by anyone on inspection.

The lumpenisation of politics is limited at four levels. First, the aggregation of spontaneous demands does not necessarily generate cogent programmes or viable platforms for social change.

Second, digital communication does not lend itself easily to organisation based on class or workplace. Instead, the direct expression of demands on the web favours simplification, superficiality, 'common sense' and the formulation of demands in very broad terms. This implies the language of 'rights' (to transport, housing, work, health, education, drugs, abortion and so on) and, closely related, 'respect' for any self-identified group (women, gays, teachers, truck drivers, inhabitants of specific neighbourhoods, etc.), and 'honesty' in public life. These unobjectionable claims can deflect attention from complex, layered and historically informed transformative projects. In other words, the decomposition of the working class and the middle class under neoliberalism has channelled social discontent towards a universalist ethics mired in issues of crime and corruption rather than class action. Implicitly, they suggest that 'strong' leaders are both necessary and sufficient to 'resolve' common problems, bypassing the corrupt and inefficient institutions of the state and civil society (see Chapter 9).

Third, digital media can support mobilisation, but it is not a suitable means for debate or the build-up of trust, which is essential for the consolidation, broadening and radicalisation of protest movements.

Fourth, direct representation and 'horizontality' (i.e. the lack of hierarchies in the movement) foster individualism and disorganisation. However, dissatisfaction – without organisation – tends to explode and then evaporate, and although spontaneous mass movements with a mixed class base and fuelled by unfocused anger can be destabilising for the political system, they normally achieve little, and leave behind unsatisfied demands that can fuel further waves of protest. Although successive protests can erode the political edifice of bourgeois rule, they do not spontaneously generate feasible alternatives.

The need for organisation, delegation of power and compromise within the movement and with outside institutions in complex societies suggests that overcoming the material fragmentation of the working class and its political allies, and transcending the cultural separations imposed by neoliberalism, requires collectivity *in practice*. This means talking and doing things together, more than interacting through digital media. Twitter and Facebook are good ways to exchange discrete morsels of information, but they do not allow the exchange of ideas or the development of personal and collective links that can sustain social movements.

The new forms of mobilisation are highly plastic. They can support a politically-informed left-wing platform of restoration of collectivity and confrontation against neoliberalism, but they also offer fertile ground for the emergence of fascism. The consolidation of a new generation of mass movements along progressive lines requires new forms of mobilisation, participation and delegation, fostering a new form of democracy appropriate for a post-neoliberal age. These are difficult challenges for the left, since its social base has been extensively decomposed and disempowered through the transition to neoliberalism. The Brazilian protests have also shown that the economic, social and political fragilities of the 'new' working class can allow right-wing platforms to overwhelm existing social movements with individualistic and destructive forms of mobilisation.

Summary and Conclusion

This chapter has sketched the class structure in Brazil and its transformations following the economic transition from ISI to neoliberalism. Four classes were examined in some detail: the bourgeoisie (including the internationalised and the internal bourgeoisie), the formal working class, the informal working class and the middle class. These were examined in terms of their role in the reproduction of the system of accumulation and their shifts over time, especially across the economic transition from ISI to neoliberalism. This approach was deployed in support of a novel interpretation of the wave of protests in 2013.

These protests were highly significant for three reasons. First, they were the largest mass uprising in Brazil in a generation. Second, they signalled an irreversible break in the base of support of the PT, and the political paralysis of Dilma Rousseff's administration. Third, the protests started from the left, but were captured by the right. They underpinned the recomposition of the mass base of the far right among the middle class for the first time since the early 1980s. These significant developments were examined in detail and interpreted through the social and political implications of the change in SoA, leading to the concept of the 'lumpenisation of politics'. The next chapter deploys these conclusions in order to inform the analysis of Dilma Rousseff's impeachment and the Temer administration.

9

From the Confluence of Dissatisfactions to the Restoration of Neoliberalism

Overview

The economic slowdown that began in 2011 fed a devastating political crisis in Brazil. Perceptions of economic degradation framed a convergence of revolts that would include the mainstream media, finance, industrial capital, the middle class, the judiciary, the Federal Police and most of the government's base in Congress. While these hostile forces gathered steam, the base of support of the administration remained largely inert. Most formal and informal workers were disorganised and intimidated into inaction by the opposition and the adverse turn of the economy, while the PT, having chosen years earlier to follow the established rules of politics, found itself defenceless against an aggressive constellation of foes.

The revolt of the elite was energised by a succession of corruption scandals focusing almost exclusively on the PT. The *lava jato* (carwash) investigation led by the Federal Police gained momentum gradually, enveloped Petrobras and eventually overwhelmed the PT and Dilma Rousseff's administration. The entire government was tainted by aspersions of corruption, with the PT being accused on a daily basis of having set up a system to rob public assets and despoil the state for its own benefit. The wheels of justice turned briskly, detaining carefully chosen businesspeople and prominent politicians until they agreed to enter a plea bargain, by which they would necessarily incriminate others. Evidence was optional; hearsay was enough. Others would then be arrested, especially if they could make further allegations against the PT, and would be kept in jail until they complied. Other political parties were also caught in the net, but this did not matter too much. Only claims against the PT really counted. Despite the unrelenting pressure, no credible allegations could be made against Dilma Rousseff. No matter: the absence of guilt would not be allowed to prevent her political liquidation. Extraneous allegations were concocted, and Rousseff was dislodged from the presidency by an overwhelming majority of the Chamber of Deputies and, later, the Senate, constituted as a political court.

In order to contextualise the political implications of the Brazilian crisis, this chapter examines the background of the involvement of the PT with corruption and the party's unique vulnerability to allegations of corruption. It also reviews the role of the middle class in corruption scandals, first, because of their unique sensitivity to allegations of corruption and, second, because of Brazil's history of mobilisation of the middle class around right-wing programmes under the pretext of fighting corruption. The chapter subsequently analyses the emergence of an 'alliance of privilege' since 2013. This alliance was led by the internationalised bourgeoisie and populated, primarily, by the middle class. The alliance of privilege subsequently expanded, while Rousseff struggled to mobilise support for her administration. The attack of the alliance of privilege against the PT was fronted by the *lava jato* operation. While the judicial system and the Federal Police pretended to be looking 'impartially' for evidence of corruption in public office, they set out to implement a political programme to dismantle the PT, eviscerate the party's sources of support and paralyse Rousseff's administration. At a later stage, their efforts spread in multiple directions, with taskforces increasingly pursuing their own goals regardless of the implications for the economy and the political system. The last substantive section in this chapter tracks the impeachment of President Rousseff.

The Workers' Party Courts Political Corruption

Allegations of corruption have been part of all political upheavals in Brazil since, at least, the late nineteenth century. In recent decades, the right-wing revolt against developmental nationalist President Getúlio Vargas, in 1954, was justified by arguments that his government was corrupt. The 1964 coup claimed its legitimacy, in part, from perceptions of corruption in the Second Republic, which the military were, presumably, uniquely equipped to extirpate. Yet, corruption scandals dogged all military Presidents, especially Ernesto Geisel and João Figueiredo (1979–85), who were subjected to far closer scrutiny by the opposition, the media and social movements than their predecessors.[1]

Given the rising tide of democracy during their administrations, those scandals lent support to the view that the dictatorship was irretrievably soiled and that political liberalisation and the rule of law were essential requirements for an 'honest' Republic.[2]

Despite these pious wishes, all democratic governments were implicated in corruption scandals that were followed up selectively by the judiciary, the media and the public. Finally, since 2005 the mainstream media and the neoliberal parties have insisted that the PT had spawned a uniquely corrupt system of government. This argument has been deployed repeatedly in order to criminalise the party, support damaging legal cases against its leaders, smother the PT's sources of support in the internal bourgeoisie, remove Dilma Rousseff from office and exclude Lula from political life.[3]

It was shown in Chapter 2 that, in the 1990s, the PT decided to address the disintegration of its traditional base of support in the working class and the lower middle class by shifting the party's priorities away from class-driven goals of economic and political democracy. The party focused, instead, on a broader strategy of national development backed up by appeals to ethics and efficiency in public administration. This was meant to lure, or at least pacify, the internal bourgeoisie and two groups disconnected from the core economic relations in capitalism: the middle class and the informal workers (see Chapters 5 and 8). Although they lacked a programmatic connection with the PT's inchoate socialism, these groups could give the party both legitimacy and mass appeal. In the late 1990s, the PT's political shift deepened through the accretion of a neoliberal discourse foregrounding the importance to 'everyone' of keeping inflation low and promoting economic efficiency.[4] It was as if corruption, inflation and inefficiency were the causes of slow GDP growth and the economic malaise enveloping the middle class and the poor (rather than, say, capitalism, neoliberalism or the relations of exclusion at the core of the Brazilian state).[5]

The political repositioning of the PT was successful in the short term, but it created a lethal contradiction. In order to become a 'normal' party, committed to the democratic institutions and enjoying cross-class appeal, the PT had to dismiss most of its left-wing commitments and traditions of class-based mobilisation and rely, instead, on conventional tools to promote a social-democratic programme. These tools included contingent funding by the internal bourgeoisie, which would be provided to the PT against economic returns. In the meantime, the middle class was expected to support the PT because of the party's commitment to honesty and efficiency in office, expectations of greater equality at the margin, and the pursuit of broad-based economic growth. It would be *impossible* for the PT to live up to these conflicting expectations, not least because the party would be permanently vulnerable to damaging disclosures by disgruntled funders or hostile media outlets. In this sense, *the PT gained electoral viability at the expense of a unique vulnerability to charges of corruption.*

Corruption and the Middle Class

The middle class is highly sensitive to allegations of corruption for three reasons (see Chapter 8). From the angle of democracy, the middle class tends to feel that its privileged status derives from individual merit rather than inherited privilege, as is the case with the bourgeoisie. Consequently, there are material reasons why the middle class longs for a society in which a level playing field supports the rise of the best, and prevents them from being held back 'unfairly' by hereditary wealth, preferential treatment bought for cash, a corrupt state or other 'artificial' hindrances.[6] From the angle of class mobility, the middle class understands that corruption feeds upon *and* concentrates power and resources, and provides unmerited political and economic advantages to the bourgeoisie. From the angle of ethics, corruption breaks the law and offends public morality.

Middle-class concerns with democracy, justice and fairness went into overdrive, first, because of the frenzy of media allegations of corruption against the PT since the *mensalão*. Second, the industrial policies implemented by the PT administrations were vulnerable to neoliberal objections that they privileged vested interests to the detriment of the (presumably) 'neutral' and (consequently) 'meritorious' outcomes that would have emerged through the (mythical but ideologically powerful) 'free market'. Third, the PT's social policies were susceptible to conservative attack because they allegedly taxed the 'creators of wealth' (a distinction that the middle class wishes to share with the bourgeoisie, despite the implicit conflation between the creation and appropriation of riches), in order to benefit the undeserving poor, opportunists and other unproductive members of society. Middle-class opposition to the PT tended to harden as the party leaned towards neodevelopmentalism, and it turned bitter as the poorest and the richest were both perceived to be gaining ground, while the middle class was losing out in relative and, to some extent, absolute terms (see Chapters 6 and 8).[7]

In 2013, abhorrence of corruption supported a moralising attack by the 'people as a whole' against public policy in general and the PT specifically, because of allegations that the party had hijacked the state for selfish reasons. Egregious stories were banded around, focusing on apocalyptic insufficiencies in public provision and scabrous tales of corruption, as if the appropriate response to these scandals could be 'less state intervention' rather than, say, greater accountability in public policy.[8] These complaints, dressed up as incontrovertible 'facts' inviting common-sense solutions, fed destructive outcomes at several levels.

First, the emerging mass movement against corruption, the PT and Dilma Rousseff's government suggested that corruption and state inefficiency were the most important problems in Brazil while, at the same time, suggesting that these evils derived from the perverse behaviour of specific individuals and parties, regardless of the country's history, institutions, political practices and social structures. It follows that the moralising goals of the anti-corruption campaign are unachievable, and that mobilisation in an attempt to 'confront corruption' is bound to feed personal frustration. These feelings of disbelief in collective action foster the lumpenisation of politics (see below, and Chapter 8).

Second, the campaign suggested that there are two possible 'solutions' to corruption. One is the transposition of capitalist rules of behaviour to the public sphere (conventional measures of accountability, micro-economic efficiency, cost minimisation and so on). This would lead the state to be governed by the rationality of finance as the embodiment of capital in general; that is, the radicalisation of neoliberalism. The other is the suggestion that the conflicts of interest that breed corruption can be contained only by a 'strong' leader; that is, fascism.

Third, every achievement of the PT administrations was tarnished by the deluge of allegations. At the same time, the anti-corruption campaign overlooked the self-evident truth that improvements in public service provision will take time, cost huge sums of money and cannot be achieved without state policy.

Fourth, the protests drew strength from a mainstream media that, for years, had been subliminally claiming the position of the begetter as well as the *only* legitimate channel of expression of the public interest. All other structures of representation were presumably corrupt, as if private newspapers and TV stations were not self-interested and ideologically committed profit-making enterprises, constantly swapping stories for cash, selling misleading publicity and negotiating deals with elected officials as part of their duty to shareholders.[9]

Fifth, the power of the media was reinforced by its alliance with the judiciary. The synergies between carefully staged leaks from ongoing investigations, media-led worship of telegenic judges and prosecutors and plentiful coverage of Federal Police raids fed TV ratings and newspaper sales. In turn, media attention empowered the judiciary and the police to act outrageously in the interests of self-promotion, regardless of the law. This symbiotic arrangement fed middle-class outrage against the political system, which became destructive not only for the PT, but also for the Constitution.[10]

Sixth, the middle class was nurtured for several years on a media-led diet of hatred for the PT.[11] Unsurprisingly, they ended up blaming the party for more or less tangible but presumably vast damages suffered by the state, and for the loss of income, privilege and authority by the middle class itself.[12] The middle class ignored the impact of neoliberal reforms on the material reproduction of society, and projected its own discontent, in a lumpenised fashion, onto the state and the political system. In doing this, it blamed its misfortunes on corruption, inefficiency and the domination of politics by the PT, despite the party's extraordinary political moderation and unreasonable attachment to neoliberalism.

The Alliance of Privilege

The 2013 protests were the catalyst for the emergence of an *alliance of privilege*, building upon the neoliberal alliance that had opposed the PT for many years (see Chapter 8).[13]

The alliance of privilege expanded gradually. It eventually included, first, the internationalised and the internal bourgeoisie, who were suffering losses due to government policy and the economic crisis, and resented their perceived loss of control of state policy because of Rousseff's push for neodevelopmentalism (see Chapter 7).[14] Second, most of the middle class, who were ideologically committed to neo-liberalism or otherwise alienated from the PT because of the ascent of the broad working class, and tormented by income losses and dislocation from the outer circle of power since Lula's election and the change in social composition of the state. Third, large sections of the youth, the judicial system, most of the government's base in Congress, segments of the informal working class and the members of competing protestant sects that, for religious, ideological or financial reasons, opposed the expansion of civil rights and progressive values, with flashpoints around Rousseff's move towards the liberalisation of abortion and recognition of citizenship rights for homosexuals.[15] The organised and informal workers were mostly passive, partly because of the economic pressures due to the economic crisis and, partly because of the political shackles imposed by political disorganisation for many years and the pressure of the corruption scandals (it is exceedingly difficult to take a public stance in support of someone accused of such crimes).

The alliance of privilege bonded ideologically and acquired an aggressive edge in the mainstream media (see Chapter 8), which drew upon a strident discourse bringing together right-wing values, neoliberal economics and allegations of mismanagement and corruption. The government was hemmed in. It became paralysed politically, and its popularity evaporated.

The emergence of the alliance of privilege bred mass support for the far right for the first time in five decades. Just as in the early 1960s, the 'new' right-wing movement is populated by the middle class, and it has coalesced against a left-leaning administration battered by accusations of economic incompetence (allegedly demonstrated by falling GDP growth and rising fiscal deficits and inflation), left-wing populism (due to their distributional efforts) and rampant corruption. Even though these cycles of the right are separated by decades, they suggest that the powerful tend to rise up against the government if their wealth is threatened, or if economic privilege fails to secure political prominence.[16]

The similarities between these right-wing movements go further. The selective anti-corruption discourse of the alliance of privilege closely mirrors the campaign against Presidents Getúlio Vargas, in 1954, and João Goulart, in 1964.[17] The movement against Vargas collapsed when he committed suicide rather than be overthrown; the rebellion against Goulart culminated in a military coup (see Chapter 1). Other right-wing movements fronted by anti-corruption propaganda include the successful bid to elect as President the populist right-winger Jânio Quadros, in 1960. He promised to clean up the country, but ended up resigning after only seven months, after failing to blackmail Congress into gifting him emergency powers. Finally, the neoliberal right elected Fernando Collor, the presumably incorruptible 'hunter of Maharajahs' (i.e. highly paid or corrupt civil servants) in the first presidential elections after the fall of the dictatorship. Collor was forced to resign after two years because of his staggering incompetence and hair-raising scandals involving thievery and much else (see Chapter 1). Although the campaign to impeach Collor was led by the left, his own election included right-wing mobilisations centred, in part, on corruption, as a distraction from his crash programme of neoliberal reforms. These episodes suggest that right-wing movements against corruption can have mass appeal, and can serve to throttle the left.[18]

Despite these commonalities with earlier right-wing mobilisations, and their broader similarities as lumpenised forms of protest, the alliance of privilege did not appeal centrally to traditional anti-communist discourses of Cold War vintage, and it was not inspired by traditional Catholic values. Instead, it proclaimed its rejection of the (poorly defined) dangers of 'Bolivarianism', and the closely related (but chimerical) threat of 'left-wing authoritarianism'. Beyond its vacuous calls for 'the end of corruption', which was code for 'the destruction of the PT', the strategic goal of the alliance of privilege was the elimination of government autonomy from the privileged classes, and the imposition of an excluding variant of neoliberalism.[19] The mainstream media was explicit about the need for an economic policy shift including the reaffirmation of the policy tripod, sharp fiscal adjustment, drastic liberalisation of the labour market, the reversal of Brazil's independent foreign policy, the 'reform' of Petrobras, and the rollback of the neodevelopmental aspirations of BNDES.

The Lava Jato Operation

A small number of state institutions is centrally important for the determination of policy outcomes in Brazil. They are constantly being fought over by rival groups aiming to create, entrench and project their power and to challenge rival programmes.[20] The most important institutions are the presidency and the economic and political ministries conceiving, implementing and monitoring the country's accumulation strategy. Subordinate institutions can also be influential. For example, during the PT administrations, the internal bourgeoisie established a power centre in large SOEs, especially BNDES, Petrobras and two state-owned banks, *Banco do Brasil* and *Caixa Econômica Federal*. In contrast, the internationalised bourgeoisie and the middle class dominated the Central Bank, the judiciary, the Attorney General's office (*Procuradoria Geral da*

República, PGR) and the Federal Police. They became the main institutional base for the attack on the PT by the alliance of privilege.

Two features of the judiciary, the Federal Police and the PGR, have led them to support the alliance of privilege against the internal bourgeoisie, the PT and their associates. First, those institutions employ some of the most privileged civil servants in the country. Brazil's 40,000 judges, prosecutors, attorneys and top bureaucrats in the judiciary are comfortably at the top of the middle class. The starting salary of a public prosecutor is between 29 and 38 times the monthly minimum wage for a working week of only 25 hours, with additional work counting as overtime. Their perks and holidays are exceptionally generous. Judges, who earn around 40 times the minimum wage, also receive generous food allowances and housing subsidies. Even though the top managers at BNDES and Petrobras are also well paid, their salaries are far lower, and these institutions have very little autonomy when compared with the judiciary, the Federal Police and the PGR. Second, since the structural role of these institutions is to maintain public order, their staff tends to oppose governments that promote popular organisation or accommodate 'illegal' struggles, for example, roadblocks, or occupations of land or urban dwellings, as the PT often did.

The mainstream media, judges, prosecutors, attorneys and the senior levels of the Federal Police supported the PSDB in increasingly vicious attacks on the PT administrations, with corruption eventually emerging as the ideal pretext (see above). Their investigations targeted key institutions of neodevelopmentalism, especially Petrobras, BNDES and industries closely connected to the internal bourgeoisie, particularly construction, oil, nuclear energy and processed meats.[21] Those assaults were facilitated by the deference of the PT towards the media and the judiciary: the PT governments provided unyielding support, inordinate autonomy and abundant funding for the judiciary, rejected any form of regulation of the media, and refused to mobilise their social base to counter the flagrantly biased treatment of their party.[22]

The *lava jato* operation revealed that a cartel of engineering and construction companies had bribed a small number of politically appointed directors of Petrobras, in order to secure a virtual monopoly of oil and related contracts.[23] The Brazilian construction sector is heavily concentrated around 15 large (mostly family-owned) firms that emerged in the late 1950s. Those firms expanded rapidly during the dictatorship, eventually dominating the market for public works.[24] Bribes paid to senior Petrobras executives allegedly allowed those companies to control hundreds of contracts and distribute them to members of the cartel; in turn, the directors of Petrobras received large amounts of cash for personal use and for distribution to the parties that kept them in post, including the PT.

High-ranking Federal Police managers and public prosecutors made overt political use of these investigations.[25] For long periods, they ignored clues suggesting that the PSDB was involved in similar cases of corruption, selectively leaked classified or inaccurate information to the media, and sought to compromise the PT whenever possible. In 2014, the PSDB created a congressional committee to investigate corruption at Petrobras, escalating the confrontation. The media started speculating about the impeachment of Dilma Rousseff immediately after the 2014 elections while, simultaneously, claiming that the only way to end corruption at Petrobras was to eliminate the domestic procurement policy and remove the legal requirement that Petrobras must participate in every oilfield. The PSDB immediately proposed new legislation to that effect, which was approved shortly after Rousseff's impeachment.

In turn, European capital rushed to claim the construction industry. In an article in the newspaper *O Estado de S. Paulo*, EU Trade Commissioner Cecilia Malmström pontificated about corruption in Brazilian public works and concluded that the EU would only sign a trade deal with Mercosur if its firms had greater access to this (presumably tainted) market.[26] Interestingly, the commissioner failed to mention the cases of Siemens and Alstom, which admitted making large payments to the PSDB in order to win contracts for the São Paulo rail and metro systems. This scandal raised no media, judicial or police eyebrows.[27]

The *lava jato* operation catalysed a lumpenised right-wing mass movement populated by the middle class, demanding the 'end of corruption' and Rousseff's impeachment. Their grievances included a laundry list of deeply felt, unfocused and conflicting dissatisfactions articulated by expletives rather than logic, let alone law. Their agitation was both partial and misleading, for three reasons.

First, both *lava jato* and the anti-corruption discourse of the alliance of privilege were highly selective. Primarily, they targeted the institutions and parties aligned with neodevelopmentalism, suggesting that their most important aim was to change government policy, rather than eliminate corruption.[28] Second, the charge of corruption provides a convenient excuse to avoid serious debate on economic policy and the accumulation strategy. For example, the internationalised bourgeoisie would find it difficult to campaign for its *actual* goals – to weaken domestic industry, cripple Petrobras, eliminate the local content policy and reduce labour rights. However, if these goals were concealed by the commonsensical banner of 'fighting corruption', policy changes could be smuggled in later, regardless of the interests of the vast majority. Third, the scandals and the persecution of selected individuals disconnected the PT from its mass base and sources of funding in the internal bourgeoisie. Under the threat of indefinite imprisonment, the internal bourgeoisie was forced to distance itself from the PT, stop funding the party and accept the neoliberal hijacking of the state. The loss of millions of jobs and billions of dollars in output and investment were treated as collateral damage in the war for the economic and political hegemony of neoliberalism.[29]

Lava jato was remarkable for another reason, unrelated to corruption: it was indicative of a distortion in Brazil's judicial system, by which the constitutional guarantees of independence of the judiciary supported the rise of investigators claiming the right to clean up the political system. They set out to do this partly through an attack on corruption and partly by punishing violations of the LRF.[30] Their mission was fortuitously supported by the animosities towards the PT's progressive programme, the fragilities and distortions of Brazil's political system, the sensitivities of the middle class, the economic crisis and the paralysis of the administration. In seeking to 'save' Brazil, this group of judges, prosecutors and Federal Police managers judicialised Brazilian politics to an unprecedented degree, and severely damaged the Constitution and the country's institutional fabric.[31]

The PT failed miserably to respond in the only potentially effective way, that is, by leading a mass campaign against corruption including a national debate, institution-building, transparency, the reform of political finance, the elimination of expectations of impunity and controls on flight capital.[32] Such an initiative could have highlighted the fact that corruption is systemic in Brazil, and that it cannot be extricated from political life one criminal, firm or Swiss bank account at a time. Finally, while punishment must be part of the package, meaningful change must start with legal reforms addressing the funding and operation of all political parties and any other structures of representation.

This ambitious programme was unfeasible; the PT was already unravelling, and it collapsed politically after the 2014 elections. Dilma Rousseff's administration was demolished. In its place, rose a government whose commitment to political malfeasance was matched only by its staggering incompetence. In the meantime, *lava jato* and other corruption investigations trundled along, obsessively seeking to convict Lula of *something*.[33]

Dénouement: Impeachment and the Debacle of the PT

Dilma Rousseff faced severe political and economic difficulties in the wake of her re-election. She was hated by the middle class, rejected by capital, faced an unrelentingly hostile media campaign and was being hounded by *lava jato*. She was also hemmed in by the growth of the right in Congress.[34]

In order to repair her base of support, Rousseff abandoned the 'left turn' promised in her campaign and sacked Guido Mantega, the long-standing neodevelopmentalist Minister of Finance inherited from Lula.[35] She appointed a banker chosen by Bradesco, one of Brazil's largest financial conglomerates (see Chapter 7). Joaquim Levy was tasked with implementing a conventional adjustment policy that chimed with the neoliberal policy tripod; it was also aligned with bourgeois expectations of a prolonged global contraction, and the perceived need to limit inflation in order to contain the devaluation of capital located in Brazil.

The government parroted the neoliberal discourse that the public sector had become 'too big' and 'too interventionist', and that the social programmes had become 'too expensive'. Fiscal austerity was imperative. Public spending, investment and services were cut, followed by pensions and unemployment benefits. These cuts were dangerously similar to what the PT had suggested that the opposition would do, if the PSDB had won the elections. Yet the policy shift came too late – since capital had been demanding a contractionary strategy for at least four years – and included important exceptions, for example the preservation of key social programmes, among them *Bolsa Família* and MCMV, and the protection of most social rights and entitlements. A 'proper' fiscal adjustment would also require higher taxes on capital, which were rejected outright by the mounting rebellion against the President. In the meantime, increases in SOE prices and tariffs (petrol, electricity, and so on), drought, and the oscillations of the exchange rate led inflation to rise and GDP to contract strongly in 2015. As the economy imploded, interest rates rose and the tax intake fell sharply. The fiscal deficit and the ratio between the DPD and GDP shot up, regardless of the fiscal restraint.[36]

Even though the government tried to find common ground with capital and the middle class, its policies failed to satisfy the radicalising demands of the opposition. The fury of the privileged was fanned, daily, by venomous media attacks, backed up by the supplications of mainstream economists, who pleaded for harsh adjustment policies to create 'market confidence'. The result was that the government's contortions never satisfied the opposition, but they alienated Rousseff's base of support in the formal and informal working class. The economy went into a tailspin because of the contraction of domestic as well as external demand. It was impossible for the government to cut its way to growth, and its policies irked all constituencies.

The government was never supported by the internationalised bourgeoisie and the media, and it was not about to win them over now. It had lost most of the middle class after the *mensalão* and because of its initiatives to expand citizenship and improve the distribution of income. It had alienated the organised workers because of the worsening economic situation, corruption scandals, the policy turnaround towards neoliberalism and the failure to address key demands of the working class: the 40-hour working week, reduction of subcontracting and improved pensions. Although Rousseff's support held better among the informal workers, many were alienated for the same reasons. Finally, the government lost the internal bourgeoisie because of the economic slowdown, perceptions that the President was excessively autonomous, disagreements over public policy (see Chapter 8), and the pressure of *lava jato*. The administration also earned the hostility of Congress because of its unwillingness to dish out favours through the established channels of pork-barrel politics.

The opposition was given a semblance of coherence by an antagonistic media claiming that the government was incompetent, the state was out of control and the fiscal deficit would sink the nation. After Rousseff's re-election, political pragmatism and attempts to do 'deals' with the opposition became counterproductive: with each round of concessions, more allies were lost. The haemorrhage had become uncontrollable. Each demonstration of flexibility was met by aggressive opposition and escalating demands, as the PSDB, the PMDB and the government's foes in the Federal Police and the judiciary spotted successive opportunities to paralyse the administration, destabilise the government and, eventually, overthrow Dilma Rousseff through a judicial-parliamentary coup.

The coup could have been pursued in multiple ways, and they were all tried as part of the search for a silver bullet against the PT. They included the rejection of the outcome of the 2014 elections, attempts to invalidate Rousseff's campaign accounts, the defeat or disfigurement of every government initiative in Congress, a barrage of accusations against key politicians and civil servants that criminalised policy-making even retrospectively, making it extremely risky to take decisions in the public sector, the imprisonment of prominent funders of the PT, and allegations of transgression of the Fiscal Responsibility Law by the Treasury and the Ministry of Finance (no personal gain was suggested). Any weapon could be used, regardless of cost to the economy, social welfare or social cohesion, as long as it worked.

Although finance had initially supported Rousseff's neoliberal policy shift, it ceased to support the government when it became clear that Levy would be unable to restore orthodox neoliberalism because the PT was sceptical about his mission and Rousseff's own support for him was conditional.[37] Persistent policy failures, unremitting opposition in Congress, repeated embarrassments and growing impotence pushed Levy to resign in December 2015. He was replaced by Nelson Barbosa, a heterodox academic economist, unwavering Rousseff loyalist and, formerly, second-in-command at the Ministry of Finance under Mantega. The opposition and the 'business community' rejected Barbosa because he was too heterodox, while the left shunned him because he insisted on the need for contractionary fiscal policies. Barbosa's tenure was sterile.

In the melee, the economic crisis, spiralling unemployment and a torrent of corruption scandals became thoroughly enmeshed. The mainstream media trumpeted daily that the PT was at the centre of a web of thievery without precedent, with Lula and Rousseff robbing the Republic during the day while, at night, they conspired to turn Brazil into a satellite of Venezuela. The left split down the middle; the PT lost its legitimacy and Rousseff's popularity tumbled into single digits.

Despite these converging threats and the menace of impeachment, the PT and the left reacted only slowly and weakly, and spent a considerable amount of time fighting each other. Most social movements had long been captured by the PT administrations or demobilised as part of the PT's effort to win elections and govern by the established rules (see

Chapter 2); the party was crippled by fear, shame, political confusion and popular misgivings, and its base of support was melting away.[38] The far left remained small and scattered and, since it had always defined itself in opposition to the PT, most far-left organisations found it hard to support Rousseff in her hour of need. Finally, the media had campaigned implacably against the left since 2013, making it difficult to mobilise the population in support of Rousseff's mandate. She lost an impeachment vote in the Chamber of Deputies by 367–137, on 17 April 2016, and had to step down 'provisionally'. She lost in the Senate by 61–20, on 31 August and was removed from office.[39]

Dilma Rousseff's impeachment on questionable grounds (in the end, it was the fiscal technicality that did it) was a grotesque piece of political theatre. The trial was overtly political, all legal niceties having been abandoned long before, and it was orchestrated by a self-serving cabal of thieving politicians. They claimed the right to impose an unconstitutional vote of no confidence on a President who had made mistakes, but committed no crime.[40] The impeachment itself was driven by an alliance between the leadership of the PSDB, bitterly regretting their four consecutive defeats in presidential elections, leading figures in the judiciary, Rousseff's treacherous Vice President and leader of the PMDB, Michel Temer, and the Machiavellian Speaker of the Chamber of Deputies, Eduardo Cunha, who was struggling against corruption charges in Brazil and in Switzerland (he would end up in prison only a few weeks later, his usefulness to the coup destroyed by the political cost of the allegations against him). They were trailed by business leaders and a motley crew of minor politicians, many of them accused of egregious crimes, not least corruption, who were cheered on by the mainstream media as national saviours. Allegedly, several bourgeois pillars of the community disembarked in Brasília before the impeachment vote carrying bags of cash for distribution among the undecided while, simultaneously, keeping their private jets ready to hunt down any absconding Deputies.[41] To cap this destructive process, the PT suffered a crushing defeat in the local elections, in October 2016.

In the following months, Temer's administration engaged in the relentless imposition of an accumulation strategy based on an unprecedentedly excluding and internationalised variety of neoliberalism. Key initiatives included, first, the change in oil exploration contracts to privilege transnational capital at the expense of Petrobras, and the partial break-up and denationalisation of the company (October 2016). Second, a constitutional amendment freezing primary fiscal spending (i.e. not counting interest payments on the DPD) in real terms for 20 years. It passed in December 2016 by an overwhelming majority of the Chamber of Deputies and the Senate. Third, a reform of labour law liberalising the labour market almost entirely (July 2017). Fourth, the reform of pensions and social security (still pending in late 2017).

The administration's achievements were limited only by the severity of the economic crisis, the unpopularity of the 'reforms' and the incompetence, venality and endless tribulations of Temer and his staff. They were constantly stumbling against the law, *lava jato* and other investigations of corruption, emerging mass opposition, parliamentary greed, crass disputes for political space and the continuing threat of disintegration of their base of support.[42]

Brazil finds itself immersed in political confusion to an exceptional degree even by the standards of Latin American folklore. Public administration is in chaos; the left is fragmented, demoralised and under tremendous pressure from the government and the judicial system, and the right is fraught with conflict and, surprisingly, given their institutional and ideological power, divided and unable to field a viable presidential candidate. The economy has stopped contracting, but there is no prospect of sustained recovery. There are simply no drivers of growth.

A long period of political impasse and economic paralysis is inevitable, until a new hegemony is imposed. If, as is likely, a neoliberal hegemony becomes consolidated, it will come into sharp conflict with the social clauses in the Constitution. This will reveal the government's implacable hostility to the workers and the poor, which will deepen the political dislocations in the country for years to come. This is also likely to lead to a protracted battle, including strong pressures for a new, leaner and unambiguously neoliberal Constitution. This would be the end of the social democratic experiment in Brazil, and it would return the country to the exclusionary swamp of the neoliberal Latin American periphery.

The political tragedy unfolding in Brazil is symptomatic of something much bigger than a factional squabble over corruption. Similarly, Rousseff's impeachment was not merely the tortured end of a failing government or the outcome of a savage attack on the PT. These developments are symptomatic of the effort of the neoliberal elites to destroy the fragile balance in the Constitution between the expansion of citizenship and the reproduction of privilege, and their attempt to upset the fragile equilibrium between democracy and neoliberalism that has defined Brazilian political life since 1988. The Constitution has become too small to hold two contradictory principles, and the Brazilian elites have sensed that the time is right to impose their choice.

Summary and Conclusion

Corruption was the ideal pretext to destroy the PT. During the 1990s, the PT had thrived in opposition, presenting itself as the only honest party in Brazil. This strategy worked, but it contained a contradiction that turned out to be deadly for the party. In order to win expensive elections with a politically moderate platform, manage local governments efficiently and sustain a majority in Congress through sprawling coalitions boosted by case-by-case deals, the PT would *have* to get involved in questionable practices. Yet the party succeeded for several years, winning elections at all levels. As the PT prospered, it became increasingly concerned with 'governance' and 'stability', and began to avoid confrontations with current, prospective, necessary or potential allies, in contradiction with the party's originally combative approach to politics. Its accommodating position required the abandonment of earlier commitments to reform campaign finance, the media and electoral law, expand the influence of the workers in their place of employment, and democratise the SOEs. When Lula was elected President, the PT was already a shadow of its former self.

Even this was not enough. Once in power, the PT was confronted by the hostility of the internationalised bourgeoisie and the mainstream media and, increasingly, the middle class. The neoliberal alliance used the global economic crisis, dissatisfaction with the provision of public services and other insufficiencies of the PT administrations to mount a savage attack on Dilma Rousseff. Corruption provided the ideal pretext, but its deployment in those circumstances was part of a pattern going back decades. In Brazil, the political right has been able to create a mass base for itself only by enveloping the middle class and in campaigns against inflation or corruption. This approach was first attempted against Lula during the *mensalão*, but failed to gain traction. The next attempt, against Dilma Rousseff, was more careful and systematic; it also confronted a weaker political leader facing adverse global circumstances. This time it was successful.

It goes without saying that the left must reject corruption and repress corrupt practices; the left must also reject neoliberalism as a system of accumulation. However, revulsion against neoliberalism must not be reduced to matters of corruption, since neoliberalism ought to be opposed even if it is implemented honestly. By the same token, political or administrative initiatives focusing on 'corruption in general' should be rejected because they are vulnerable to capture by the political right. Instead, progressive initiatives against corruption must have concrete content, including legal arrangements increasing transparency and accountability in the state, and empowering the public to lead challenges against dishonesty, rather than vesting power in the judiciary and the police. There was an opportunity to do this during Lula's administration and after Rousseff's first election. When the PT finally woke up to its vulnerabilities, it was already too late and its leadership was too compromised. In the end, there was no one left to lead the resistance.

Conclusion: Crisis of Neoliberalism, Crisis of Democracy

Brazil is going through an unprecedented economic and political crisis. Several years of slowing growth rates followed by successive contractions of national output reduced income per capita back to its level in the early 2000s: the gains during the PT administrations have evaporated. Open unemployment has risen dramatically; the fiscal deficit and the DPD are mounting; and Petrobras and several 'national champions' are in deep trouble. On the political front, the Constitution lies in shreds. The legitimate President was impeached by a coalition of the privileged, and a large number of political leaders are implicated in an array of corruption scandals fuelled by the media. The judiciary has gone rogue. Congress is demoralised, and the Executive is disorganised. Policy-making has become bogged down, except where it concerns the imposition of a highly excluding form of neoliberalism.[1]

This book has examined the reasons for the attack on Dilma Rousseff and the PT, why that attack succeeded and the consequences of that success for neoliberalism, democracy and the fortunes of the PT. The main conclusions are summarised below.

Limitations of Neoliberalism, Limitations of Democracy

Neoliberalism has created extraordinarily favourable conditions for the accumulation of capital and the concentration of power, income and wealth worldwide. However, in Brazil and elsewhere this system of accumulation has been accompanied by declining rates of investment and GDP growth, a deteriorating pattern of employment, a tendency towards the concentration of income and wealth, and frequent finance-driven crises. These outcomes derive from the dismantling of earlier systems of provision, the reduction of the space for the coordination of economic activity through industrial policy, greater vulnerability of the balance of payments to fickle international flows of capital, and the ability of the financial institutions to shift resources from production into speculation at will.

The social consequences of neoliberalism include the decomposition of the working class and the dilution of its culture and forms of solidarity, making it much harder to organise against the imposition of neoliberalism. The political implications of these processes include a worldwide tendency towards the implosion of traditional left parties, trade unions and mass organisations, and the dislocation of the political spectrum to the right. The decline of the left has facilitated the capture and virtual elimination of democracy by neoliberalism, in order to shield market processes from political intervention and social accountability. In a neoliberal democracy, popular participation tends to be limited to choosing between shades of neoliberalism in a sterilised political market, policed by the right-wing media.

Neoliberal democracies are, then, contradictory. On the one hand, they have political legitimacy because, presumably, democracies are inclusive, respond to popular pressure and create opportunities for the poor to seek improvements to their daily lives. On the other hand, neoliberalism requires a strong state hostile to the majority. A neoliberal democracy can address this contradiction. The institutions of the state are hijacked and transformed in order to insulate the interests of the privileged from political accountability; in the meantime, the legitimacy of democracy draws a veil over the imposition of exclusionary economic and social policies. It follows that acclaim for democracy must be tempered by recognition that it is compatible with deepening economic inequalities. This arrangement can be efficient from the point of view of capital, but it remains vulnerable to political challenges focusing on demands for the expansion of democracy: *this is the most efficient way to challenge the hegemony of neoliberalism.*[2]

Brazil offers four examples of the limitations of neoliberal democracy. First, the political transition to democracy was successful because of mass mobilisations against the dictatorship, but it was completed only through a political deal in which the country's elite accepted the dilution of its political power, the extension of citizenship rights and the legitimacy of new political actors and pressure groups. In exchange, there would be no major shifts in the pattern of economic exclusion, and no significant distribution of resources. These limitations to democracy were reinforced by the economic transition to neoliberalism, which drastically reduced the space for economic processes at variance with neoliberalism.

Second, the transition to neoliberalism secured the concentration of economic power through the transnationalisation of production, changes in the composition of the working class, higher unemployment and labour turnover, rising personal debt and economic insecurity, contractionary fiscal and monetary policies and threats of inflation or balance of payments crises should the distributive conflict get out of hand.[3] These limitations overwhelmed the reformist inclinations of the PT and its countervailing initiatives, for example, participatory budgets.[4]

Third, the economic transition to neoliberalism and the political transition to democracy became mutually reinforcing and, eventually, democracy became the political form of neoliberalism in Brazil.[5] This is why, once neoliberalism was undermined by the policies of the PT governments, powerful fractions of capital attacked the edifice of democracy in order to remove the government and eliminate the perceived threats to neoliberalism.

Fourth, the economic consequences of neoliberalism and the political encroachment of democracy drove the middle class into a (lumpenised) hatred of the PT, the left, the poor and minorities. Their disorderly hatred became so intense that even PSDB politicians were booed in demonstrations against the PT, which morphed seamlessly into an anti-political movement prone to capture by the far right.

Yet, there are important counter-tendencies to the degradation of democracy under neoliberalism that help to explain the four consecutive elections of PT leaders to the presidency and the emergence of strong mobilisations against the Temer administration in the wake of the impeachment. For example, the struggle for democracy led to the inclusion of civil, social and political rights and welfare guarantees in the Constitution. These rights are markers of ambition, sources of inspiration and a reminder of the achievements of earlier generations. They also provide a platform for struggles to limit the neoliberalisation of the economy and society.

Contradictions of the Workers' Party

Significant gains for the majority were achieved during the administrations of Lula and Rouseff, at least while the external conditions were permissive. These gains included the expansion of citizenship, social inclusion driven by the expansion of social programmes (transfers, benefits, admissions quotas for universities and the civil service, the expansion of provision of public goods and so on) and, to a limited extent, the democratisation of the state itself, especially through changes in its social composition. The majority also benefitted from faster economic growth because of the flexibilisation of neoliberalism and improvements in distribution through a higher minimum wage, the creation of millions of low-paid jobs and the formalisation of labour. The government also supported 'national champions', rebuilt the oil sector and much else.[6] Finally, even after Brazil was engulfed by economic crisis, the PT governments managed to shelter the workers until 2014, when unemployment rates touched on the historical minimum of 4 per cent and real wages peaked, *despite* the continuing deterioration of the economy. This was a remarkable achievement, given the expanding external deficit, the competitivity lag and the overvaluation of the currency.

In this context, the impeachment of Dilma Rousseff can be interpreted at four levels. They suggest that *the PT was caught in the pincers of the contradictions between neoliberalism and democracy.*

First, the government's vulnerability to impeachment derived from the escalating economic crisis, which crept through the faultlines of a process of growth overdetermined by neoliberalism and the ambitions of the PT. These faultlines radiated from the role of the neoliberal policy tripod as the foundation of macroeconomic policy. Given the limitations that the tripod imposed on aggregate demand, GDP growth had to be led by exports at least initially, and it remained highly vulnerable to fluctuations in the balance of payments. The PT administrations channelled the proceeds of the commodity boom to transfers, public and SOE investment and consumer credit. However, the neoliberal tripod and the Brazilian financial system kept interest rates much higher than the global norm. This differential rewarded speculation and depressed investment, fostering deindustrialisation, currency overvaluation and an increasing reliance on primary commodity exports.[7]

These perverse outcomes were not helped by the discovery of vast oil reserves in the South Atlantic. Even though it helped Brazil's balance of payments, the expansion of the oil sector ran counter to the economy's need for diversification and the creation of millions of well-paid high productivity jobs. Brazil ended up inserting itself into the global division of labour below China: while China became the world's assembly hub, Brazil became one of the world's largest suppliers of unprocessed inputs for industry based overseas.[8] It became impossible for the government to raise investment levels or improve the pattern of job creation. Economic growth eventually faltered, inflation increased, the fiscal and current account deficits rose and GDP growth rates declined. Brazil was battered by successive waves of QE from the advanced economies, and the space for developmental neoliberalism evaporated.

In retrospect, the Rousseff administration underestimated the severity of the global crisis, either because of the successful bounce-back of Brazil and other middle-income countries in 2009–10, or because they believed that the advanced economies would address their own difficulties rapidly and restore the earlier pattern of global growth. The government also failed to appreciate its growing isolation from capital and the contraction of its policy space. Instead, it insisted on a bold activism ungrounded in political reality, which turned into mere voluntarism. Economic growth stalled. Shockingly, prominent businesspeople started complaining about 'excessive' state intervention and 'lack of access' to a government that was following a growth strategy determined by the interests of capital. The neoliberal fraction of the bourgeoisie, the mainstream media and the middle class escalated a confrontation that led to political paralysis. Every initiative of Rousseff's administration not only failed, but also carried heavy political costs for the PT, rupturing the alliance of winners built by Lula that had carried Rousseff to victory in 2010.

Secondly, vulnerabilities of a different order emerged because of the attempt by the Rousseff administration to transcend the neoliberal SoA through marginal policy changes and the expansion of citizenship grounded on the Constitution. However, the Constitution had already become a hybrid document that *also* supported neoliberalism, for example, through its fiscal clauses and the privileges of the Central Bank. The impeachment found its (flimsy) legal grounding in these clauses. At a later stage, the administration led by Michel Temer would seek to impose an excluding modality of neoliberalism through changes in the Constitution, in order to reinforce privilege at the expense of citizenship.[9] In retrospect, the balance that the PT maintained between the opposing principles of neoliberalism and democracy depended *entirely* on a strategy of class conciliation and political accommodation that could work only when the economy was growing. However, given the economic limitations of neoliberalism, growth could be maintained only with a favourable external environment. When growth faltered, the administration lost all its sources of support and disintegrated.

Third, the impeachment signalled the exhaustion of the political project of the PT. Over time, the party shifted from a radical to a moderate version of social democracy; in sequence, it was the keystone of the alliance of losers, the hub of the alliance of winners, and the leader of the progressive alliance. Finally, it became the disintegrating core of a collapsing government. The trajectory of the PT encapsulates a cycle of the Brazilian left that has come to its end. This historical arch suggests that Rousseff's impeachment is more than a temporary reversal in the forward march of the PT and the Brazilian left. This is a long-term reversal of fortune, based on deep structural and historical weaknesses that defy simple resolution.

Fourth, the impeachment illustrates the disintegration of the pact framing Lula's election in 2002, whereby the PT was allowed to govern and tweak neoliberalism at the margin, but the defining features of the system of accumulation could not be challenged. Lula abided by this pact, and global prosperity and Lula's exceptional political talent allowed his administration to temper the neoliberal policy framework at the margin. He introduced more expansionary policies and unleashed a virtuous cycle of growth that increased profits, created jobs, distributed income, improved participation and appeared to build a new political culture. Unsurprisingly, when Lula stepped down in January 2011, his popularity rate approached 90 per cent.[10]

Dilma Rousseff strayed from this pact when she attacked financial interests by reducing interest rates; her administration added insult to injury by seeking to control the profitability of some capitals. The government seemed to believe that more aggressive intervention-ism would be tolerated because neodevelopmentalist policies would benefit capital as a whole, for example, opening new opportunities for accumulation in infrastructure, oil and other sectors. This technocratic approach was misguided because *capital will sacrifice economic growth for political control*. The administration also misjudged the global conjuncture, failed to deliver growth and campaigned from the left in 2014, raising the spectre of ideological confrontation and the intensifi-cation of class conflict. Capital became alienated from the government and, in rapid sequence, hostile to it. Capital sought solace in a renewed commitment to neoliberalism and financialisation. In the meantime, Rousseff's government alienated its own mass base, which was substantial but disorganised and, for the most part, unable to intervene politically. This limitation of the workers and the poor was partly due to the economic and social consequences of neoliberalism, and partly due to the PT's political choices as it followed its path to power.

In summary, under favourable external circumstances the developmental neoliberal policies implemented by the PT, and the greater legitimacy of the state which accompanied Lula's election, disarmed the neoliberal camp and the political right, consolidated the alliance of the PT with the internal bourgeoisie, demobilised the workers and disconnected the radical left from the working class. The PT achieved political hegemony both within the left and in the country as a whole during Lula's second administration and the first half of Rousseff's first administration. However, under unfavourable economic circumstances the limitations of the PT administrations and their accommodation of neoliberalism fostered a confluence of dissatisfactions that destroyed the alliances supporting the PT's all-too-brief double hegemony. In addition, the debacle created the conditions for the emergence of a vicious new right that would grip the middle class, propel the impeachment of Dilma Rousseff and support the reversal of the economic, distributive and social advances of the 2000s.

This dénouement *shows that what was lasting in the federal administrations led by the PT was their neoliberal economic base, and what was untenable was the neodevelopmental policies superimposed onto the neoliberal model.*

The impeachment also shows that the PT was not destroyed for being 'too bold' or 'too leftist'. Instead, its double hegemony buckled because of the party's attachment to pragmatism even when it had become counterproductive, and because of the PT's obsessive attempts to triangulate towards a political centre that was collapsing into the far right.[11]

With the media and the judiciary in hot pursuit, and the opposition choosing the line of intransigence and conflict, no amount of concessions could have kept the PT in power. Yet the party refused to mobilise its mass base; it preferred to try to do deals at the top. However, the implementation of neoliberal austerity policies after the 2014 elections, in flagrant contradiction of its own campaign rhetoric, destroyed the remaining credibility of the PT and left the party vulnerable to attack under the pretexts of corruption, conspiracy to subvert the Constitution, fiscal malfeasance, electoral lies and much else. The PT lost its supporters, and did not gain any allies. Pragmatism had run its course.

The experience of the PT suggests that transformative projects in Brazil are bound to face escalating resistance by conservative interests.

The form and effectiveness of these attacks will depend on the global environment, the government's response and the alliances supporting the administration. Experience in Brazil and elsewhere suggests that reformist pragmatism has limited efficacy, and the cultivation of wider and wider circles of increasingly unreliable allies can support the administration in good times but, in adverse circumstances, it fosters instability and political paralysis. Experience also suggests that the class, political and institutional sources of conservative power must be targeted openly, rapidly and decisively, through the mobilisation of those groups with the most to gain, especially the urban poor. The PT failed to do this, and the party was severely damaged as a result. The Brazilian left is paying a heavy price for the PT's flawed strategy.

The Journey Thus Far

The impeachment of Dilma Rousseff derives from the crises surrounding the reproduction of neoliberalism in Brazil in the wake of the global economic slowdown, the limitations of neodevelopmentalism as its purported counterweight, and the collapse of the political project of the PT, as it became impossible to keep expanding citizenship while, simultaneously, delivering economic gains to everyone. The Brazilian crisis suggests that the incompatibility between neoliberalism and neo-developmentalism was only temporarily suspended by a constellation of favourable economic and political factors. In turn, the political crisis shows that the elite will not surrender control of public policy. Finally, the PT's inability or unwillingness to transform the modalities of economic and social reproduction while in office limited the scope for the party's own survival.

Given these mutually reinforcing deadlocks, an alliance of traditional economic and political elites and the middle class emerged, and attacked the government in order to regain control of the state and disable the PT as a political force.[12] The alliance of privilege succeeded; meanwhile, and partly because of that onslaught, Brazil's economic and political crises became intractable. The deepest economic contraction in the country's history and the worst political impasse in living memory have degraded Brazilian democracy and made it impossible for any plausible composition of forces to stabilise the SoA in the short term.

It follows that the impeachment was not the inevitable outcome of historical forces. It was not the expression of the crisis of neoliberalism as the dominant modality of social reproduction, the outcome of the objective limitations of developmental neoliberalism, the result of an impasse within the bourgeois state as the condensation of the class relations of capital(ism), or the unavoidable outcome of the PT's contradictory political practices. The ouster of Dilma Rousseff was neither logically necessary nor historically inevitable. It was, instead, the contingent outcome of shifting political disputes and economic conflicts: *the coup was avoidable.*[13]

Similarly, the imposition of an extraordinarily excluding form of neoliberalism fronted, initially, by Michel Temer, was not the necessary outcome of relentless historical forces. Temer's government struggled to achieve political stability, was only partially able to re-establish the hegemony of neoliberalism, failed to restore economic growth and could not deliver the economic prosperity demanded by the middle class. Those outcomes depended on the stabilisation of the alliance of privilege, the strength of popular resistance and economic circumstances beyond the control of the administration.

The political and economic crises in Brazil defy easy resolution. First, Brazil must confront its external difficulties and the persistent failure of its development projects despite the country's size, population, resources and earlier economic achievements. These difficulties have been intensified by the worldwide shift of manufacturing to East Asia in recent decades. This process has placed at the core of global capitalism a highly-integrated region offering capital better infrastructure, higher productivity, larger populations, lower wages and political systems more attuned to the demands of accumulation than in Brazil.

This world-historical transformation has pushed Brazil away from the dynamic core of the world economy and from the technological frontier, except in a few narrowly-defined fields (e.g. tropical seeds and pesticides, hydroelectric dams, mid-sized aircraft and deep-sea oil extraction). The consequence has been the long-term decline of Brazilian manufacturing industry for reasons that are only partly related to domestic mismanagement. Closely related, the country has slipped down the hierarchy of the international division of labour.[14] While in the second half of the twentieth century Brazil could dream of converging with the USA, today the country's economy is firmly locked behind China's. It provides the Asian giant with unprocessed primary inputs, in exchange for manufactured goods worth tens of billions of dollars every year:

The rise of Brazil's exports to China ... has been stunning. It grew ... from US$ 1bn in 2000 to US$ 44.3bn in 2011, with nearly all exports to China being based on commodities ... This gives an emblematic illustration of Brazil's integration into the world economy. While Brazil's main exports to China over the last decade have been predominantly resource-based products, notably iron ore, soya and oil (81% of all Brazilian exports to China), its three main imports from China are ... at the other end of the value chain, notably engines and electrical equipment, furnaces, nuclear reactors and chemicals (58.2% of all imports from China) ... This could be regarded as a minor issue if China had not become Brazil's biggest trading partner. Brazil faces the prospect of becoming a net exporter of commodities, while other large developing economies are consolidating their position as net suppliers of manufactured goods.[15]

Brazil's external deficit in manufactured goods is covered by the sale of domestic assets and with resources borrowed, in different forms, from the advanced Western economies. Brazil's response to these challenges will determine the country's trajectory for the next few decades, but there is no sign that the Brazilian political system and the dominant SoA have the coherence, dynamism, planning capacity or resources to forge a path to the global 'core'.

Second, domestically, the coup and the crisis of social reproduction in which it took place point to a rupture in the constitutional order. The contradictions between neoliberalism and democracy, embodied in the incompatibility between the progressive social chapter of the 1988 Constitution and the conservative fiscal clauses newly embedded in the Charter, will become increasingly acute.[16] These tensions are unlikely to be resolved without a revision of the Constitution. While this is likely to support the imposition of a renewed neoliberal hegemony, this will not be a simple or stable process.[17] Since these constitutional changes will require the restriction of the rights of citizenship, they can only be imposed by authoritarian means. Alternatively, the preservation of citizenship may be secured by efforts to inaugurate a new SoA in which democracy prevails over economic and social exclusion.

Neoliberalism can be transcended only if its material basis is systematically dismantled, initially through democratic economic policy initiatives supporting a model of development generating more equal distributions of income, wealth and power, and improved material welfare for the poor.[18] This is a fundamental condition for democracy. These alternative policies must be supported by controls on capital flows, coordinated trade, financial and industrial policies, the expansion of non-revenue-generating social programmes financed by progressive taxation, and the reallocation of government spending.

These initiatives require the support of a politically rearticulated working class, as one of the main levers for its *own* economic recomposition. The difficulty is that this virtuous circle cannot be wished into being. Its elements cannot be addressed purely academically, the organisation of another political party or through alliances between existing forces. The construction of a democratic economy, society and political system will require mass mobilisations sufficiently strong not only to demand change *from* governments, or even changes *of* government, but also to *embed popular organisations within the state*, while preserving their political integrity, mass roots and accountability to the majority of the population. The construction of this new wave of popular movements is likely to be one of the most important challenges for the Brazilian left in the next decade.

Notes

Introduction

1. O'Donnell (1989) discusses the social costs of 'development' in Brazil; Torras (2001) reviews the environmental costs.
2. In order to avoid confusion, in this book the name 'Real stabilisation plan' is capitalised; the name of the currency introduced with the plan, the *real*, is italicised. When pronounced, the word 'real' is stressed on the letter 'a'.
3. 'Grand' theory is used here in the sense of Gallie (1956) and Merton (1968); see also Saad-Filho (2000).
4. The SoA is obviously a more concrete form of the mode of production. For the latter, see Banaji (2010), Byres (1995), Lenin (1899) and Ste. Croix (1984).
5. For an overview, see Saes (2001). Primary goods are unprocessed agricultural and mining products (manufacturing is the secondary sector; the tertiary sector is services).
6. See Fiori (1992, p. 181), Martins (1977) and the detailed analysis in Rose (2006).
7. See Ianni (1988, p. 7).
8. See Martins (1985) and Ianni (1988).
9. The most influential Brazilian economist, Celso Furtado, stated that 'there can be no other explanation to the misery of the greater part of the population than the resistance of the ruling classes against any change which might endanger their privileges' (quoted in Fagnani 2005, p. 556).
10. Brazil's relative youth and large size, the diversity of its natural resources and economic activities and the relative isolation of large areas have contributed to the emergence of strong local elites and distinct social structures over time and across the country (see Karavaev 1987, pp. 212–14).
11. For an extended analysis, see Martins (1985).
12. See Martins (1985, ch. 3).
13. Contractionary fiscal policy, or 'fiscal austerity', is the systematic imposition of cuts in government spending as part of a conventional (orthodox or mainstream) economic policy response to an economic downturn, or simply for ideological reasons. Contractionary monetary policy is the imposition of high interest rates by the Central Bank, in order to reduce private spending in consumption and investment.
14. Reprimarisation is a form of economic involution in which an industrialised economy gradually loses part of its manufacturing base, while the share of primary production in GDP expands.
15. The PT's socialism is examined in Branford and Kucinski (2003, pp. 46–9).
16. Developmentalism is an interpretation of ISI that evolved in connection with the UN Economic Commission for Latin America (ECLAC or, in Spanish, CEPAL) between the 1950s and the 1980s. Neodevelopmentalism

emerged in the 2000s. For simplicity, and given the temporal separation between theses approaches, the prefix 'neo' may be dropped in what follows. Paulani (2017) examines the differences between developmentalism and neodevelopmentalism.

Chapter 1

1. For a historical review of the development of technology in Brazil, see Motoyama (1994).
2. In 1982 BNDE would become BNDES, with the addition of the suffix 'Social'.
3. See Cardoso and Faletto (1979).
4. For an overview, see Gowan (1999) and Panitch and Gindin (2012).
5. Import-substituting industrialisation is assessed by Bruton (1981, 1998), Gereffi and Wyman (1990) and Hirschman (1968). For an overview of ISI in Latin America, see Bulmer-Thomas (2003), FitzGerald (2000) and Thorp (1992). The Brazilian case is reviewed by Baer (2013), Cano (2015), Evans (1979), Furtado (1972), Hewitt (1992), Ianni (1988), Lessa (1964), Oliveira (1977), Versiani and Mendonça de Barros (1978) and Tavares (1978).
6. For an overview, see Coutinho and Reichstul (1977).
7. For a description, see Silva (1979, pp. 22–5).
8. Estimates of the sectoral composition of Brazilian GDP have been debated in a vast literature; for various approximations, invariably leading to similar trends, see Abreu, Bevilacqua and Pinho (2000), Bonelli and Pessôa (2010), Feijó and Carvalho (1998), Nassif (2008), Oreiro and Feijó (2010) and Torres and Cavalieri (2015).
9. Fiori (1992).
10. See Martins (1985, pp. 23–5).
11. The balance-of-payments constraint expresses the limits imposed by the scarcity of foreign currency on the capacity to import, save, invest and finance the state (see McCombie and Thirlwall 1994). Bértola, Higachi and Porcile (2002) and Alencar and Strachmann (2014) provide estimates of the balance-of-payments constraint for Brazil.
12. See Hurtienne and Sperber (1983, p. 121).
13. See Oliveira (1977). Portugal (1994) and Silva (2003) examine the implications of ISI for Brazilian trade policy.
14. For a detailed analysis, see Baer (1986), Oliveira (1977) and Studart (1995). See also Fiori (1990), Goldsmith (1984), Lees Botts and Cysne (1990) and Tavares (1978, pp. 125–52).
15. These are dedicated (usually subsidised) credit lines offered by the commercial banks to priority sectors, by order of the Central Bank or the Ministry of Finance.
16. See Fiori (1990, p. 47).
17. For an overview of industrial policies under ISI, see Amann and Chang (2004), Auty (1991), Boschi (1978), Evans (1979), Laffer (1984), Moreira (1991), Nembhard (1996), Saad-Filho (1998), Suzigan and Villela (1997, ch. 2) and Théret (1993). The SOEs are examined by Dain (1977).
18. See Baracho (1982) and Fiori (1992).

19. For detailed studies of the Brazilian state, see Oliveira (1977), Martins (1985) and Saes (2001).
20. For an overview, see Coutinho and Reichstul (1977, section 2) and Schneider (2015).
21. See Boschi (1978, p. 115), Cardoso and Faletto (1979, chs. 5–6) and Ianni (1988, p. 155).
22. See Diniz (1978) and Ianni (1988).
23. See Saad-Filho, Iannini and Molinari (2007) and Skidmore (1973).
24. See Martins (1985) and Saes (2001, pp. 120–6).
25. See Briones (1978, p. 127), di Tella (1997, p. 189), Fiori (1992, p. 181) and Oliveira (1977, pp. 118–19).
26. See Chauí (1994) and Weffort (1980).
27. Fiori (1992, p. 181) rightly argues that 'the conservative pact which sustained the Brazilian developmentalist state never included democratic participation in any of its forms, and consequently never sponsored the institutionalisation of structures which could respond to pressures by expanding political and social citizenship'. See also Saes (2001, pp. 64–79).
28. Briones (1978, p. 27).
29. O'Donnell (1982) rightly argues that the military coups were responses to hegemonic impasses across Latin America. They responded to 'a static equilibrium ... [in which] no group, neither the conservatives nor the progressives, has the strength for victory, and [in which] the conservative group needs a master' (Gramsci, 1971, p. 451). The cases of Argentina and Brazil are reviewed by Saad-Filho, Iannini and Molinari (2007).
30. See Cardoso and Faletto (1979, pp. 167–9, 207–12) and O'Donnell (1982).
31. See Furtado (1972) and Tavares (1978).
32. For a review, see Varaschin (2015).
33. For an overview, see Pereira (2016a).
34. See Oliveira (1977).
35. For a review of the coup, see Demier (2013, pp. 212–17), Ridenti (2016) and, especially, Dreifuss (1981).
36. See Fiori (1992) and Karavaev (1987, p. 222).
37. Sader (2013, Kindle locations 3153–6) rightly argues that 'The military coup in Brazil had a peculiarity vis-à-vis the other coups in the [Latin American] region. The [Brazilian] coup took place during the long expansive cycle of global capitalism and, on that basis, the regime could, through the repression of the trade unions and the compression of wages, impose an expansive rhythm to the economy. In the other countries in the region ... the repressive regime was installed in the long recessive cycle of the global economy, and it coincided with economic contraction and early forms of transition to neoliberalism ... It was only with the [international] debt crisis that the economic situation in Brazil became similar to that of other countries.'
38. For an overview of the military period, see Skidmore (1988). The economic angle is examined by Boschi (1978, pp. 118–19), Fiori (1992) and Karavaev (1987, p. 222). The renewal of Brazilian agribusiness is reviewed by Hopewell (2016).
39. See Alves (1984, pp. 239–45).

40. Political folklore suggested that the difference between them was that MDB was the 'Party of Yes', while ARENA was the 'Party of Yes, Sir!'.
41. For a review, see Cysne (1993), Lara-Resende (1982) and Moraes (1987).
42. See Martone (1970).
43. See Itoh and Lapavitsas (1999) and Zysman (1983).
44. See Oliveira (1978).
45. For example, the National Monetary Council and the Central Bank of Brazil were both created in 1964.
46. See Hermann (2002), Studart (1995) and Studart and Hermann (2001).
47. For a detailed review of the Brazilian economy during this period, see Baer and Kerstenetzky (1975).
48. See Hurtienne and Sperber (1983, pp. 117–18) and Silva (1979, pp. 37–43).
49. See Hurtienne and Sperber (1983, p. 120), Martins (1985, p. 80), Oliveira (1977) and Tavares (1978, pp. 211–63). In São Paulo, the remuneration of managers increased 75 per cent in real terms between 1964 and 1985, while the wages of skilled workers rose 83 per cent. In contrast, the wages of unskilled workers rose 38 per cent, the wages of office workers 33 per cent and the minimum wage fell 43 per cent (Sabóia, 1991).
50. See Alonso (2003, pp. 83–7) and Baer and Kersternetzky (1975).
51. See, for example, Furtado (1972), Tavares (1978), Oliveira (1977) and Singer (1978).
52. See Coes (1994), Coutinho and Ferraz (1995), Hurtienne and Sperber (1983, p. 120) and Motoyama (1994).
53. See Moraes (1987, pp. 146–7). Bresser-Pereira (2015a, pp. 107–9) reviews the successful growth of Brazilian manufacturing exports. For an examination of the export subsidies provided by the government, see Baumann and Braga (1988).
54. In the sense of Studart (1995) and Paula (2013).
55. Studart and Hermann (2001, p. 61) rightly argue that: 'Until the late 1980s … the Brazilian model of financing was very different from other private systems – both in capital markets and credit markets. During this period, the state remained the only domestic provider of long-term loans for industry and infrastructure, both through BNDES and by less conventional fiscal channels.' Hurtienne and Sperber (1983, p. 119) add that the state banking system held 50 per cent of demand deposits and 75 per cent of savings deposits, distributed 80 per cent of funding for long-term investment and 44 per cent of all credit in the economy. See also Baer (1986) and Silva (1979, pp. 14–20).
56. For detailed analyses, see Carneiro (1977) and Fishlow (1986).
57. See Bacha (1978a, 1978b) and Singer (1978).
58. The policy decisions taken in this period are outlined by Cysne (1993).
59. Castro and Souza (1984, p. 30), quoting the plan.
60. The nuclear programme was especially important. It was based on a 1975 agreement signed with West Germany, that included the purchase of eight light-water reactors and equipment for uranium enrichment and the reprocessing of nuclear fuel. The programme was expected to lead to the internalisation of the production of equipment for the nuclear industry, creating an estimated US$1 billion market for high-tech Brazilian industry in the following decade. The ultimate goal was to position Brazil among the

leading exporters of nuclear technology. See Gaspari (2004, pp. 373, 388–9; 2016, pp. 35–7) and Hurtienne and Sperber (1983, p. 124).

61. For a detailed review of PND2, see Castro and Souza (1985); see also Fiori (1990).

62. See Villela (1984) and Werneck (1987).

63. For a detailed analysis, see Alonso (2003, pp. 89–90).

64. Belluzzo (2013, Kindle location 2382–5) rightly points out that 'in the 1970s … [the government] built infrastructure (to produce non-tradable services) on a mountain of debts in foreign currency. In other words: they financed the construction of roads, hydroelectric dams, metro systems and telecommunications networks in dollars, even though they knew that the tariffs and tolls would be paid in domestic currency.'

65. For a review, see Fishlow (1986).

66. For descriptions and analyses of the Volcker shock, see Gowan (1999) and Panitch and Gindin (2012).

67. See Cruz (1984).

68. The impact of the international debt crisis in Brazil is reviewed by Cruz (1984) and Gaspari (2016, pp. 174–9).

69. For a detailed analysis of the DPD, see Casa (2004) and Silva, Carvalho and Medeiros (2009).

70. See Bontempo (1988), Cavalcanti (1988) and Cohen (1987).

71. For an examination of the decline of public sector investment, see Bresser-Pereira (2015a).

72. Belluzzo (2013, Kindle locations 2427–30) rightly argues that 'during the years 1950, 1960, 1970 there were synergies … between public investment, led by the SOEs, and private investment. Privatisation dismantled this virtuous relationship. A high volume of public investment in infrastructure is vital for … growth … Investment by multinationals is important to generate hard currency and for the technological upgrading of exports, but not for the aggregate volume of investment.'

73. Annual interest rates were limited by law to a maximum of 12 per cent per annum. Since inflation often exceeded this level, there was no scope for the development of a deep financial system in the country. The way around that restriction was to index-link the returns on financial assets, starting with government securities, so the 12 per cent limit would apply only to real, rather than nominal gains (Studart, 1995).

74. The indexation of the exchange rate avoided the overvaluation of the Brazilian currency and the loss of trade competitivity that would occur if Brazilian prices rose faster than US prices under a fixed exchange-rate system. For example, suppose that Brazilian inflation was 100 per cent and US inflation was zero, with a fixed exchange rate. By the end of the year, Brazilian goods would cost 100 per cent more *both* in Brazilian currency *and* in US dollars, making them uncompetitive. In order to compensate domestic inflation, the exchange rate could be indexed, in which case it would automatically fall by 50 per cent, neutralising the increase in domestic prices in dollar terms. The same principle applies to other prices and wages. Bontempo (1989) examines Brazil's exchange-rate policy during this period.

75. Nominal wages increased once a year until 1979, twice yearly until 1985, approximately every three months until 1987 and monthly thereafter. At that point, workers would only know their nominal wages *after* they were paid (see Balbinotto Neto, 1991, Barbosa and McNelis, 1989, and Macedo, 1983).

76. Imagine the national income as a fixed 'cake'. If, suddenly, 5 per cent of the cake had to be transferred to the external creditors every year, some pre-existing claimant would have to lose a corresponding share.

77. See Arida and Lara-Resende (1985, 1986), Bresser-Pereira and Nakano (1985), Dornbusch and Simonsen (1983), Lopes (1986) and Simonsen and Barbosa (1989).

78. Munhoz (1988, pp. 25–6) rightly argues that '[o]rthodox adjustment is based on the hypothesis of excess aggregate demand, which is destabilising ... because it is based on mechanisms to transfer real income to the government, the financial institutions, savers, exporters and/or consumers of exported goods. *Inflation is the mechanism that, in market economies, makes this adjustment of incomes*, triggering losses especially for the groups with contractual incomes, by an amount equivalent to the incomes transferred to others because of the policy measures introduced by the adjustment programme' (see also p. 31).

79. See Bresser-Pereira (1981, 1992), Lafer (1984) and Saad-Filho and Mollo (2002).

80. For a review, see Banco Central do Brasil (1995, pp. 37–8), Carvalho (1993), Hermann (2002), Pastore (1990), Paula (1996) and Ramalho (1995).

81. See Boismery (1996) and Garcia (1996).

82. The banks gradually relaxed the conditions for the supply of index-linked accounts, but always excluded the majority of the population, who were too poor to qualify. Kane and Morisett (1993) estimate that the asset gains of the higher income brackets more than compensated their losses due to inflation between 1980–9; in contrast, inflation reduced the annual income of the poorest quintile by 19 per cent. See also Cysne (1993, pp. 219–22).

83. Celso Furtado is the best-known critic of this aspect of ISI, see Furtado (1972).

84. See Amadeo and Camargo (1991).

85. See Pochmann (2010, pp. 640, 648; 2011, pp. 23, 38).

86. See Pomar (2013, p. 34).

87. The 1989 Lorenz curve envelops that of 1970 completely, showing an unambiguous deterioration in the distribution of income; see Bonelli and Sedlacek (1991), Cacciamali (1997) and Ferreira and Litchfield (1996).

88. See Calvo (1992) and Végh (1992). Silva and Andrade (1996) survey the debate about the causes of Brazilian inflation. Carvalho (1993) and Parkin (1991) provide stimulating non-mainstream analyses.

89. Judicial challenges against government intervention in private contracts eventually led to heavy penalties being imposed against the state.

90. The most important inflation stabilisation plans were the Cruzado (1986), Bresser (1987), Summer (1989), Collor I (1990), Collor II (1991) and Real (1994). They are examined, from different angles, by Arida and Lara-Resende (1985), Bresser-Pereira (1987), Bresser-Pereira and Nakano (1985), Cardoso and Dornbusch (1987), Carvalho (1993), Feijó and Carvalho (1992), Lopes (1986, 1989), Munhoz (1988) and Paulani (1997).

91. For an examination of the failure of the Cruzado plan, see Solnik (1987). Bresser-Pereira (2015, pp. 102–3) rightly argues that '[t]he collapse of the Cruzado plan, in 1987, was a major political and economic disaster, that demonstrated that the opposition that had fought against the military regime lacked a theory and a project of development'.

92. See Camargo and Ramos (1988) for a detailed examination of the distributional implications of the Cruzado plan.

93. Fiori (1992, p. 184).

94. For an overview of the Collor plan and its implications, see Carvalho (2000, 2006), Faro (1990) and Martuscelli (2015, pp. 56–8).

95. Collor never achieved his goal of dismissing 360,000 civil servants, and his attempt to axe as many as possible was largely reversed. However, in the meantime it disorganised the public administration and demoralised the civil service, facilitating the reorganisation of the state along neoliberal lines in the following years (see Martuscelli, 2015, pp. 63–5).

96. See Auty (1991, p. 158), Baracho (1982) and Rodrik (1998).

Chapter 2

1. The imperative of legitimacy pushed the military regime towards a strategy of economic growth; see above and Gaspari (2003, pp. 437–8).

2. For an overview of the armed resistance against the dictatorship, see Mir (1994) and Rollemberg (2003).

3. For an overview of these elections, see Alves (1984, pp. 188–9) and Gaspari (2016, p. 237).

4. See Alves (1984, pp. 230–1) and Gaspari (2004, pp. 181–4, 327–32).

5. See, for example, Diniz (1978, p. 188) and Hurtienne and Sperber (1983, pp. 124–6).

6. For an expanded analysis, see Alves (1984, pp. 323–4).

7. The death of journalist Vladimir Herzog is reviewed in Gaspari (2004, pp. 172–87).

8. The campaign of terror is described in Alves (1984, pp. 316–21) and Gaspari (2004, pp. 280–3). For the Riocentro affair, see Gaspari (2016, pp. 183–210).

9. See Alves (1984, pp. 246–51).

10. For an overview, see Alves (1984, p. 186), Kucinski (1982), Mir (1994, p. 667) and Silva (2003).

11. See Alves (1984, p. 200).

12. See, for example, Alves (1984, pp. 202, 229).

13. See, for example, Schneider (2016).

14. See Alves (1984, pp. 220–1).

15. In what follows, 'consensus' refers to a substantial measure of agreement on a strategic political and economic project by social groups that, by virtue of their institutional power and political influence, can implement these projects through the institutions of the state. This concept is related to the Gramscian notion of hegemony. Neither of them presume unanimity.

16. There was much talk about the creation of 302 SOEs by the military regime; in contrast, only 14 SOEs were founded before the 1930s, 15 between 1930 and 1954, 23 under Kubitscheck and 33 under Goulart (see Fiori, 1990, p. 42).

17. See, for example, Diaz-Alejandro (1985).

18. See Gaspari (2004, pp. 54–9, 334–5) and Markoff and Baretta (1990, p. 429).

19. See Gaspari (2004, pp. 342–51).

20. For an overview of the campaign for democracy, see Alves (1988), Gaspari (2016, pp. 267–75) and Leonelli and Oliveira (2004). The implications of the democratic transition are reviewed in Kinzo and Dunkerley (2003) and Stepan (1989).

21. See Gaspari (2016, pp. 298–311).

22. For a similar analysis, see O'Donnell (1992). For Diniz (1999, p. 163), when Sarney was sworn in as president, 'there was a consensus about the need to make democratic political reforms in order to eliminate the authoritarian legacy … [but] there was no agreement, within the government itself, about the breakdown of the previous model of development, either with respect to its economic aspects, or with respect to its institutional support … [This model] was being gradually eroded since the mid-seventies … *but its destruction was not yet the subject of deliberate government policies*' (emphasis added).

23. The decline of the Catholic Church was partly compensated by the growth of a myriad of (mostly right-wing) evangelical sects (see Alves, 2014, p. 106).

24. See Fiori (1997).

25. Sader (2013, Kindle locations 3171–3) rightly argues that '[t]he democratic transition was completed without the democratisation of economic power in Brazil. The banking system was not democratised; neither was the media, or landed property, or large industrial and commercial conglomerates. The end of the dictatorship did not represent the democratisation of Brazilian society.'

26. For a similar approach, see Coutinho (2013), Lavinas (2013, 2017) and Sánchez-Ancochea and Mattei (2011).

27. See Câmara Neto and Vernengo (2007, p. 80), Leubolt (2013) and Sánchez-Ancochea and Mattei (2011).

28. For a review of the process of writing up the Constitution, see Sampaio (2009).

29. See Amorim (2009, p. 21), Bercovici (2009) and Sampaio (2009, p. 44).

30. See Castro *et al.* (2009), Coutinho (2013, pp. 89–91), Fagnani (2005, pp. xv–xvi, 219, 541–5), Leubolt (2013, p. 72) and Trubek, Coutinho and Shapiro (2013). Sampaio (2009) examines the political context of these social policy achievements.

31. See Sampaio (2009, p. 46).

32. Leubolt (2013, p. 73).

33. For a description of these funding mechanisms, see Fagnani (2005, p. 546) and Mattei (2012).

34. BPC is a non-contributory transfer awarded to those aged over 65 or unable to work or lead an independent life, and whose per capita household income is 25 per cent below the minimum wage. BPC transfers are constitutionally set at one minimum wage (see IPEA, 2012 and Leubold, 2013).

35. See Castro (2009, pp. 68–72), Fagnani (2005, p. 547), Sader (2013, Kindle locations 3163–9) and Santos and Gentil (2009, pp. 124–8).

36. President Cardoso famously called young retirees *vagabundos* ('bums' or 'layabouts'); see http://www2.uol.com.br/JC/_1998/1205/br1205n.htm (accessed 7 July 2017).

37. See Leubold (2013) and Mattei (2012).

38. See Fagnani (2005, pp. 547–55).

39. See Amorim (2009, p. 21), Fagnani (2005, pp. 440 *et seq.*) and Santos and Gentil (2009).
40. 'Pauperist' welfare regimes are described by Seekings (2012).
41. For a detailed critique of social policy in Brazil, especially during the PT administrations, see Lavinas (2017); see also Saad-Filho (2015a).
42. Three important organisations were the Women's Movement for Amnesty (*Movimento Feminino pela Anistia,* MFA), the Brazilian Committee for Amnesty (*Comitê Brasileiro de Anistia* CBA) and the Movement Cost of Living (*Movimento Custo de Vida* MCV), which collected millions of signatures demanding inflation control and real wage increases for the low-paid.
43. For a detailed analysis, see Alves (1984, pp. 248–51) and Gaspari (2016, pp. 47–57). The strike waves in 1979 and 1980 are reviewed in Alves (1984, pp. 253–4 and 261–4) and Bourne (2008, ch. 2).
44. 'Lula' was a nickname. He changed his legal name to Luiz Inácio Lula da Silva, for electoral reasons, in 1982.
45. Del Roio (2004) contrasts the politics and social composition of the PT with the PCB.
46. The history of the PT is reviewed in Amaral (2003), Bourne (2008), Branford and Kucinski (1995, 2003), Gadotti and Pereira (1989), Sader (2003), Sader and Silverstein (1991), Secco (2011) and Singer (2012, ch. 2). Party documents are collected in PT (1998). For the history of CUT, see Costa (1995).
47. Radical left parties have found it difficult to prosper under the twin pressures of neoliberalism and PT political hegemony among the left. The recomposition of the working class in recent decades has increased social heterogeneity and reduced the workers' organisational and political capacities (see Chapter 8), while the dissolution of socialist alternatives worldwide and Brazil's integration into 'global' culture have deprived the proletariat of points of reference on the far left. Since the early 1980s, despite repeated attempts, no party has prospered to the left of the PT, and debates about the desirability and feasibility of revolutionary alternatives to capitalism have largely died down.
48. For an overview of these pressures, see Jessop (2016, pp. 24, 83–5).
49. This process is reviewed in Branford and Kucinski (2003, ch. 1).
50. See Branford and Kucinski (2003, pp. 32–4) and Saad-Filho and Mollo (2002).
51. For a review of the programme of privatisations, see Bérzin (2002) and Biondi (2014). The case of public utilities is examined by Pinheiro and Fukasaku (2000).
52. See Bianchi and Braga (2003) and Lacerda (2002).
53. Medeiros (2013, p. 65).
54. Robaina (2003, p. 109) rightly calls it the 'vicious circle of electoralism'.
55. See Machado (2003, 2005).
56. See Branford and Kucinski (2003, ch. 4).
57. Branford and Kucinski (2003, pp. 34–5).
58. For detailed analyses of the 'moderation' of PT, see Bianchi and Braga (2003), Branford and Kucinski (2003), Coggiola (2004), Machado (2003), Ribeiro (2014), Robaina (2003, ch. 4) and Sader (2004, 2005).
59. Gorender and Lorent (1998) discuss the elections of 1994 and their impact on the PT.
60. See Branford and Kucinski (2003, pp. 45–52).

Chapter 3

1. See Mollo and Saad-Filho (2006) and Saad-Filho (2007b).
2. Transitions to neoliberalism were connected to inflation stabilisation in Argentina, Bolivia, Chile, Uruguay and elsewhere, and transitions to neoliberalism were articulated with democratic transitions in Eastern Europe, South Africa and South Korea.
3. All macroeconomic data mentioned in this book are from www.ipeadata.gov.br, unless stated otherwise.
4. See Fine and Saad-Filho (2017) and Saad-Filho (2017); for a broader overview, see Saad-Filho and Johnston (2005).
5. Sader (2013, Kindle locations 3185–6) argues that '[i]n Brazil, neoliberalism promoted two central phenomena, both adverse: the financialisation of the economy and the precarisation of labour relations'.
6. See Sader (2013, Kindle locations 3174–7).
7. See Laplane and Sarti (1999, p. 198), Moreira and Correa (1998) and Tauile (2001, pp. 222–3).
8. Fiori (1992, p. 174) rightly argued that: 'With a decade of delay, neoliberalism is ... mounting an unprecedented ideological offensive against the Brazilian State, which is seen as the main culprit of the stagflation and economic losses of the 1980s ... [S]ometimes ... a new ideological hegemony succeeds in temporarily sweeping away the knowledge accumulated in the past, replacing history and theory with pure and simple ideology capable of suddenly convincing intellectuals and politicians that only the market holds the secret of economic success and universal happiness.'
9. See Auty (1991), Bresser-Pereira (1996), Franco (1995), Kingstone (1999), Kormann (2015, part III) and Moreira (1991). For a critique, see Fiori (1990), Lessa and Fiori (1991) and Martins (1985). Machado (2002) and Bianchi (2004) trace the construction of the neoliberal consensus among the São Paulo bourgeoisie.
10. See Weeks (2000).
11. See, for example, Chang and Yoo (2000), Felder (2013) and Valle Baeza and Martínez González (2011).
12. See Banco Central do Brasil (1993). The liberalisation of the exchange rate turned it from a trade policy tool into a macroeconomic stabilisation tool increasingly dependent on the level of interest rates.
13. For an overview of the liberalisation of trade, see Hay (2001), Kume (1988), Kume, Piani and Souza (2000) and Suzigan and Villela (1997, pp. 67–76). The liberalisation of finance is reviewed by Paula (2011).
14. See Squeff (2015, p. 15).
15. For a detailed analysis of Brazil's external debt and the Brady plan, see Cerqueira (2003); see also Alonso (2003, pp. 97–8).
16. Martuscelli (2015, pp. 46, 89–90) reviews the relationship between the bourgeoisie and Fernando Collor. The alliance supporting Lula is examined on pp. 48–9.
17. See Figueiredo (2000) and Valença (2002) for a description of the Collor administration and the scandals that brought its downfall.

18. This was partly justified by the conviction that any successful inflation stabilisation programme would require substantial balance-of-payments support (Levy and Hahn, 1996).

19. See Sampaio (2009, pp. 47–8).

20. For an overview of the privatisations and the industrial policies under Collor and Franco, see Orair (2015, pp. 118–19) and Suzigan and Villela (1997, chs. 6–7).

21. See Gonçalves (1999, pp. 125–8).

22. In his youth, Cardoso was an influential contributor to the dependency school. His intellectual profile changed in the 1980s, and his political trajectory can be described as a steady shift upwards and to the right (not necessarily in that order). For a review of his administration, see Purcell and Roett (1997).

23. Governo do Brasil (1993); see also Amadeo (1996), Andrade *et al.* (1997), Bacha (1997), Cintra (2015), Dornbusch (1997), Dornbusch and Simonsen (1983), Franco (1995), Lopes (1986), Nogueira Batista (1996), Saad-Filho and Maldonado-Filho (1998), Saad-Filho and Mollo (2002), Saad-Filho and Morais (2000, 2002), Saad-Filho, Morais and Coelho (1999) and Sachs and Zini (1996). Although its paternity is disputed, the Real plan was outlined in Arida and Lara-Resende (1986), possibly inspired by a failed experiment in Hungary in 1946 (see Anderson, Bomberger and Makinen, 1988 and Bomberger and Makinen, 1983).

24. See Saad-Filho (2005).

25. See, for example, Baumann, Rivero and Zavattiero (1997).

26. See Saad-Filho and Morais (2004).

27. See Nogueira Batista (1996, p. 34). For other estimates of the overvaluation of the *real*, see Bacha (1997, p. 201), Dornbusch (1997, p. 375), Fishlow (1997) and Kilsztajn (1996). Ironically, early supporters of the stabilisation plan had highlighted the dangers of the overvaluation of the currency; see, for example, Bonelli, Franco and Fritsch (1992).

28. Source: Banco Central do Brasil, séries históricas.

29. See Nakatani (1999) and *Conjuntura Econômica*, Maio (1996).

30. *Gazeta Mercantil*, 24 October 1994. Edmar Bacha, one of the economists in charge of the programme, claimed that in 'its first stage, the Plan had to be supported by a policy of exchange rate revaluation in order to guarantee the rapid convergence of inflation to around two per cent per month. It is difficult to imagine this success if there had not been an additional policy of trade liberalisation' (cited in Troster and Solimeo, 1997, pp. 3–4); see also Franco (1998, p. 141).

31. For a detailed analysis, see Freitas and Prates (2001).

32. The methodology used to calculate the rate of investment changed in 2000, and two series are available in Ipeadata until 2013. The new series provides slightly higher values along a similar trend.

33. See Bresser-Pereira (2003).

34. See Casa (2004) and Silva, Carvalho and Medeiros (2009).

35. See Giambiagi (2007).

36. Source: Ipeadata.

37. See Sicsú (1996).

38. See, for example, the revealing statement by Banco Central do Brasil (1995, p. 103, emphasis added): 'At the beginning of the year [1995] the *policy of maintaining trade deficits was reviewed*, in light of the uncertainty in foreign financial markets ... [T]he government sought to define a strategy aimed at balancing trade flows. Initially, special attention was given to the export sector ... Later on, steps were taken to regulate imports in sectors less detrimental to the process of price stabilisation and industrial modernisation. However, on several occasions, the priority accorded [to] the fight against inflation made it necessary to facilitate imports in order to offset supply deficiencies on the domestic market.'

39. For an overview of the distributional impact of the plan, see Galvão (2007, pp. 51–3). These gains were ephemeral, since the share of national income of the poorest half of the population declined from 12.2 per cent to 11.6 per cent between 1993 and 1995 (Neri and Considera, 1996, pp. 52–4, and Simonsen, 1994).

40. See Cardoso (2003, pp. 51–2).

41. For an overview of industrial policy during the Real plan, see Suzigan and Villela (1997, ch.8).

42. For a review of the role of the Real plan in Cardoso's election, see Martuscelli (2015, pp. 135–9).

43. For an exploration of the reasons for high interest rates in Brazil, see Modenesi and Modenesi (2012) and World Bank (2006).

44. For a similar interpretation, see Medialdea (2013).

45. Data from: https://fred.stlouisfed.org/series/INTDSRUSM193N (accessed 18 July 2017).

46. See Bacha (1997, p. 183).

47. Nogueira Batista (1996, p. 48); see also Dornbusch (1997, p. 375).

48. See Cinquetti (2000). The nominal fiscal deficit (or public sector borrowing requirements, PSBR) is the difference between total government expenditures and total revenues, including all levels of public administration and the SOEs. The primary fiscal deficit is the difference between non-financial expenditures (that is, excluding interest on the DPD) and government revenues.

49. See Cintra (2015, p. 134).

50. In 1998 the manufacturing leader Eugênio Staub declared that '[the] dialogue of the private sector with the government is at its lowest level. The state bureaucracy has become self-sufficient and arrogant ... [T]hey do not listen to us and, when they listen, they do not believe us'. His colleague Roberto Nicolau Jeha was more incisive: 'We are on our knees. We are facing extinction. Brazilian manufacturers are finished and we have no dignity left. We are being taken to the slaughterhouse but keep praising "modernisation"' (Diniz, 1999, pp. 172–3).

51. See Amann and Baer (2000) and Morais, Saad-Filho and Coelho (1999).

52. For a critical review of Cardoso's administration, see Amann (2000), Flynn (1999) and Lesbaupin (1999).

53. See Morais, Saad Filho and Coelho (1999).

54. Annual bank profit rates in Brazil were in the region of 11 per cent, and total bank profits in 1998 were R$1.8 billion. In January 1999, several banks

reached profit rates of 200–400 per cent, and total bank profits that month alone were R$3.3 billion (*Folha de S.Paulo*, 6 March 1999, p. 2–2).

55. Banco Central do Brasil (1999, table IV.13).
56. See Saad-Filho and Morais (2000).
57. Fine and Saad-Filho (2014) and Saad-Filho (2007b). For the case of Brazil, see Cintra (2015, p. 135).
58. See Saad-Filho and Morais (2002).
59. Officially, *Lei Complementar* 101/2000. The history of the LRF is examined by Afonso (2016).
60. After successive 'adjustments' the inflation target eventually settled on 4.5 (plus or minus 2.0) per cent in 2005. In 2017, the target for 2019 was reduced to 4.25 per cent and 4 per cent in 2020, with margins of 2.0 per cent.
61. See Gentil (2015, p. 57).
62. These trends and the reasons for divergence are examined by Bonelli (2015).
63. The 1988 Constitution originally had 245 articles and 80 transitional paragraphs (*disposições transitórias*). By 2014 the text had been amended 86 times: 6 in 1994, 35 under Cardoso, 28 under Lula and 17 under Rousseff.

Chapter 4

1. For a detailed discussion, see Laplane (2015).
2. See Coutinho, Baltar and Camargo (1999). Gonçalves (1999, p. 76) shows that some Brazilian conglomerates benefitted from the purchase of state-owned assets (for example, Grupo Vicunha, which acquired a large part of the steel industry and part of the electricity industry). Foreign firms also expanded their operations, such that 'virtually no industrial sector has escaped from the advance of foreign companies in the Brazilian economy'.
3. By definition, average productivity will rise if the least productive firms close down. Similarly, if a general dismisses his shortest soldiers the average height of the army will increase, but this outcome is unrelated to the general's expertise in military affairs. In economic terms, eliminating the weakest firms does not spontaneously generate a sustainable growth path, but it does imply that capital will be destroyed and unemployment will rise at least in the short term.
4. Bonelli (1999, pp. 95–7).
5. PricewaterhouseCoopers (*Folha de S.Paulo*, 21 January 2000, p. 2–1). For similar estimates, see Diniz (2004, p. 92), Gonçalves (1999, pp. 138–42) and Moreira (2000).
6. See Diniz (2004, pp. 91–4), Kormann (2015, parts I and IV) and Gonçalves (1999, pp. 74–5). For a detailed analysis of the internationalisation of Brazilian industry during this period, see Laplane and Sarti (1999).
7. Machine imports increased from US$6.0 billion in 1990 to US$26.2 billion in 1997 (*Conjuntura Econômica*, November 1998). Their growth was partly due to the dislocation of domestic production (the capital goods sector was one of the worst hit by foreign competition, takeovers and 'rationalisation'). For a detailed analysis of productivity changes and shifts in import coefficients during the 1990s, see Britto (2003), Cacciamali and Bezerra (1997), Coutinho

and Ferraz (1995), Moreira and Correa (1998), Salm, Saboia and Carvalho (1997) and Squeff (2015).

8. Squeff (2015, pp. 34–5).

9. See Cano (1999), Laplane and Sarti (1999, pp. 222–4) and Leal and Silva (2008). Machado and Markwald (1997, p. 197) argue that: '[Brazilian] exports to the Argentine market are [disproportionately] concentrated on medium-high and medium-low technological intensity products, which include 70–75% of the sales of Brazilian industrial goods. The participation of these products in Brazilian exports to the rest of the world is less than 40%.' Sawaya (2014, p. 143) highlights that 45 per cent of Brazilian manufactured exports go to Latin America.

10. For detailed analyses of the changes in productivity, employment, labour 'flexibility' and unemployment under the Real plan, see CNI/Cepal (1997), Paes de Barros, Camargo and Mendonça (1998) and Ramos and Almeida Reis (1998). For a long-term analysis, see Bonelli and Gonçalves (1998) and Urani (1998).

11. Coutinho, Baltar and Camargo (1999, pp. 66, 73).

12. Paraphrasing Schumpeter, Gustavo Franco, the Central Bank president, called this process 'creative destruction'. However, Tavares (1999) was closer to the truth when she criticised government-sponsored 'non-creative destruction'.

13. See Nassif, Feijó and Araújo (2015a) and Pochmann (2016).

14. Nassif (2013) reports that Brazil's imports have a much higher income elasticity than the country's exports. While 1 per cent growth in Brazilian GDP raises imports by 3.4 per cent, 1 per cent GDP growth in the rest of the world raises Brazil's exports by only 1.3 per cent. For alternative estimates, see Araújo and Marconi (2015, p. 290) and Schettini, Squeff and Gouvêa (2012).

15. Diniz (1999, p. 172); see also Coutinho, Baltar and Camargo (1999, p. 75).

16. See Cacciamali (1992), Coutinho, Baltar and Camargo (1999), Feijó and Carvalho (1998), Pochmann (2006, p. 137), Saad-Filho and Morais (2000, pp. 14–18) and Santos (2001). Bonelli (2015) and Sarti (2015) provide detailed estimates of employment in manufacturing.

17. Laplane and Sarti (1999, p. 263).

18. See Lacerda (1996, p. 19).

19. Pochmann (2011, p. 16).

20. See Santos (2001). He argues that there are: 'significant wage differences between the informal and formal labour markets, even when controlling for individual worker attributes. There is a very high wage flexibility in the country.'

21. Different data sources are reported in Ipeadata. According to the trade union research institute, DIEESE, total (open and disguised) unemployment in São Paulo reached 20.3 per cent in April 1999. Pochmann (1999) reviews the dismantling of the formal labour markets under neoliberalism.

22. São Paulo, Rio de Janeiro, Belo Horizonte, Porto Alegre, Recife and Salvador.

23. See Santos (2001).

24. See Antunes and Pochmann (2008, pp. 5–6), Carvalho (2015), Pochmann (2003, p. 7), Pomar (2013, pp. 41–5) and Santos (2001).

25. For a detailed analysis, see Fon (2013) and Pochmann (2012).

26. See Santos (2001).

27. Source: Ipeadata.

28. See Saad-Filho and Mollo (2006); see also Bonelli (1999, p. 89).
29. See Pochmann (2011, p. 16).
30. For an overview, see Coslovsky, Pires and Bignami (2017), Diniz (1999, p. 168), Pochmann (2003, p. 7; 2006, p. 131), Singer (2010, p. 103). Because of its political significance and heavy-handed government tactics, the oil workers' strike was often compared with the British coalminers' strike in 1984–5; see, for example, Cardoso (2003, pp. 44–5) and Santana (2003, pp. 302–3).
31. See Calvo (1996) and Palma (1998).
32. For an extended discussion, see Kregel (2014).
33. See also Calvo (1996), Calvo, Leiderman and Heinhart (1996) and Feldstein and Horioka (1980).
34. For a review of economic stagnation in Brazil after ISI, see Bresser-Pereira (2015a).
35. See Ayers and Saad-Filho (2014) and Saad-Filho (2011).

Chapter 5

1. See Morais and Saad-Filho (2003) and Saad-Filho (2003a). Singer (2012) offers a similar approach in his analysis of 'Lulismo'.
2. For a similar interpretation, see Coggiola (2004). For a leftist interpretation of Lula's election, see Genro and Robaina (2006).
3. See Machado (2003) and Martuscelli (2015, pp. 153–4).
4. See Singer (2010, p. 109).
5. For a detailed analysis, see Barbosa (2013, Kindle location 1593–601). Paulani (2003) argues that the crisis was not as severe as it was being presented.
6. The Brazilian press has been dominated for several decades by four virtually identical newspapers, two based in São Paulo (*Folha de S. Paulo* and *O Estado de S. Paulo*), and two in Rio de Janeiro (*O Globo* and *Jornal do Brasil*, of which the latter is now online only and much diminished in relevance). TV ownership is also heavily concentrated, with the Globo network (the parent company of the newspaper of the same name) commanding the largest audience. Other networks include Record (controlled by the Universal Church of the Kingdom of God since 1990), SBT and Band. Although their audience has been diluted by the new cable and satellite channels, the main networks retain a virtual monopoly of the national news programmes, which are substantively indistinguishable.
7. See Lula da Silva (2002). Lula da Silva (2013, Kindle locations 341–5) claims that: 'we wrote the Letter to the Brazilian People, that was a necessary document. I was against it. Actually, I was completely against the letter because it said things that I did not want to say, but today I recognise that it was extremely important. It was necessary to try and build alliances.'
8. IMF (2002, paragraph 26, emphasis added).
9. The election is reviewed by Panizza (2004).
10. Sader (2013) offers an alternative interpretation, in which Lula led a 'post-neoliberal' administration. For an alternative view, see Saad-Filho and Morais (2005).
11. Lula's centre-left alliance, including PT, PSB, PL, PCdoB, PPS, PV and PDT, elected 177 deputies (35 per cent of the house) and 25 senators (31 per cent).

The centrist and right-wing PMDB, PTB and PP joined the coalition in 2003, while the PDT left. Then, the government could count, notionally, on 368 deputies (72 per cent) and 48 senators (59 per cent).

12. In their Article IV consultation with Brazil in March 2005, the IMF executive board 'welcomed Brazil's impressive economic achievements over the last two years, and the remarkable track record of performance … which reflected the [Brazilian] authorities' continued pursuit of strong macroeconomic policies and steady progress with structural reforms … [IMF] Directors [also] congratulated the authorities for consistently achieving high primary fiscal surpluses … Looking ahead, the authorities' reform agenda – including central bank autonomy, reform of the state-level VAT, and further measures to enhance the business environment – covers important areas. Other critical reforms would include measures to increase budget flexibility, address the large remaining imbalances in the pensions system, promote financial intermediation, and reduce labour market informality through reforms of the labour code, so as to substantially increase flexibility in labour contracts' (IMF 2005a). IMF first deputy managing director, Anne Krueger, added that the 'impressive track record of program implementation [under the stand-by arrangement], together with the continued pursuit of sound macroeconomic policies and steady progress with structural reforms are clearly paying off … The central bank's steady tightening of monetary policy in recent months has been prudent … Reflecting recent developments, financial market sentiment is very positive … The government's agenda for 2005 includes important tax reforms and further measures to strengthen the business environment' (IMF, 2005b).

13. Meirelles is an ambitious policy-maker. His years of service to Lula did not prevent him from joining the cabinet of President Michel Temer after the impeachment of Dilma Rousseff (see Chapter 9).

14. See Martuscelli (2015, pp. 170–1).

15. For a critical overview of the neoliberal policies adopted in Lula's first administration, see Coggiola (2004), Filgueiras and Gonçalves (2007), Genro and Robaina (2006) and Paula (2005).

16. Data source: www.sidra.ibge.gov.br.

17. See Cintra (2005, pp. 135–6) and Santos and Gentil (2009, p. 140).

18. See Boito (2003), Martuscelli (2015, pp. 155–6), Pereira (2016b) and Singer (2010, p. 109). Marcelino (2017, p. 11) suggests that 1,300 trade unionists were appointed to government positions.

19. See, for example, Wu (2010).

20. For a more extended analysis, see Morais and Saad-Filho (2011).

21. The only notable exceptions were the MST, which was always close to the PT but never allowed its leaders to join the administration, and the Trotskyite parties, who opposed the PT.

22. See Bourne (2008, pp. 108–18, 176–95), Martuscelli (2015, pp. 214–16) and Singer (2009) .

23. See, for example, the editorial of *Folha de S. Paulo* on 13 April 2006 (FSP, 2016).

24. Singer (2010, p. 94). The crisis is discussed by Martuscelli (2016, pp. 16–21).

25. For a detailed analysis, see Boito and Galvão (2012). For a critical overview of Lula's first administration, see Arestis and Saad-Filho (2007) and *Monthly Review* (2007).

Chapter 6

1. See, for example, Bresser-Pereira (2003, 2005), Sicsú (2006) and Sicsú, Paula and Michel (2005); for a review, see Amado and Mollo (2015), Paula, Fritz and Prates (2017), Mattei (2013) and Mollo and Fonseca (2013).
2. See Bresser-Pereira (2005, 2015).
3. Sicsú, Paula and Michel (2005: xxxv).
4. Barbosa and Souza (2010, p.11).
5. For an analysis of the significance of Lula's social programmes for his re-election, see Marques *et al.* (2009).
6. 'Among Brazilians with higher education, the rejection of Lula jumped 16 percentage points, rising from 24 per cent in August to 40 per cent today' (*Folha de S. Paulo*, 23 October 2005, cited in Singer, 2009, p. 84).
7. See Boito (2003) and Martuscelli (2015, pp. 249–56).
8. Singer (2009); see also Singer (2010, p. 98) and Tible (2013).
9. The alliance of winners had an uncanny similarity to the popular fronts proposed by pro-Soviet communist parties in Brazil and elsewhere in the 1950s-1960s (see Boito, 2013 and Sader, 2013, Kindle locations 3246–59).
10. Singer (2012, pp. 223 *et seq.*, 2014).
11. Singer (2010, pp. 96–7).
12. Morais and Saad-Filho (2011, 2012); see also Barbosa and Souza (2010).
13. Ban (2013) has a similar approach. He calls this hybrid model 'liberal neo-developmentalism'.
14. Boito and Saad-Filho (2016).
15. Saad-Filho (2014b).
16. Boito (2012).
17. For an overview of PAC, see Barbosa (2013, Kindle location 1737–42) and Dweck and Teixeira (2017, p. 22).
18. See Barbosa and Souza (2010, p. 73).
19. Barbosa (2013) examines the macroeconomic implications of MCMV; Rolnik (2015) reviews the programme in the context of Brazilian housing policy.
20. See Barbosa (2013, Kindle locations 1742–3).
21. See Bastos and Hiratuka (2017), Berringer (2015), Boito and Berringer (2014), Garcia (2013) and Pomar (2014). The transnationalisation of Brazilian firms is examined in detail by Garcia (2012).
22. See Lievesley and Ludlam (2009).
23. See Barbosa (2013, Kindle location 1848–51).
24. Pochmann (2011, pp. 25–7). For a review of personal credit policy, see Barbosa (2013, Kindle locations 1719–25).
25. See Freitas (2009) for an overview of the immediate impact of the crisis and Brazil's monetary policy response. Orair (2015, pp. 119–26) examines public sector investment in detail and shows its positive correlation with economic growth between 1948 and 2010.
26. See Loureiro and Saad-Filho (2018), Santos *et al.* (2012) and Santos *et al.* (2016b).
27. See Cintra (2015, p. 156).
28. See Morais and Saad-Filho (2011, 2012), Paula, Oreiro and Basílio (2013), Saad-Filho (2007a) and Saad-Filho and Morais (2014). For an overview of

poverty and distribution under neoliberalism, see Henriques (2000) and Hoffmann (2013).

29. For detailed studies of the distributional changes under Lula and Rousseff, see Calixtre, Biancarelli and Cintra (2014).

30. See Castro *et al.* (2012, p. 29) and Chaves and Ribeiro (2012, p. 11).

31. See Castro *et al.* (2012, p. 14).

32. See Pomar (2013, p. 42) and www.ibge.gov.br, monthly employment survey.

33. For a more detailed breakdown of occupations, see Carvalho (2015, p. 101).

34. Between 2001 and 2011 the income of the poorest 10 per cent rose, on average, 6.3 per cent annually, in contrast with 1.4 per cent per annum for the richest 10 per cent (Paes de Barros, Grosner and Mascarenhas, 2012, p. 15).

35. For more detailed analyses, see Jannuzzi and Sousa (2016, p. 27) and Morais and Saad-Filho (2011). See also Bastos (2012), Pochmann (2010, pp. 640, 648; 2011, p. 38; 2012, p. 32) and Tible (2013, p. 68).

36. This is the number of people in households with per capita income below the poverty line, which is defined as twice the line of extreme poverty. The latter is determined by the cost of a food basket including the minimum calories recommended by FAO and WHO (see www.ipeadata.gov.br).

37. The income of the poor in Brazil grew 2.5 times faster than that of the non-poor during this period. This is less than in other Latin American countries with left-of-centre governments. Using the international US$2.50/day poverty line, Argentina had a much higher pro-poor growth indicator of 5.5, Bolivia of 6.2 and Ecuador of 7.3 between 2007 and 2011 (see CEDLAS and World Bank, 2016 and Loureiro and Saad-Filho, 2018).

38. Saad-Filho (2015a).

39. Source: Ipeadata. The Gini coefficient ranges from 0 to 1, and it measures income inequality. A Gini of zero implies complete equality, and 1 implies that one person earns all the income. Gini coefficients usually range between 0.3 and 0.45, with extreme cases of inequality (e.g. South Africa) near 0.7.

40. See Hall (2008, p. 812) and Mattei (2012, pp. 167–8).

41. At the end of his administration, President Lula famously insisted that, during the previous decade, a lot had changed in the homes of the poor in terms of their access to consumer goods. However, once they stepped outside, they found that nothing had changed in terms of infrastructure provision and public goods and services (see Saad-Filho, 2013, p. 668).

42. Safatle (2012) rightly argues that the 'economic upward mobility, with the ensuing feeling of achieving citizenship, did not include the expansion of quality social services. Aside from the significant expansion of federal universities, upward mobility implied being able to pay for private schools, private health insurance, mobile phones, household appliances, and attending a private university. In other words, the rights of citizenship were translated into consumer rights.'

43. See Gobetti and Orair (2016, 2017) and Medeiros, Souza and Castro (2015a, 2015b). For an extended discussion, see Loureiro and Saad-Filho (2018).

44. Pomar (2013, p. 42).

45. See Oreiro (2015, pp. 140–1) and Souza (2015, p. 10).

46. See Almeida (2004) and Tavares (2003).

47. For a detailed analysis, see Saad-Filho (2015a).

48. See Barrientos (2007, p. 67), Hall (2008) and Molyneux (2007).
49. See Marques (2013, p. 304) and Soares *et al.* (2010). For alternative estimates leading to similar results, see Mattei (2012, pp. 166–8).
50. IPEA (2012, pp. 16, 21).
51. Hall (2008, p. 815); see also Castro and Modesto (2010, p. 21), Lavergne and Beserra (2016), and the detailed study by Leichsenring (2010).
52. See Marques *et al.* (2009). Singer (2009) claims that PBF is at the root of '*Lulismo*'.
53. Ghosh (2011, p. 68); see also Coleman (2003).
54. See Loureiro and Saad-Filho (2018) and Rugitsky (2016).

Chapter 7

1. So-called because oil is locked underneath several kilometers of South Atlantic water, rock and a thick layer of salt.
2. Nobre (2017, pp. 142–3) rightly points out that this transformative project was imposed from above, by technocratic means, without negotiation with civil society. The consequences would be disastrous, as is shown below.
3. See Seabra (2009).
4. See Ribeiro and Novaes (2014, pp. 45–6).
5. Brazilian presidents can be re-elected only once, but they are allowed to run again for the same position after an interruption of one term.
6. The left 'core' government coalition, including PT, PCdoB, PDT and PSB, had 165 seats out of 513 in the Chamber of Deputies and 23 in the Senate out of 81. Its 'outer circle' of centre-right allies had 186 deputies and 37 senators. The left-wing opposition PSOL (*Partido Socialismo e Liberdade*, Socialism and Freedom Party) had 3 Deputies and 2 Senators, while the right-wing opposition (PSDB and the so-called Democrats) had 108 Deputies and 19 Senators. The remaining 51 seats in the Chamber of Deputies were held by 'undecided' or wavering parties.
7. Nobre (2017) reviews the political manoeuvring underpinning Rousseff's first administration.
8. The difficulties surrounding the improvements in competitivity are reviewed in detail by Souza (2015); see also Marconi (2015). Barbosa (2013) reviews the first two years of Rousseff's administration.
9. See FIESP *et al.* (2011); see also CNI (2014), which reiterates FIESP's arguments about lack of competitivity. For example: 'Brazil has lost [competitive] positions in [the rankings of] infrastructure and logistics and macroeconomic environment. On the former, the country fell from 13th to 14th place [out of 15 countries] … This outcome is due to the country's low competitivity in … transport and customs infrastructure and operations … In all modes of transportation – roads, rail, ports and air transport – Brazil receives a negative assessment' (CNI, 2014, pp. 15, 36). See also Singer (2015a, pp. 43–5, 55–6).
10. For a detailed analysis, see Nassif, Feijó and Araújo (2015b).
11. For an overview of exchange-rate policy and the market for foreign currency in Brazil, see Rossi (2016).
12. See MF (2013).
13. See Cintra (2015, p. 141), Kaltenbrunner and Painceira (2017) and Palma (2015).

14. See Braga (2015), Giovannetti and Carvalho (2015) and Santos *et al.* (2016a).
15. See Carvalho and Rugitsky (2015) and Serrano and Summa (2015).
16. See, for example, Soares (2013) and Herédia (2013); see also Sawaya (2014, p. 143).
17. For an overview of this policy challenge, see Singer (2015a, pp. 39–49).
18. For a detailed study of Brazilian inflation between mature and developmental neoliberalism, see Summa and Serrano (2015).
19. See Singer (2015a, pp. 43–5, 49–50).
20. The government was frequently criticised for its inability to establish a constructive dialogue with the 'business community'; see, for example, Rovai (2013).
21. For a detailed study of the case of the auto industry, see Schapiro (2017).
22. For a comprehensive analysis, see SEP-PPS (2016).
23. See Orair, Siqueira and Gobetti (2016, p. 17).
24. Deindustrialisation can be highly problematic for a country like Brazil. Belluzzo (2013, Kindle locations 2412–4) rightly argues that '[a]n urban-industrial economy formed many years ago cannot base its stability and growth on commodity exports, since they have a limited impact upon employment and income'. For estimates of deindustrialisation, see Bonelli and Pessôa (2010).
25. This argument has been made, insistently, by Bresser-Pereira; see www.bresserpereira.org.br.
26. See, for example, Akyüz (2013).
27. See Cintra (2015, p. 140).
28. See www.ipeadata.gov.br. For an examination of the causes of this deterioration, see Cintra (2015, pp. 136–43) and Souza (2015, pp. 16–21).
29. See Akyüz (2013) and Palma (2015).
30. For a similar analysis of the failure of Rousseff's economic policies, see Carneiro (2017).
31. For an analysis of the composition of Congress between 2002 and 2014, see Dias (2014).
32. Singer (2015b).
33. See Matais and Morais (2017).
34. See Singer (2015a, p. 40).
35. For a review of economic policy during this period, see Belluzzo and Bastos (2016), Paula and Pires (2017), Pereira and Mattei (2016) and Rossi and Mello (2016, 2017a).
36. See Saad-Filho (2014b); see also Laplane (2015).
37. See Loureiro and Saad-Filho (2018).
38. See Corrêa and Santos (2013).
39. For a review, see Calixtre and Fagnani (2017) and Souza (2015, pp, 16–19); see also World Bank (2016).
40. Sallum Jr and Kugelmas (2004).
41. The number of automobiles in circulation in Brazil rose from 42 million in 2005 to 86 million in 2014 and 95 million in mid-2017 (http://www.denatran.gov.br/frota.htm). The number of passengers using the country's 63 largest airports rose from 96 million in 2005 to a peak of 193 million in 2012;

passenger numbers subsequently declined to 104 million in 2016 (http://www. infraero.gov.br/index.php/br/estatisticas/estatisticas.html).

42. For details, see Kaltenbrunner and Painceira (2017).
43. The fiscal deterioration in Brazil after the global crisis is reviewed by Dweck and Teixeira (2017) and SEP-PPS (2016).
44. See Alves (2014, pp. 174–6), Boito and Saad-Filho (2016) and Martuscelli (2015, pp. 205–6).
45. Domingues (2015a) reports that, when the PSB (*Partido Socialista Brasileiro,* Brazilian Socialist Party) turned sharply right, in 2013, Lula explained that this was because the PT did not leave any political space to its left.
46. Singer (2010, pp. 110–11).
47. Detailed studies showing the extent of media bias against the PT can be found in: http://www.manchetometro.com.br/, http://observatoriodaimprensa.com. br/ and https://www.facebook.com/desmascarandoglobo/. For a particularly egregious example, see ESP (2010). Kitzberger (2016) discussed why the PT never sought to reform the media, despite their strong opposition to the party and its administrations.
48. Lula da Silva (2013, Kindle locations 286–8). Note the absence of the middle class in this summary.

Chapter 8

1. '[A] class ... is a group of persons ... identified by their position in the whole system of social production, defined above all according to their relationship ... to the conditions of production ... and to other classes. The individuals constituting a given class may or may not be wholly or partly conscious of their own identity and common interests as a class, and they may or may not feel antagonism towards members of other classes as such' (Ste. Croix,1984, p. 94).
2. For similar analyses, see Boito (2012), Chauí (2013a) and Pomar (2013). Singer (1981) examines the Brazilian class structure during ISI.
3. Pomar (2013, p. 32). The analysis below draws upon Saad-Filho (2014a).
4. The following analysis of the material interests of broad social groups does not imply that individual proclivities can be read off from fixed class positions, or suggest that social classes or strata ought to be either self-conscious or politically united. Instead, it seeks to illustrate how economic interests can support contrasting political programmes that tend to be expressed through distinct political parties, organisations and movements.
5. See Alves (2014, pp. 175–6) and Martuscelli (2015, pp. 92–3).
6. See Boito (2012, 2013).
7. For an overview of these tensions and their political implications, see Galvão (2007, pp. 54–5, 72–4).
8. See Saad-Filho (2002, chs. 3–4).
9. Pomar (2013, p. 3).
10. Brazil has one of the highest labour turnover rates in the world, and an extremely flexible labour market; see Alves (2014, pp. 68–81) and Pomar (2013, p. 42).
11. See Boito (2003, p. 12). This contradiction came to the fore during the Cardoso administration. However, it will be ignored in what follows because

it did not play a political role either immediately before or after Rousseff's impeachment.

12. Boito and Marcelino (2011, p. 62).

13. See Boito and Marcelino (2011) and Marcelino (2017). Kalecki (1943, p. 326) presciently argues that 'full employment would cause social and political changes which would give a new impetus to the opposition of the business leaders ... [because] "the sack" would cease to play its role as a disciplinary measure. The social position of the boss would be undermined and the self assurance and class consciousness of the working class would grow ... It is true that profits would be higher under a regime of full employment than they are on the average under *laissez-faire* ...But "discipline in the factories" and "political stability" are more appreciated by the business leaders than profits. Their class instinct tells them that lasting full employment is unsound from their point of view and that unemployment is an integral part of the "normal" capitalist system.' This insight might help to explain the growing opposition of 'business' to the Rousseff administration.

14. Medeiros (2013, p. 64).

15. The Brazilian population is 85 per cent urban; large-scale rural-urban migration was largely completed in the 1980s.

16. For an original assessment of this social group, see Standing (2011); see also the critique in Breman (2013) and Palmer (2014).

17. See Singer (2012).

18. For details, see Saad-Filho (2007a).

19. A large part of Fernando Collor's appeal was due to mass hostility to strikes; his rival Lula was the symbol of strikes in Brazil. For example, there was a clear correlation between lower incomes and agreement with the statement that 'military force should be used to break strikes' (supported by 9 per cent of respondents in households earning more than 20 times the minimum wage, and 42 per cent of those in households earning up to twice the minimum wage) (Singer, 2009, p. 87).

20. See Demier (2013).

21. See Chauí (2013b) and Pomar (2013, p. 48).

22. 'Within capitalism ... scope is created for the self-employed to emerge and for "professionals" to prosper because, for different reasons, they are able to retain the full fruits of their labour despite being paid a wage or, more exactly, a salary, although this can take different forms including fees, commissions, and so on' (Fine and Saad-Filho 2016, p. 164).

23. This phenomenon was highlighted by Lenin (1920).

24. See Chauí (2013a), Pomar (2013, pp. 43–4) and Saad-Filho (2014).

25. Surveys have shown a negative relationship between years of schooling and support for distributive federal programmes. These programmes were supported by 56 per cent of illiterate respondents, 49 per cent of those with basic education, and only 38 per cent of those with university degrees. Years of schooling were also closely associated with greater respect for the rights of women and minorities (Tible, 2013, p. 74).

26. For a detailed analysis, see Bianchi and Braga (2015).

27. See Medeiros (2013, p. 59).

28. The middle class became increasingly conservative and intolerant during the 2000s, especially in the economic powerhouses in the Centre-South. An opinion poll in 2012 showed that 55 per cent of the middle class supported

different products for 'rich' and 'poor' customers; 48 per cent were unhappy with the queues following the expansion of the domestic market, 17 per cent believed that poorly dressed people should be barred from certain places, and the same percentage favoured separate lifts in public places. 26 per cent of the inhabitants of Higienópolis, a prosperous neighbourhood in São Paulo, were against a new metro station because it might increase the number of 'undesirables' in the area (see Ricci, 2012).

29. See Fon Filho (2013).

30. For a detailed review of the protests, see Saad-Filho (2013, 2014) and Saad-Filho and Morais (2014); see also Domingues (2015b, ch. 5) and Singer (2014).

31. See, for example, http://acervo.folha.com.br/fsp/2013/06/07/15/ (accessed 7 July 2017). Note the changing tone of the coverage in the following days.

32. http://noticias.terra.com.br/brasil/cidades/globo-deixa-de-exibir-novelas-para-cobertura-de-protestos,ffc24201aea5f310VgnVCM5000009ccceb0aR CRD.html and http://www.conversaafiada.com.br/brasil/2013/06/20/globo-derruba-a-grade-e-o-golpe/ (accessed 20 July 2017).

33. An opinion poll in eight state capitals on 20 June (a day of large demonstrations) suggested that 63 per cent of the demonstrators were aged 14–29, 92 per cent had completed at least secondary school, 52 per cent were students, 76 per cent were in paid employment and only 45 per cent earned less than 5 times the minimum wage. In other words, they had attended school for much longer and had much higher incomes than the population average; see Saad-Filho (2013).

34. See, for example, Alonso and Mische (2017).

35. http://noticias.uol.com.br/politica/ultimas-noticias/2013/03/19/dilma-cni-ibope.htm (accessed 7 July 2017).

36. For a trenchant examination of the (lack of) ideology of PMDB, see Nobre (2013), Saes (2016) and Sampaio Jr (2017, p. 232).

37. See, for example, CB (2013) and Simões (2013).

38. For an overview of the social composition and political alignment of Brazilian trade unions, see Galvão, Marcelino and Trópia (2015).

39. For an analysis of the position of the middle class, see Sampaio (2014).

40. In March 2010, the chairwoman of the National Association of Newspapers declared that, given the weakness of the mainstream opposition, the media must fulfil this political role; see Farah (2010) and LEMEP (2016).

41. In the first page of its edition of 26 June, after the President's pronouncement on TV proposing constitutional and policy changes in the wake of the mass protests, the largest Brazilian newspaper found it essential to inform the nation about the cost of Dilma Rousseff's make-up and hair-styling; see http://acervo.folha.com.br/fsp/2013/06/26/ (accessed 3 July 2017).

42. See Ayers and Saad-Filho (2014).

43. See Saad-Filho (2015a).

44. See Fine and Saad-Filho (2017) and Saad-Filho (2017).

45. This was evident on TV and it was widely reported at the time. It was also witnessed by one of the authors [ASF] on 1, 2 and 3 July 2013, at Avenida Paulista, São Paulo's main thoroughfare.

46. See Marx (1852) for the classic interpretation of the political role of the lumpen-proletariat.

Chapter 9

1. For an overview of the corruption scandals during the dictatorship, see Gaspari (2004, p. 298; 2016, pp. 119–22).
2. See Boito (2017) and Sampaio Jr (2017, p. 204).
3. For a detailed analysis, see Rocha (2017).
4. See Singer (2009).
5. See Medeiros (2013, pp. 59, 65).
6. See, for example, Boito (2017) and Cavalcante and Arias (2017).
7. See Boito (2015).
8. The privatisation programme under the PSDB was riven with large-scale corruption, but these scandals were rarely investigated and, even then, never thoroughly. See, for example, Braga (2015) and Ribeiro Jr (2011). The privatisations eventually became highly unpopular; see Cardoso (2003, p. 46).
9. See Chauí (2013b).
10. See Avritzer (2015).
11. See, for example, Nepomuceno (2015). Former Minister L.C. Bresser-Pereira (2015) remarked in an interview that 'the national-popular political pact ... evaporated. The bourgeoisie unified itself. Then came something I had never seen in Brazil. Suddenly I saw this collective hatred of the upper class, the rich, against a party and a President. It was not worry or fear. It was hatred.'
12. See Boito (2015).
13. For a similar approach, see Singer (2015a, pp. 54, 57), where this group is called the 'united front of the bourgeoisie'.
14. See Singer (2015a, pp. 57, 64–6).
15. See Boito and Saad-Filho (2016), Pochmann (2012), Saad-Filho and Boito (2016) and Singer (2015a).
16. See Fortes (2016) and Singer (2015b).
17. See Martuscelli (2015, pp. 114–17).
18. The significance of corruption in the mobilisations against Dilma Rousseff is undeniable; see, for example, Ferraz (2015) and Martuscelli (2016).
19. The debates surrounding the last wave of right-wing demonstrations against Dilma Rousseff were polarised by a photograph taken in Rio de Janeiro, in March 2016. It shows an evidently well-off white couple going to the anti-government march, followed by a uniformed black nanny with the couple's baby (see, for example, 247, 2016a). Debates about the meaning and significance of this image triggered furious reactions on both sides of the political divide. Greenwald, Fishman and Miranda (2016) report memes with such captions as: 'Speed it up, there, Maria [the generic 'maid name'], we have to get out to protest against this government that made us pay you minimum wage.'
20. This section draws on Boito and Saad-Filho (2016).
21. For an examination of the lending criteria of BNDES, see Hochstetler and Montero (2013), Pochmann (2013) and Trindade, Ferraz and Marques (2015). Cyrino (2017) examines in detail the impact of developmentalism on the meat industry.
22. Dilma Rousseff has expressed her regret about these mistakes; see, for example, Rousseff (2017).

23. Graphic summaries are available at http://infograficos.estadao.com.br; http://www.estadao.com.br; and http://estadaodados.com. For a description of *lava jato*, see FSP (2017). For a critique of the operation, see Lassance (2017).

24. See Sabença (2013).

25. For the most chilling example of a legal licence to do virtually anything in support of *lava jato*, see Pizzolatto (2016). For an overview of the legal context of *lava jato*, see Lopes and Maranhão (2016) and *Revista Consultor Jurídico* (2016). For a critique, see Damous (2017a, 2017b), Hochuli (2017) and Sampaio (2017, pp. 249–50). In contrast, Michener and Pereira (2016) claim that *lava jato* had no political motives.

26. See Boito and Saad-Filho (2016, p. 203).

27. For a list of corruption scandals involving the PSDB but never adequately investigated, see Carlotti (2016) and 247 (2017).

28. See Campos (2015) and Nobre and Rodriguez (2011).

29. In mid-2016 it was estimated that the firms under investigation for corruption represented 14 per cent of Brazilian GDP; see 247 (2016b). A manifesto of trade unions released in July 2017 claimed that: 'The *lava jato* operation has contributed to the destruction of the productive sector and of Brazilian engineering. It helped to destroy 740,000 jobs and nearly paralysed the construction industry that, for 10 years, created around 14 per cent of GDP.' Belluzzo (2017) claims that *lava jato* and similar investigations led to the loss of 5–7 million jobs.

30. Conti (2017) examines the judicialisation of fiscal policy in Brazil.

31. For an overview of the judicialisation of politics, see Avendaño (2017), Carlotti (2017), Fonseca (2017) and Nobre (2017, p. 140).

32. See, for example, Guimarães (2015); for a debate within the left, see Pinto, Filgueiras and Gonçalves (2015).

33. For a critique of the charges against Lula, see Tardelli (2017).

34. 'The Parliament voted in 2014 includes the largest number of millionaires in Republican history, chosen in the most expensive elections since the restoration of democracy, that brought in the largest number of business people, bishops and preachers, military and police. The outcome is that the progressive agenda of promoting freedom and equality has been blocked, and the regressive agenda has taken over. In less than 60 days the Christian Family [Parliamentary] Group ... submitted proposals including a Day of Heterosexual Pride, punishment against heterophobia, the prohibition of adoption by homosexual couples, the proscription of abortion even in the [small number of] cases currently permitted by law, and the [creation of a] "rape grant" [for victims of rape who get pregnant and choose to have the baby]' (Nozaki, 2015).

35. See Singer (2015a, pp. 40, 53).

36. For a review of this period, see Carvalho (2016).

37. 'One of the businessmen [interviewed for the specialist newspaper *Valor Econômico*] argues that the appointment of Joaquim Levy to the Ministry of Finance was welcomed [by business] and brought the expectation that the government would correct the mistakes of the first [Rousseff] administration and build a more consistent economic policy. "With him, there was a subtle uptick in confidence, the hope that the fiscal [side] could be fixed", he says. "When the PT started to attack Levy, then the flight [away from

the government] became a stampede. The President was re-elected lying to the population, and she became unviable when she tried to lie to business'" (Neumann, 2016). See also Castro (2016) for an illuminating analysis of the reasons why the bourgeoisie shifted against Dilma Rousseff.

38. For a critique of the passivity of the PT, see Dias (2016) and Sampaio Jr (2017, p. 246).

39. Rousseff's argumentation to the Senate is available in Rousseff (2016).

40. For detailed accounts of Rousseff's impeachment, see Amaral (2016, part I), Gentili (2016), Nassif (2015), Saad-Filho (2015b, 2016b, 2016c, 2016d, 2017), Saad-Filho and Boito (2017), Snider (2017) and van Dijk (2016). For Rousseff's own analysis, see Rousseff (2017). Nobre (2017, p. 139) argues that Rousseff fell because her government could no longer function according to the rules of the Brazilian political system: it was incapable of protecting allied politicians from judicial attack, and unable to secure access to public funds for the parties in her coalition. The point is that Brazilian politicians do not simply want 'posts' in government; they must be able to appropriate and distribute funds. When this became impossible, Rousseff's coalition disintegrated.

41. See Maciel (2016) for a detailed review of the role of business federations in the impeachment.

42. For an overview of the Temer administration, see Carvalho (2017), Proner (2016) and Rossi and Mello (2017b). The implications of the 'reforms' for the working class are examined by Marcelino (2017). The fiscal policies of the Temer administration are reviewed by Dweck (2017), Dweck and Teixeira (2017) and SEP-PPS (2016). The reform of social security is discussed by Fagnani (2017).

Conclusion

1. For examples of erratic policy-making, see Nobre (2017).

2. See Saad-Filho (2003b, 2011).

3. For an overview of the ways in which neoliberalism imposes a particular modality of social discipline, see Dardot and Laval (2013). For the latter (p. 14), 'the originality of neoliberalism is precisely its creation of a new set of rules defining not only a *different* "regime of accumulation", but, more broadly, a *different* society.'

4. For a review of participatory budgeting and its limitations, see Albert (2016) and Marquetti, Campos and Pires (2008).

5. See Ayers and Saad-Filho (2014) and Saad-Filho and Morais (2014).

6. The Cardoso administration had reduced drastically the funding available to the oil and shipbuilding industries, and it compelled Petrobras to import most of its equipment and shipping services. By 2003, the Brazilian shipbuilding industry employed only 4,000 workers. The policy reversal under Lula drove a strong recovery of the shipyards and related firms in mechanical and electrical engineering, construction and other sectors. They employed 100,000 workers in 2014; mothballed shipyards in Rio de Janeiro were reopened, and new ones started operating in the Northeast and South of the country (Gomes, 2015 and Sabença, 2014). The recovery of the oil and shipbuilding chains provides

a textbook example of the success of neodevelopmentalist policies supported by a multiclass political front.

7. For a detailed analysis, see Bresser-Pereira (2015b).

8. See Ferraz, Gutierre and Cabral (2015, p. 219), Schymura (2015), Silva (2016) and Souza (2015).

9. See, for example, Fagnani (2017).

10. http://blogandonoticias.com/presidente-lula-tem-quase-90-de/ (accessed 7 July 2017).

11. For a similar interpretation, including the proposal for a healthy self-criticism by the PT, see Boff (2016).

12. The role of the US government in the coup remains to be brought to light. In the meantime, see Braun (2016), Engdahl (2014), Farias and Zero (2017) and Rocha (2017). See also https://wikileaks.org/plusd/cables/06SAOPAULO30_a. html#efmAJZAKWAKfAK-ARrASHAS1ATbCf0Cf9CgLCgZDOLDO-VDWDDX7EgjEHl (accessed 13 July 2017) and https://www.youtube.com/watch?v=JqLK6dD1_kU&feature=youtu.be (accessed 17 July 2017).

13. In earlier times, the military would have moved in to remove an inconvenient but popular President confronting difficult political challenges. In the age of mature neoliberalism, even *coups d'état* must follow legal niceties. Moreover, the Brazilian military distinguish themselves more by their nationalism than their (unquestionable) commitment to the political right. However, the Soviet Union is no more, while neoliberalism poses a continuing challenge to the idea of the nation. The incompatibility between, on the one hand, an internationalising and subordinate right-wing neoliberalism and, on the other hand, a nationalist programme defended only by the left may have contributed to the political paralysis of the Brazilian military.

14. 'Brazil's top eight net exports (non-metallic minerals, agribusiness, steel, pulp and paper, furniture, oil and gas, leather and footware, wood products and tobacco) are ... restricted to low value-added sectors. To a large extent, these are the sectors ... behind Brazil's trade surpluses in recent years. This continuous dependence on low dynamic commodity sectors places ... a strong hindrance on long-term economic development. Incapable of building a stronger position on the value-chain, Brazil's trade balance remains uncomfortably sensitive to the ups-and-downs of commodity prices ... Brazil's largest deficits are predominantly in medium and high technology intensive products. The sector that leads Brazil's list of imports is chemical products, ... followed by IT, electronic and medical equipment. Brazil remains a committed net importer of machinery, oil products, automotive vehicles and electrical equipment ... This is an intriguing outcome to a country like Brazil whose set of reforms originally had the main aim of modernising the economy' (Kormann, 2015, pp. 27, 40).

15. Kormann (2015, pp. 18–22).

16. For a similar approach, see Santos (2017).

17. See Amaral (2017), Pinto *et al.* (2017) and Pochmann (2017).

18. For an outline, see Saad-Filho (2007b).

References

247 (2016a) 'Banqueiro é Quem Aparece na Foto-Símbolo dos Protestos', www.brasil247.com/pt/247/rio247/220891/Banqueiro-%C3%A9-quem-aparece-na-foto-s%C3%ADmbolo-dos-protestos.htm (accessed 3 July 2017).

247 (2016b) 'Lava Jato e Zelotes: Empresas Investigadas Representam 14% do PIB', www.brasil247.com/pt/247/economia/239094/Lava-Jato-e-Zelotes-empresas-investigadas-representam-14-do-PIB.htm (accessed 3 July 2017).

247 (2017) 'Requião: "Nunca Vi Cabeça de Bacalhau, Enterro de Anão e Tucano Preso"', www.brasil247.com/pt/247/parana247/304205/Requi%C3%A3o-%E2%80%9CNunca-vi-cabe%C3%A7a-de-bacalhau-enterro-de-an%C3%A3o-e-tucano-preso%E2%80%9D.htm (accessed 3 July 2017).

Abreu, M., Bevilaqua, A. and Pinho, D. (2000) 'Import Substitution and Growth in Brazil, 1890s–1970s', in: E. Cárdenas, J. Ocampo and R. Thorp (eds) *An Economic History of Latin America*, vol.3. London: Palgrave.

Afonso, J.R. (2016) 'Uma História da Lei Brasileira de Responsabilidade Fiscal', *Revista de Direito Público*, 13, pp. 126–54.

Akyüz, Y. (2013) 'Waving or Drowning: Developing Countries after the Financial Crisis', *South Centre Research Paper*, No.48, https://g24.org/wp-content/uploads/2014/03/RP48_Waving-or-drowning_EN.pdf (accessed 7 July 2017).

Albert, V. (2016) *The Limits to Citizen Power: Participatory Democracy and the Entanglements of the State*. London: Pluto Press.

Alencar, D.A. and Strachman, E. (2014) 'Balance-of-Payments-Constrained Growth in Brazil: 1951–2008', *Journal of Post Keynesian Economics*, 36 (4), pp. 673–98.

Almeida, M.H.T. (2004) 'A Política Social no Governo Lula', *Novos Estudos*, 70, pp. 7–17.

Alonso, A. and Mische, A. (2017) 'Changing Repertoires and Partisan Ambivalence in the New Brazilian Protests', *Bulletin of Latin American Research*, http://onlinelibrary.wiley.com/wol1/doi/10.1111/blar.12470/full (accessed 17 July 2017).

Alonso, P.P.S.A. (2003) 'Uma Análise da Origem e Evolução da Dívida Externa no Período 1968–2000', *Cadernos de Finanças Públicas*, 4 (4), pp. 59–119.

Alves, G. (2014) *Trabalho e Neodesenvolvimentismo*. Bauru: Canal 6 Editora.

Alves, M.H.M. (1984) *Estado e Oposição no Brasil, 1964–1984*. Rio de Janeiro: Vozes.

Alves, M.H.M. (1988) 'Dilemmas of the Consolidation of Democracy from the Top in Brazil: A Political Analysis', *Latin American Perspectives*, 15 (3), pp. 47–63.

Amadeo, E.J. (1996) 'The Knife-Edge of Exchange-Rate-Based Stabilization: Impact on Growth, Employment and Wages', *UNCTAD Review*, pp. 1–25.

Amadeo, E.J. and Camargo, J.M. (1991) 'Mercado de Trabalho e Dança Distributiva', in: J.M. Camargo (ed.) *Distribuição de Renda no Brasil*. Rio de Janeiro: Paz e Terra.

Amado, A. and Mollo, M.L.R. (2015) 'The "Developmentalism" Debate in Brazil: Some Economic and Political Issues', *Review of Keynesian Economics*, 3 (1), pp. 77–89.

Amann, E. (2000) *Economic Liberalisation and Industrial Performance in Brazil*. Oxford: Oxford University Press.

Amann, E. and Baer, W. (2000) 'The Illusion of Stability: The Brazilian Economy under Cardoso', *World Development*, 28 (10), pp. 1805–19.

Amann, E. and Chang, H-J. (eds) (2004) *Brazil and South Korea: Economic Crisis and Restructuring*. London: ILAS.

Amaral, O.E. (2003) *A Estrela Não é Mais Vermelha: As Mudanças do Programa Petista nos Anos 90*. São Paulo: Ed Garçoni.

Amaral, R. (2016) *A Serpente sem Casca: Da 'Crise' à Frente Brasil Popular*. São Paulo: Fundação Perseu Abramo.

Amaral, R. (2017) 'A República Inaugurada em 1988 está de Joelhos', www.cartacapital.com.br/politica/a-republica-inaugurada-em-1988-esta-de-joelhos (accessed 8 July 2017).

Amorim, R.L.C. (2009) 'A Constituição Brasileira de 1988 Revisitada', in: J.C. Cardoso Jr (ed.) *A Constituição Brasileira de 1988 Revisitada*. Brasília: IPEA.

Anderson, R., Bomberger, W.A. and Makinen, G.E. (1988) 'The Demand for Money, the Reform Effect, and the Money Supply Process in Hyperinflation: The Evidence from Greece and Hungary Reexamined', *Journal of Money, Credit and Banking*, 20 (4), pp. 653–72.

Andrade, J.P., Mollo, M.L.R. and Silva, M.L.F. (1997) 'Os Programas de Estabilização na América Latina: Traços Ortodoxos e Heterodoxos'. *Anais da Sociedade Brasileira de Economia Política*, pp. 337–50.

Antunes, R. and Pochmann, M. (2008) 'Dimensões do Desemprego e da Pobreza no Brasil', *Revista Interfacehs*, 3 (2), pp. 1–10.

Araújo, E. and Marconi, N. (2015) 'Estrutura Produtiva e Comércio Exterior no Brasil', in: N. Barbosa, N. Marconi, M.C. Pinheiro and L. Carvalho (eds) *Indústria e Desenvolvimento Produtivo no Brasil*. Rio de Janeiro: FGV.

Arestis, P. and Saad-Filho, A. (eds) (2007) *Political Economy of Brazil: Recent Economic Performance*. London: Palgrave.

Arida, P. and Lara-Resende, A. (1985) 'Inertial Inflation and Monetary Reform: Brazil', in: J. Williamson (ed.) *Inflation and Indexation: Argentina, Brazil and Israel*. Cambridge, Mass.: MIT Press.

Arida, P. and Lara-Resende, A. (eds) (1986) *Inflacao Zero: Brasil, Argentina e Israel*. Rio de Janeiro: Paz e Terra.

Auty, R.M. (1991) *Economic Development and Industrial Policy: Korea, Brazil, Mexico, India and China*. London: Mansell.

Avendaño, T.C. (2017) 'Brasil, el País en el que los Jueces Tomaron el Poder', https://internacional.elpais.com/internacional/2017/07/15/america/1500148296_237219.html (accessed 19 July 2017).

Avritzer, L. (2015) 'Eleitor de Dilma Não Foi às Ruas Nesse Domingo', https://noticias.uol.com.br/opiniao/coluna/2015/03/15/eleitor-de-dilma-nao-foi-as-ruas-neste-domingo.htm (accessed 3 July 2017).

Ayers, A. and Saad-Filho, A. (2014) 'Democracy Against Neoliberalism: Paradoxes, Limitations, Transcendence', *Critical Sociology*, 41 (4–5), pp. 597–618.

Bacha, E. (1978a) *Os Mitos de Uma Década*. Rio de Janeiro: Paz e Terra.

Bacha, E. (1978b) *Política Econômica e Distribuição de Renda*. Rio de Janeiro: Paz e Terra.

Bacha, E. (1997) 'Plano Real: Uma Segunda Avaliação', in: IPEA/CEPAL (eds) *O Plano Real e Outras Experiências Internacionais de Estabilização*. Brasília: IPEA.

Baer, M. (1986) *A Internacionalização Financeira do Brasil*. Petrópolis: Vozes.

Baer, W. (2013) *The Brazilian Economy: Growth and Development*, 7th ed. Boulder, CO: Lynne Rienner.

Baer, W. and Kerstenetzky, I. (1975) 'A Economia Brasileira dos Anos 60', in: *A Industrialização e o Desenvolvimento Econômico do Brasil*. Rio de Janeiro: FGV.

Balbinotto Neto, G. (1991) *A Indexação Salarial: Teoria e Evidência*. Rio de Janeiro: BNDES.

Ban, C. (2013) 'Brazil's Liberal Neo-Developmentalism: New Paradigm or Edited Orthodoxy?', *Review of International Political Economy*, 20 (2), pp. 298–331.

Banaji, J. (2010) *Theory as History: Essays on Modes of Production and Exploitation*. Leiden and Boston: Brill.

Banco Central do Brasil (1993) *O Regime Cambial Brasileiro: Evolução Recente e Perspectivas*. Brasilia: Banco Central do Brasil.

Banco Central do Brasil (1995) *Relatório Anual*. Brasília: Banco Central do Brasil.

Banco Central do Brasil (1999) *Boletim Mensal, December*. Brasília: Banco Central do Brasil.

Baracho, M.A.P. (1982) *O Processo de Acumulação de Capital no Brasil: Um Estudo da Tendência à Crise Fiscal – Período 1947/80*. MSc Dissertation, Departamento de Economia, UFMG.

Barbosa, F.H. and McNelis, P. (1989) 'Indexation and Inflationary Inertia: Brazil 1964–1985', *World Bank Economic Review*, 3 (3), pp. 339–57.

Barbosa, N. (2013) 'Dez Anos de Política Econômica', in: E. Sader (ed.) *10 Anos de Governos Pós-Neoliberais no Brasil: Lula e Dilma*. São Paulo: Boitempo (Kindle edition).

Barbosa, N. and Souza, J.A.P. (2010) 'A Inflexão do Governo Lula: Política Econômica, Crescimento e Distribuição de Renda', in: E. Sader and M.A. Garcia (eds) *Brasil Entre o Passado e o Futuro*. São Paulo: Boitempo.

Barrientos, A. (2007) 'Understanding Conditions in Income Transfer Programmes: A Brief(est) Note', *IDS Bulletin*, 3 8 (3), pp. 66–8.

Bastos, E.K.X. (2012) 'Distribuição Funcional da Renda no Brasil: Estimativas Anuais e Construção de Uma Série Trimestral', *Texto para Discussão IPEA*, No. 1702, Brasília: IPEA.

Bastos, P.P.Z. and Hiratuka, C. (2017) 'A Política Econômica Externa do Governo Dilma Rousseff: Comércio, Cooperação e Dependência', *Texto Para Discussão* No.306, I.E.-UNICAMP, www.eco.unicamp.br/docprod/downarq. php?id=3535&tp=a (accessed 8 July 2017).

Baumann, R. and Braga, H.C. (1988) 'Export Financing in LDCs: The Role of Subsidies for Export Performance in Brazil', *World Development*, 16 (7), pp. 821–33.

Baumann, R., Rivero, J. And Zavattiero, Y. (1997) 'As Tarifas de Importação no Plano Real', *Pesquisa e Planejamento Econômico*, 27 (3), pp. 541–86.

Belluzzo, L.G. (2013) 'Os Anos do Povo', in: E. Sader (ed.) *10 Anos de Governos Pós-Neoliberais no Brasil: Lula e Dilma*. São Paulo: Boitempo (Kindle edition).

Belluzzo, L.G. (2017) 'Lava Jato Produziu 7 Milhões de Desempregados', www.brasildefato.com.br/2017/07/19/belluzzo-lava-jato-e-carne-fraca-produziram-5-a-7-milhoes-de-desempregados/ (accessed 20 July 2017).

Belluzzo, L.G. and Bastos, P.P.Z. (eds) (2016) *Austeridade para Quem? Balanço e Perspectivas do Governo Dilma Rousseff*. São Paulo: Carta Maior.

Bercovici, G. (2009) 'Os Princípios Estruturantes e o Papel do Estado', in: J.C. Cardoso Jr (ed.) *A Constituição Brasileira de 1988 Revisitada*. Brasília: IPEA.

Berringer, T. (2015) *A Burguesia Brasileira e a Política Externa nos Governos FHC e Lula*. Curitiba: Editora Appris.

Bértola, L., Higachi, H. and Porcile, G. (2002) 'Balance-of-Payments-Constrained Growth in Brazil: A Test of Thirlwall's Law, 1890–1973', *Journal of Post Keynesian Economics*, 25 (2), pp. 123–40.

Bérzin, I. (2002) *O Investimento Estrangeiro Direto e a Desnacionalização da Economia Brasileira: O Caso das Privatizações nos Anos 1990*. MSc dissertation, Departamento de Economia, UNESP-Araraquara.

Bianchi, A. (2004) *O Ministério dos Industriais: A Federação das Indústrias do Estado de São Paulo na Crise das Décadas de 1980 e 1990*. PhD thesis, IFCH-UNICAMP.

Bianchi, A. and Braga, R. (2003) 'Le PT au Pouvoir: la Gauche Brésilienne et le Social-libéralisme', *Carré Rouge*, 26, pp. 49–60.

Biondi, A. (2014) *O Brasil Privatizado: Um Balanço do Desmonte do Estado*. São Paulo: Geração Editorial.

Boff, L. (2016) 'Nós Erramos', https://leonardoboff.wordpress.com/2016/10/01/nos-erramos-frei-betto/ (accessed 8 July 2017).

Boismery, H. (1996) 'Substitution Monétaire et Dollarisation: Aspects Socio-économiques', *Economies et Sociétés* série P, 33 (1), pp. 13–39.

Boito, A. (2003) 'A Hegemonia Neoliberal no Governo Lula', *Crítica Marxista*, 17, pp. 10–36.

Boito, A. (2012) 'Governos Lula: a Nova Burguesia Nacional no Poder', in A. Boito and A. Galvão (eds) *Política e Classes Sociais no Brasil dos Anos 2000*. São Paulo: Alameda.

Boito, A. (2013) 'O Lulismo é um Tipo de Bonapartismo?', *Crítica Marxista*, 37, pp.171–81.

Boito, A. (2015) 'A Reação em Ponto de Fervura', www.consultapopular.org.br/noticia/rea%C3%A7%C3%A3o-em-ponto-de-fervura (accessed 7 July 2017).

Boito, A. (2017) 'A Corrupção como Ideologia', *Crítica Marxista*, 44, pp. 9–19.

Boito, A. and Berringer, T. (2014) 'Social Classes, Neodevelopmentalism, and Brazilian Foreign Policy under Presidents Lula and Dilma', *Latin American Perspectives*, 41 (5), pp. 94–109.

Boito, A. and Galvão, A. (eds) (2012) *Política e Classes Sociais no Brasil dos Anos 2000*. São Paulo: Alameda.

Boito, A. and Marcelino, P. (2011) 'Decline in Unionism? An Analysis of the New Wave of Strikes in Brazil', *Latin American Perspectives*, 38 (5), pp. 62–73.

Boito, A. and Saad-Filho, A. (2016) 'State, State Institutions and Political Power in Brazil', *Latin American Perspectives*, 43 (2), pp. 190–206.

Bomberger, W.A. and Makinen, G.E. (1983) 'The Hungarian Hyperinflation and Stabilization of 1945–1946', *Journal of Political Economy*, 96 (5), pp. 801–24.

Bonelli, R. (1999) 'A Reestruturação Industrial Brasileira nos Anos 90: Reação Empresarial e Mercado de Trabalho', in: OIT (ed.) *Abertura e Ajuste do Mercado de Trabalho no Brasil*. São Paulo: Editora 34.

Bonelli, R. (2015) 'Comparações Internacionais de Produtividade na Indústria e Tendências Setoriais: Brasil e EUA', in: N. Barbosa, N. Marconi, M.C. Pinheiro and L. Carvalho (eds) *Indústria e Desenvolvimento Produtivo no Brasil*. Rio de Janeiro: FGV.

Bonelli, R. and Gonçalves, R. (1998) 'Para Onde Vai a Estrutura Industrial Brasileira?', in: IPEA (ed.) *A Economia Brasileira em Perspectiva*. Brasília: IPEA.

Bonelli, R. and Sedlacek, G.L. (1991) 'Desigualdade Salarial: Resultados de Pesquisas Recentes', in: J.M. Camargo (ed.) *Distribuição de Renda no Brasil*. Rio de Janeiro: Paz e Terra.

Bonelli, R., Franco, G.B. and Fritsch, W. (1992) 'Macroeconomic Instability and Trade Performance in Brazil: Lessons from the 1980s to the 1990s', *The Bangladesh Development Studies*, 20 (2–3), pp. 127–54.

Bonelli, R. and Pessôa, S.A. (2010) 'Desindustrialização no Brasil: Um Resumo da Evidência', *Texto para Discussão No.7*, IBRE-FGV, http://bibliotecadigital.fgv.br/dspace/handle/10438/11689 (accessed 23 July 2017).

Bontempo, H.C. (1988) 'Transferências Externas e Financiamento do Governo Federal e Autoridades Monetárias', *Pesquisa e Planejamento Econômico*,18 (1), pp. 101–30.

Bontempo, H.C. (1989) 'Politica Cambial e Superávit Comercial', *Pesquisa e Planejamento Economico*, 19 (1), pp. 45–64.

Boschi, R.R. (1978) 'Empresário Nacional: Alguns Problemas Teóricos e sua Caracterização Econômica nos Anos 70', in: E. Diniz and R.R. Boschi (eds) *Empresariado Nacional e Estado no Brasil*. Rio de Janeiro: Forense Universitária.

Bourne, R. (2008) *Lula of Brazil: The Story so Far*. London: Zed Books.

Braga, J.M. (2015) 'A Inflação Brasileira na Década de 2000 e a Importância das Políticas Não Monetárias de Controle', *Economia e Sociedade*, 22 (3), pp. 697–727.

Braga, S. (2015) 'Onda Moralista Não Combaterá a Corrupção; é Seletiva e Partidária', http://cartamaior.com.br/?/Especial/A-direita-nas-ruas/Onda-moralista-nao-combatera-a-corrupcao-e-seletiva-e-partidaria/196/33067 (accessed 7 July 2017).

Branford, S. and Kucinski, B. (1995) *Brazil Carnival of the Oppressed – Lula and the Brazilian Workers' Party*. London: Latin America Bureau.

Branford, S. and Kucinski, B. (2003) *Politics Transformed – Lula and the Workers' Party in Brazil*. London: Latin American Bureau.

Braun, E. (2016) 'Wikileaks Confirms: Brazil's New President Is a US Asset', http://russia-insider.com/en/politics/wikileaks-confirms-brazils-new-president-us-asset/ri14332 (accessed 8 July 2017).

Breman, J. (2013) 'A Bogus Concept', *New Left Review*, 84, pp. 130–8.

Bresser-Pereira, L.C. (1981) 'A Inflação no Capitalismo de Estado e a Experiência Brasileira Recente', *Revista de Economia Política*, 1 (2), pp. 3–41.

Bresser-Pereira, L.C. (1987) 'Inertial Inflation and the Cruzado Plan', *World Development*,15 (8), pp.1035–44.

Bresser-Pereira, L.C. (1992) 'A Lógica Perversa da Estagnação: Dívida, Déficit e Inflação no Brasil', in: L.G. Belluzzo and P.N. Batista Jr (eds) *A Luta pela Sobrevivência da Moeda Nacional*. Rio de Janeiro: Paz e Terra.

Bresser-Pereira, L.C. (1996) *Economic Crisis and State Reform in Brazil*. Boulder, CO: Lynne Rienner.

Bresser-Pereira, L.C. (2003) 'Macroeconomia do Brasil pós-1994', *Análise Econômica*, 21 (40), pp. 7–38.

Bresser-Pereira, L.C. (2005) 'Macroeconomia Pós-Plano Real: As Relações Básicas', in: J. Sicsú, L.F. Paula and R. Michel (eds) *Novo-Desenvolvimentismo: um Projeto Nacional de Crescimento com Eqüidade Social*. Rio de Janeiro: Fundação Konrad Adenauer.

Bresser-Pereira, L.C. (2015a) 'A Quase Estagnação Brasileira e sua Explicação Novo-Desenvolvimentista', in: N. Barbosa, N. Marconi, M.C. Pinheiro and L. Carvalho (eds) *Indústria e Desenvolvimento Produtivo no Brasil*. Rio de Janeiro: FGV.

Bresser-Pereira, L.C. (2015b) 'Ricos Nutrem Ódio ao PT', *Folha de S.Paulo*, 1 March.

Bresser-Pereira, L.C. and Nakano, Y. (1985) *The Theory of Inertial Inflation: The Foundation of Economic Reform in Brazil and Argentina*. Boulder, CO: Lynne Rienner.

Briones, A. (1978) *Economía y Política del Fascismo Dependiente*. Mexico D.F.: Siglo XXI.

Britto, G. (2003) 'Abertura Comercial e Coeficientes de Conteúdo Importado na Indústria', in: M. Laplane, L. Coutinho and C. Hiratuka (eds) *Internacionalização e Desenvolvimento da Indústria no Brasil*. São Paulo: Editora Unesp.

Bruton, H.J. (1981) 'The Import-Substitution Strategy of Economic Development: A Survey', *Pakistan Development Review*, 10 (2), pp. 123–46.

Bruton, H.J. (1998) 'A Reconsideration of Import Substitution', *Journal of Economic Literature*, 36, pp. 903–36.

Bulmer-Thomas, V. (2003) *The Economic History of Latin America since Independence*, 2nd ed. Cambridge: Cambridge University Press.

Burle, L.L. (1993) 'A Internacionalização do Sistema Financeiro:1990–1992', *Análise*, 4 (2), pp. 111–30.

Byres, T.J. (1996) *Capitalism from Above and Capitalism from Below: An Essay in Comparative Political Economy*. London: Macmillan.

Cacciamali, M.C. (1992) 'Mudanças Estruturais e o Ajustamento do Mercado de Trabalho no Brasil na Década de Oitenta', *Estudos Econômicos*, 22, pp. 133–50.

Cacciamali, M.C. (1997) 'The Growing Inequality in Income Distribution in Brazil', in: M. Willumsen and E. Fonseca (eds) *The Brazilian Economy: Structure and Performance in Recent Decades*. Miami: North-South Center Press.

Cacciamali, M.C. and Bezerra, L.L. (1997) 'Produtividade e Emprego Industrial no Brasil', in: L. Carleial and R. Valle (eds) *Reestruturação Produtiva e Mercado de Trabalho no Brasil*. São Paulo: Hucitec-ABET.

Calixtre, A.B. and Fagnani, E. (2017) 'A Política Social e os Limites do Experimento Desenvolvimentista (2003–2014)', *Texto para Discussão No.295*, I.E.-UNICAMP, www.eco.unicamp.br/docprod/downarq.php?id=3524&tp=a (accessed 5 July 2017).

Calixtre, A.B., Biancarelli, A.M. and Macedo Cintra, M.A. (eds) (2014) *Presente e Futuro do Desenvolvimento Brasileiro*. Brasília: IPEA.

Calvo, G.A. (1992) 'Are High Interest Rates Effective for Stopping High Inflation? Some Skeptical Notes', *The World Bank Economic Review*, 6 (1), pp. 55–69.

Calvo, G.A. (1996) 'The Management of Capital Flows: Domestic Policy and International Cooperation', in G.K. Helleiner (ed.) *The International Monetary and Financial System*. London: Macmillan.

Calvo, G.A., Leiderman, L. and Reinhart, C. (1996) 'Inflows of Capital to Developing Countries in the 1990s', *Journal of Economic Perspectives*, 10 (2), pp. 123–39.

Câmara Neto, A.F. and Vernengo, M. (2007) 'Lula's Social Policies: New Wine in Old Bottles?', in: P. Arestis and A. Saad-Filho (eds) *Political Economy of Brazil*. London: Palgrave.

Camargo, J.M. and Ramos, C.A. (1988) *A Revolução Indesejada: Conflito Distributivo e Mercado de Trabalho*. Rio de Janeiro: Campus.

Campos, P.H.P. (2015) 'Pagamento de propina na Petrobras transcende o PT e o PSDB', https://brasil.elpais.com/brasil/2015/03/18/politica/1426706268_112230.html (accessed 7 July 2017).

Cano, W. (1999) 'América Latina: do Desenvolvimentismo ao Neoliberalismo', in: J.L. Fiori (ed.) *Estados e Moedas no Desenvolvimento das Nações*. Petrópolis: Vozes.

Cano, W. (2015) 'Crise e Industrialização no Brasil entre 1929 e 1954: A Reconstrução do Estado Nacional e a Política Nacional de Desenvolvimento', *Revista de Economia Política*, 35 (3) 140, pp. 444–60.

Cardoso, A.M. (2003) *A Década Neoliberal e a Crise dos Sindicatos no Brasil*. São Paulo: Boitempo.

Cardoso, E. and Dornbusch, R. (1987) 'Brazil's Tropical Plan', *American Economic Review*, 77 (2), pp. 288–92.

Cardoso, F.H. and Faletto, E. (1979) *Dependency and Development in Latin America*. Berkeley: University of California Press.

Carlotti, T. (2016) 'Operação Abafa: Como o Tucanato se Mantém no Poder', www.cartamaior.com.br/?/Editoria/Politica/-Operacao-Abafa-como-o-tucanato-se-manteve-no-poder/4/35428 (accessed 3 July 2017).

Carlotti, T. (2017) 'A "Justiça Pacificadora" do STF', www.cartamaior.com.br/?/Editoria/Politica/A-u21Cjustica-pacificadora-u21D-do-STF/4/37422 (accessed 13 July 2017).

Carneiro, D.D. (1977) 'Introdução: Dificuldades no Reajuste do Modelo', in: *Brasil: Dilemas da Política Econômica*. Rio de Janeiro: Campus.

Carneiro, R. (2017) 'Navegando a Contravento (Uma Reflexão sobre o Experimento Desenvolvimentista do Governo Dilma Rousseff)', *Texto para Discussão* No.289, I.E.-UNICAMP, www.eco.unicamp.br/docprod/downarq.php?id=3509&tp=a (accessed 8 July 2017).

Carneiro, R. and Rossi, P. (2012) 'The Brazilian Experience in Managing Interest-Exchange Rate Nexus', Texto para Discussão I.E.-Unicamp No.206, www.eco.unicamp.br/docprod/downarq.php?id=3196andtp=a (accessed 5 July 2017).

Carvalho, C.E. (1993) 'Liquidez dos Haveres Financeiros e Zeragem Automática do Mercado', *Revista de Economia Política*,13 (1), pp. 25–36.

Carvalho, C.E. (2000) 'O Plano Collor no Debate Econômico Brasileiro', *Pesquisa e Debate*,1 (1) 17, pp. 112–51.

Carvalho, C.E. (2006) 'As Origens e a Gênese do Plano Collor', *Nova Economia*, 16 (1), pp. 101–34.

Carvalho, F.J.C. (1993) 'Strato-Inflation and High Inflation: The Brazilian Experience', *Cambridge Journal of Economics*, 17 (1), pp. 63–78.

Carvalho, F.J.C. (2016) 'Looking Into the Abyss? Brazil at the Mid-2010s', *Journal of Post Keynesian Economics*, 39 (1), pp. 93–114.

Carvalho, F.J.C. (2017) 'Brazil Still in Troubled Waters', *Levy Economics Institute of Bard College Public Policy Brief*, No.143, www.levyinstitute.org/publications/brazil-still-in-troubled-waters (accessed 11 July 2017).

Carvalho, L. and Rugitsky, F. (2015) *Growth and Distribution in Brazil in the 21st Century: Revisiting the Wage-Led Versus Profit-Led Debate*, FEA/USP Working Paper Series, 25.

Carvalho, S.S. (2015) 'A Evolução da Estrutura Ocupacional e os Padrões Setoriais da Informalidade no Brasil: 1995–2012', in: G.C. Squeff (ed.) *Dinâmica Macrossetorial Brasileira*. Brasília: IPEA.

Casa, C.A.L. (2004) *Dívida Interna, Inflação e Desinflação (1964–2004)*, www.scribd.com/document/167378504/TESOURO-NACIONAL-OTIMA-Estabilizacao-crescimento (accessed 5 July 2017).

Castro, A.B. and Souza, F.E.P. (1985) *A Economia Brasileira em Marcha Forçada*. Rio de Janeiro: Paz e Terra.

Castro, J.A. and Modesto, L. (eds) (2010) *Bolsa Família 2003–2010: Avanços e Desafios*, vol.1. Brasília: IPEA.

Castro, J.A., Ribeiro, J.A., Campos, A.C. and Matijascic, M. (2009) 'A CF/99 e as Políticas Sociais Brasileiras', in: J.C. Cardoso Jr (ed.) *A Constituição Brasileira de 1988 Revisitada*. Brasília: IPEA.

Castro, J.A., Ribeiro, J.A.C., Chaves, J.V. and Duarte, B.C. (2012) 'Gasto Social Federal: Prioridade Macroeconômica no Período 1995–2010', *IPEA Nota Técnica* no.9, http://repositorio.ipea.gov.br/handle/11058/5695 (accessed 7 July 2017).

Castro, J.R. (2016) 'Das Desonerações ao "Renúncia Já": Como a Fiesp Rompeu com Dilma', www.nexojornal.com.br/expresso/2016/03/17/Das-desonera%C3%A7%C3%B5es-ao-%E2%80%98ren%C3%BAncia-j%C3%A1%E2%80%99-como-a-Fiesp-rompeu-com-Dilma (accessed 24 July 2017).

Cavalcante, S. and Arias, S. (2017) 'A Divisão da Classe Média Brasileira na Crise Política de 2013–2016', unpublished manuscript.

Cavalcanti, C.B. (1988) *Transferência de Recursos ao Exterior e Substituição de Dívida Externa por Dívida Interna*. Rio de Janeiro: BNDES.

CB [Correio Brasiliense] (2013) 'Conselhos de medicina vão à justiça contra o Programa Mais Médicos', www.correiobraziliense.com.br/app/noticia/eu-estudante/tf_carreira/2013/08/14/tf_carreira_interna,382567/conselhos-de-medicina-vao-a-justica-contra-o-programa-mais-medicos.shtml (accessed 16 July 2017).

CEDLAS and World Bank (2016) *SEDLAC*. http://sedlac.econo.unlp.edu.ar/eng/ (accessed 7 July 2017).

CEPAL [UN Economic Commission for Latin America] (1999) *Panorama Social da América Latina 1998*. New York: United Nations.

Cerqueira, C.A. (2003) *Dívida Externa Brasileira*, 2nd ed. Brasília: Banco Central do Brasil.

Chang, H.-J. and Yoo, C.-G. (2000) 'The Triumph of the Rentiers?', *Challenge*, 43 (1), pp. 105–24.

Chauí, M. (1994) 'Raízes Teológicas do Populismo no Brasil: Teocracia dos Dominantes, Messianismo dos Dominados', in: E. Dagnino (ed.) *Anos 90: Política e Sociedade no Brasil*. São Paulo: Brasiliense.

Chauí, M. (2013a) *Uma Nova Classe Trabalhadora*, www.cartamaior.com.br/?/
Editoria/Politica/Uma-nova-classe-trabalhadora/4/28062 (accessed 7 July 2017).

Chauí, M. (2013b) *As Manifestações de Junho de 2013 na Cidade de São Paulo*, www.
teoriaedebate.org.br/materias/nacional/manifestacoes-de-junho-de-2013-na-
cidade-de-sao-paulo (accessed 7 July 2017).

Chaves, J.V. and Ribeiro, J.A.C. (2012) 'Gasto Social Federal: Uma Análise da
Execução Orçamentária de 2011', *IPEA Nota Técnica* no.13, http://repositorio.
ipea.gov.br/handle/11058/5687 (accessed 7 July 2017).

Cinquetti, C.A. (2000) 'The *Real Plan*: Stabilization and Destabilization', *World
Development*, 28 (1), pp. 155–71.

Cintra, M.A.M. (2015) 'O Financiamento das Contas Externas Brasileiras:
1995–2014', in: G.C. Squeff (ed.) *Dinâmica Macrossetorial Brasileira*. Brasília:
IPEA.

CNI [Confederação Nacional da Indústria] (2014) *Competitividade Brasil:
Comparação com Países Selecionados*. Brasília: CNI.

CNI/CEPAL [Confederação Nacional da Indústria and UN Economic Commission
for Latin America] (1997) *Investimentos na Indústria Brasileira 1995–1999 –
Características e Determinantes*. Rio de Janeiro: CNI.

Coes, D.V. (1994) 'Macroeconomic Stabilisation and Trade Liberalisation: Brazilian
Experience and Choices', *The World Economy*, 17 (4), pp. 433–50.

Coggiola, O. (2004) *O Governo Lula: Da Esperança à Realidade*. São Paulo: Xamã.

Cohen, D. (1987) 'External and Domestic Debt Constraints in LDCs: A Theory
with a Numerical Application to Brazil and Mexico', in: R. C. Bryant and R.
Portes (eds) *Global Macroeconomics, Policy Conflict and Cooperation*. London:
Macmillan.

Coleman, N. (2003) 'Current Debates around BIG: The Political and Socio-
economic Context', in G. Standing and M. Samson (eds) *A Basic Income Grant
for South Africa*. Cape Town: University of Cape Town Press.

Conti, J.M. (2017) 'Teori Zavascki, o Supremo Tribunal Federal e a Responsabilidade
Fiscal', www.conjur.com.br/2017-fev-07/contas-vista-teori-zavascki-supremo-
responsabilidade-fiscal (accessed 8 July 2017).

Corrêa, V.P. and Santos, C.H.M. (2013) 'Modelo de Crescimento Brasileiro e
Mudança Estrutural – Avanços e Limites', in: V.P. Corrêa (ed.) *Padrão de
Acumulação e Desenvolvimento Brasileiro*. São Paulo: Fundação Perseu Abramo.

Coslovsky, S., Pires, R. and Bignami, R. (2017) 'Resilience and Renewal: The
Enforcement of Labor Laws in Brazil', *Latin American Politics and Society*, 59
(2), pp. 77–102.

Costa, S. (1995) *Tendências e Centrais Sindicais: O Movimento Sindical Brasileiro,
1978–1994*. São Paulo: Editora Anita Garibaldi.

Coutinho, D.R. (2013) 'Decentralization and Coordination in Social Law and
Policy: The *Bolsa Família* Program', in D.M. Trubek, H.A. Garcia, D.R. Coutinho
and A. Santos (eds) *Law and the New Developmental State*. Cambridge:
Cambridge University Press.

Coutinho, L. and Ferraz, J.C. (eds) (1995) *Estudo da Competitividade da Indústria
Brasileira*. Campinas: Papirus.

Coutinho, L. and Reichstul, H.-P. (1977) 'O Setor Produtivo Estatal e o Ciclo', in:
C.E. Martins (ed.) *Estado e Capitalismo no Brasil*. São Paulo: Hucitec.

Coutinho, L., Baltar, P. and Camargo, F. (1999) 'Desemprenho Industrial e do Emprego sob a Política de Estabilização', in: OIT (ed.) *Abertura e Ajuste do Mercado de Trabalho no Brasil*. São Paulo: Editora 34.

Cruz, P.D. (1984). *Dívida Externa e Política Econômica*. São Paulo: Brasiliense.

CTB [Central dos Trabalhadores e Trabalhadoras do Brasil] (2017) 'Manifesto em defesa da Indústria Nacional' http://metalurgicosrj.org.br/manifesto-em-defesa-da-industria-nacional/ (accessed 16 July 2017).

Cyrino, T.N. (2017) *A Cadeia Produtiva da Carne e a Política Neodesenvolvimentista dos Governos Lula (2003–2010)*. MSc dissertation, Department of Politics, UNICAMP.

Cysne, R.P. (1993) 'A Economia Brasileira no Período Militar', *Estudos Econômicos* 23 (2), pp.185–226.

Dain, S. (1977) 'Empresa Estatal e Política Econômica no Brasil', in: C.E. Martins (ed.) *Estado e Capitalismo no Brasil*. São Paulo: Hucitec.

Damous, W. (2017a) 'Estado de Exceção', https://oglobo.globo.com/opiniao/estado-de-excecao-21553787 (accessed 16 July 2017).

Damous, W. (2017b) 'Fascismo e Populismo penal no "Combate à Corrupção"', www.brasil247.com/pt/colunistas/wadihdamous/291953/Fascismo-e-populismo-penal-no-%E2%80%9Ccombate-%C3%A0-corrup%C3%A7%C3%A30%E2%80%9D.htm (accessed 13 July 2017).

Dardot, P. and Laval, C. (2013) *The New Way of the World: On Neoliberal Society*. London: Verso.

Del Roio, M. (2004) 'O PCB e a Luta pela Constituição do Movimento Operário', *Margem Esquerda*, 4, pp. 50–4.

Demier, F. (2013) *O Longo Bonapartismo Brasileiro, 1930–1964*. Rio de Janeiro: Mauad X.

di Tella, T. (1997) 'Populism into the 21st Century', *Government and Opposition*, 32 (2), pp. 187–200.

Dias, M. (2016) 'Dilma Desiste de ir a Ato Contra Temer para Evitar Discursos Radicais', www1.folha.uol.com.br/poder/2016/06/1780069-dilma-desiste-de-ir-a-ato-contra-temer-para-evitar-discursos-radicais.shtml (accessed 3 July 2017).

Dias, N. (2014) 'O Novo Congresso Nacional e os Desafios para o Movimento Sindical', available at www.condsef.org.br/images/of-cir_85_filiadas_08–12–2014_anexo.pdf (accessed 3 July 2017).

Diaz-Alejandro, C. (1985) 'Good-Bye Financial Repression, Hello Financial Crash', *Journal of Development Economics*, 19, pp. 1–24.

Diniz, E. (1999) 'Globalização, Elites Empresariais e Democracia no Brasil dos Anos 90', *Ensaios FEE*, 20 (1), pp. 155–78.

Diniz, E. (2004) *Globalização, Reformas Econômicas e Elites Empresariais*, 2nd ed. Rio de Janeiro: Editora FGV.

Domingues, J.M. (2015a) 'A Esquerda no Nevoeiro', http://diplomatique.org.br/a-esquerda-no-nevoeiro/ (accessed 7 July 2017).

Domingues, J.M. (2015b) *O Brasil entre o Presente e o Futuro*, 2nd ed. Rio de Janeiro: Mauad X.

Dornbusch, R. (1997) 'Brazil's Incomplete Stabilization and Reform', *Brookings Papers on Economic Activity*, 1, pp. 367–94.

Dornbusch, R. and Simonsen, M.H. (eds) (1983) *Inflation, Debt and Indexation*. Cambridge, Mass.: MIT Press.

Dreifuss, R.A. (1981) *1964: A Conquista do Estado – Ação Política, Poder e Golpe de Classe*. Petrópolis: Vozes.

Dweck, E. (2017) 'PEC55 e Reforma da Previdência: Não Querem Mais Dividir o Bolo', http://brasildebate.com.br/pec-55-e-a-reforma-da-previdencia-nao-querem-mais-dividir-o-bolo/ (accessed 13 July 2017).

Dweck, E. and Teixeira, R.A. (2017) 'A Política Fiscal do Governo Dilma e a Crise Econômica', *Texto para Discussão 303*, I.E. Unicamp.

Engdahl, F.W. (2014) 'BRICS' Brazil President Next Washington Target', https://journal-neo.org/2014/11/18/brics-brazil-president-next-washington-target/ (accessed 13 July 2017).

ESP [*O Estado de S.Paulo*] (2010) 'Editorial: O Mal a Evitar', www.estadao.com.br/noticias/geral,editorial-o-mal-a-evitar,615255 (accessed 20 July 2017).

Evans, P. (1979) *Dependent Development: The Alliance of Multinational, State, and Local Capital in Brazil*. Princeton: Princeton University Press.

Fagnani, E. (2005) *Política Social no Brasil (1964–2002): Entre a Cidadania e a Caridade*. PhD thesis, I.E.-UNICAMP.

Fagnani, E. (2017) 'Direitos Roubados: O Fim do Breve Ciclo de Cidadania Social no Brasil', www.cartacapital.com.br/politica/direitos-roubados-o-fim-do-breve-ciclo-de-cidadania-social-no-brasil (accessed 8 July 2017).

Fagnani, E. (ed.) (2017) *Previdência: Reformar para Excluir?* Brasília: ANFIP/DIEESE.

Farah, T. (2010) 'Entidades de Imprensa e Fecomercio Estudam ir ao STF Contra Plano de Direitos Humanos', http://oglobo.globo.com/politica/entidades-de-imprensa-fecomercio-estudam-ir-ao-stf-contra-plano-de-direitos-humanos-3037045 (accessed 20 July 2017).

Farias, L. and Zero, M. (2017) 'Cooperando com os EUA, Destruindo o Brasil', http://jornalggn.com.br/noticia/cooperando-com-os-eua-destruindo-o-brasil-por-lindbergh-farias-e-marcelo-zero (accessed 8 July 2017).

Faro, C. (ed.) (1990) *Plano Collor: Avaliações e Perspectivas*. Rio de Janeiro: Livros Técnicos e Científicos Editora.

Feijó, C. and Carvalho, F.C. (1992) 'The Resilience of High Inflation: Recent Brazilian Failures with Stabilization Policies', *Journal of Post Keynesian Economics*, 15 (1), pp. 109–24.

Feijó, C.A. and Carvalho, P.G.M. (1998) *Structural Changes in the Brazilian Economy: An Analysis of the Evolution of Industrial Productivity in the 1990s*, http://isi.cbs.nl/iamamember/CD5-Mexico1998/document/CON_PA~1/Cp10apar.doc (accessed 5 July 2017).

Felder, R.S. (2013) *Neoliberal Reforms, Crisis and Recovery in Argentina (1990s–2000s)*, PhD Thesis, Department of Political Science, York University, Toronto.

Feldstein, M. and Horioka, C. (1980) 'Domestic Savings and International Capital Flows', *Economic Journal*, 90 (358), pp. 314–29.

Ferraz, L. (2015) 'Maioria Foi às Ruas Contra Corrupção, Diz Datafolha', www1.folha.uol.com.br/poder/2015/03/1603885-maioria-foi-as-ruas-contra-corrupcao-diz-datafolha.shtml (accessed 3 July 2017).

Ferraz, L.P.C. Gutierre, L. and Cabral, R. (2015) 'A Indústria Brasileira na Era das Cadeias Globais de Valor', in: N. Barbosa, N. Marconi, M.C. Pinheiro and L. Carvalho (eds) *Indústria e Desenvolvimento Produtivo no Brasil*. Rio de Janeiro: FGV.

Ferreira, F. and Litchfield, J. (1996) 'Inequality and Poverty in the Lost Decade: Brazilian Income Distribution in the 1980s', in: V. Bulmer-Thomas (ed.) *The New Economic Model in Latin America and its Impact on Income Distribution and Poverty*. London: Macmillan.

FIESP, CUT, Sindicato dos Metalúrgicos do ABC, Força Sindical, and Sindicato dos Metalúrgicos de São Paulo e Mogi das Cruzes (2011) *Brasil do Diálogo, da Produção e do Emprego*, www.fiesp.com.br/brasil-do-dialogo-pela-producao-e-emprego/ (accessed 3 July 2017).

Figueiredo, L. (2000) *Morcegos Negros*. Rio de Janeiro: Editora Record.

Filgueiras, L. and Gonçalves, R. (2007) *A Economia Política do Governo Lula*. Rio de Janeiro: Contraponto.

Fine, B. and Saad-Filho, A. (2014) 'Politics of Neoliberal Development: Washington Consensus and post-Washington Consensus' in H. Weber (ed.) *The Politics of Development: A Survey*. London: Routledge.

Fine, B. and Saad-Filho, A. (2016) *Marx's Capital*, 6th ed. London: Pluto Press.

Fine, B. and Saad-Filho, A. (2017) 'Thirteen Things You Need to Know About Neoliberalism', *Critical Sociology*, 45 (4–5), pp. 685–706.

Fiori, J.L. (1990) 'Sonhos Prussianos, Crises Brasileiras – Leitura Política de uma Industrialização Tardia', *Ensaios FEE*, 11 (1), pp. 41–61.

Fiori, J.L. (1992) 'The Political Economy of the Developmentalist State in Brazil', *Cepal Review*, 47, pp. 173–86.

Fiori, J.L. (1997) *Os Moedeiros Falsos*. Petrópolis: Vozes.

Fishlow, A. (1986) 'A Economia Política do Ajustamento Brasileiro aos Choques do Petróleo: Uma Nota Sobre o Período 1974/84', *Pesquisa e Planejamento Econômico*, 16 (3), pp. 507–50.

Fishlow, A. (1997) 'Is the Real Plan for Real?', in: S.K. Purcell and R. Roett (eds) *Brazil under Cardoso*. Boulder, CO: Lynne Rienner.

FitzGerald, E.V.K. (2000) 'ECLA and the Theory of Import Substituting Industrialization in Latin America', in: E. Cárdenas, J. Ocampo and R. Thorp (eds) *An Economic History of Latin America*, vol.3. London: Palgrave.

Flynn, P. (1999) 'Brazil: The Politics of Crisis', *Third World Quarterly*, 20 (2), pp. 287–317.

Fon Filho, A. (2013) 'A Direita Sai de Casa pela Porta da Esquerda', www.viomundo.com.br/politica/aton-fon-filho-a-direita-sai-de-casa-pela-porta-da-esquerda.html (accessed 1 July 2017).

Fonseca, F. (2017) 'Da Judicialização da Política e das Políticas Públicas à Partidarização Ativa do Poder Judiciário', www.cartamaior.com.br/?/Editoria/Politica/Da-Judicializacao-da-politica-e-das-politicas-publicas-a-parti darizacao-ativa-do-poder-judiciario/4/37904 (accessed 13 July 2017).

Fortes, A. (2016) 'Brazil's Neoconservative Offensive', *NACLA Report on the Americas*, 48 (3), pp. 217–20.

Franco, G.H.B. (1995) *O Plano Real e Outros Ensaios*. Rio de Janeiro: Francisco Alves.

Franco, G.H.B. (1998) 'Inserção Externa e Desenvolvimento', *Revista de Economia Política*, 71, pp. 121–47.

Freitas, M.C.P. (2009) 'Os Efeitos da Crise Global no Brasil: Aversão ao Risco e Preferência Pela Liquidez no Mercado de Crédito', *Estudos Avançados*, 23 (66), pp. 125–45.

Fritz, B., Paula, L.F. and Prates, D.M. (2017) 'Developmentalism at the Periphery: Can Productive Change and Income Distribution be Compatible with Global Financial Asymmetries?', *DesiguALdades.net Working Paper No.101*, https://s3.amazonaws.com/acadex.../56da2b3b856af8ea20cof01d-fileIdentified.pdf (accessed 5 July 2017).

FSP (2006) 'Um Relatório Exemplar', www1.folha.uol.com.br/fsp/opiniao/fz1304200601.htm (accessed 5 July 2017).

FSP (2017) 'Folha Explica: Operação Lava Jato', http://arte.folha.uol.com.br/poder/operacao-lava-jato/ (accessed 13 July 2017).

Furtado, C. (1972) *Análise do 'Modelo' Brasileiro*. Rio de Janeiro: Civilização Brasileira.

Gadotti, M. and Pereira, O. (1989) *Pra Que PT: Origem, Projeto e Consolidação do Partido dos Trabalhadores*. São Paulo: Cortez Editora.

Gallie, W.B. (1956) 'Essentially Contested Concepts', *Aristotelian Society*, 56, pp. 167–98.

Galvão, A. (2007) *Neoliberalismo e Reforma Trabalhista no Brasil*. São Paulo: Editora Revan.

Galvão, A., Marcelino, P. and Trópia, P.V. (2015) *As Bases Sociais das Novas Centrais Sindicais Brasileiras*. Curitiba: Editora Appris.

Garcia, A.S. (2012) *A Internacionalização de Empresas Brasileiras durante o Governo Lula: Uma Análise Crítica da Relação entre Capital e Estado no Brasil Contemporâneo*. PhD thesis, Department of International Relations, PUC-RJ.

Garcia, M.A. (2013) 'Dez Anos de Política Externa', in: E. Sader (ed.) *10 Anos de Governos Pós-Neoliberais no Brasil: Lula e Dilma*. São Paulo: Boitempo (Kindle edition).

Garcia, M.G.P. (1996) 'Avoiding Some Costs of Inflation and Crawling toward Hyperinflation: The Case of the Brazilian Domestic Currency Substitute', *Journal of Development Economics*, 51, pp. 139–59.

Gaspari, E. (2003) *A Ditadura Derrotada*. São Paulo: Companhia das Letras.

Gaspari, E. (2004) *A Ditadura Encurralada*. São Paulo: Companhia das Letras.

Gaspari, E. (2016) *A Ditadura Acabada*. São Paulo: Editora Intrínseca.

Genro, L. and Robaina, R. (2006) *A Falência do PT e a Atualidade da Luta Socialista*. Porto Alegre: LandPM Editora.

Gentil, D.L. (2015) 'Além da Macroeconomia de Curto Prazo: Notas Sobre a Debilidade Estrutural da Economia Brasileira no Período Recente', *Revista da Sociedade Brasileira de Economia Política*, 41, pp. 54–81.

Gentili, P. (ed.) (2016) *Golpe en Brasil: Genealogía de Una Farsa*. Buenos Aires: CLACSO.

Gereffi, G. and Wyman, D.L. (1990) *Manufacturing Miracles: Paths of Industrialization in Latin America and East Asia*. Princeton: Princeton University Press.

Ghosh, J. (2011) *Cash Transfers as the Silver Bullet for Poverty Reduction: A Sceptical Note*, www.epw.in/journal/2011/21/specials/cash-transfers-silver-bullet-poverty-reduction-sceptical-note.html (accessed 7 July 2017).

Giambiagi, F. (1997) *Necessidade de Financiamento do Setor Público: Bases para a Discussão do Ajuste Fiscal no Brasil – 1991/96*. Textos para Discussão BNDES No.53, ppe.ipea.gov.br/index.php/ppe/article/view/740/680 (accessed 7 July 2017).

Giovannetti, L.F. and Carvalho, L. (2015) 'Distribuição de Renda, Mudança Estrutural e Inflação de Serviços no Brasil,' *Anais do Encontro da ANPEC*, 43, pp. 1–20.

Gobetti, S.W. and Orair, R.O. (2016) Progressividade Tributária: a Agenda Negligenciada, *Textos para Discussão do IPEA*, 2190, www.ipea.gov.br/portal/index.php?option=com_contentandview=articleandid=27549 (accessed 3 July 2017).

Gobetti, S.W. and Orair, R.O. (2017) 'Taxation and Distribution of Income in Brazil: New Evidence from Personal Income Tax Data,' *Revista de Economia Política*, 37 (2), 147, pp. 267–86.

Goldsmith, R.W. (1986) *Brasil 1850–1984: Desenvolvimento Financeiro Sob Um Século de Inflação*. São Paulo: Harper and Row.

Gonçalves, R. (1999) *Globalização e Desnacionalização*. Rio de Janeiro: Paz e Terra.

Gorender, J. and Lorent, T. (1998) 'The Reestablishment of Bourgeois Hegemony: The Workers' Party and the 1994 Elections,' *Latin American Perspectives*, 25 (1), pp. 11–27.

Governo do Brasil (1993) *Exposição de Motivos No. 393 do Ministro da Fazenda*. Brasília: Congresso Nacional.

Gowan, P. (1999) *The Global Gamble: America's Faustian Bid for World Dominance*. Verso: London.

Gramsci, A. (1971) *Selections from the Prison Notebooks*. London: Lawrence and Wishart.

Greenwald, G., Fishman, A. and Miranda, D. (2016) 'Brazil is Engulfed By Ruling Class Corruption – And a Dangerous Subversion of Democracy,' https://theintercept.com/2016/03/18/brazil-is-engulfed-by-ruling-class-corruption-and-a-dangerous-subversion-of-democracy/ (accessed 3 July 2017).

Guimarães, J. (2015) 'Por Que Ainda é Possível Derrotar a Campanha Golpista do PSDB?', http://cartamaior.com.br/?/Especial/A-direita-nas-ruas/Por-que-ainda-e-possivel-derrotar-a-campanha-golpista-do-PSDB-/196/33070 (accessed 3 July 2017).

Hall, A. (2008) 'Brazil's *Bolsa Família*: A Double-Edged Sword?', *Development and Change*, 39 (5), pp. 799–822.

Hay, D.A. (2001) 'The Post-1990 Brazilian Trade Liberalisation and the Performance of Large Manufacturing Firms: Productivity, Market Share and Profits,' *Economic Journal*, 111, pp. 620–41.

Henriques, R. (ed.) (2000) *Desigualdade e Pobreza no Brasil*. Rio de Janeiro: IPEA.

Herédia, T. (2013) 'Brasil Vive o Pesadelo da Economia Estagnada com Inflação Alta,' http://g1.globo.com/platb/thaisheredia/2013/05/29/brasil-vive-o-pesadelo-da-economia-estagnada-com-inflacao-alta/ (accessed 20 July 2017).

Hermann, J. (2002) 'Financial Structure and Financing Models: The Brazilian Experience over the 1964–1997 Period,' *Journal of Latin American Studies*, 34 (1), pp. 71–114.

Hewitt, T. (1992) 'Brazilian Industrialisation,' in: T. Hewitt, H. Johnson and D. Wield (eds) *Industrialisation and Development*. Oxford: Oxford University Press.

Hirschman, A. (1968) 'The Political Economy of Import Substituting Industrialisation in Latin America,' *Quarterly Journal of Economics*, 82 (1), pp. 1–32.

Hochstetler, K. and Montero, A.P. (2013) 'The Renewed Developmental State: The National Development Bank and the Brazil Model', *Journal of Development Studies*, 49 (11), pp. 1484–99.

Hochuli, A. (2017) 'The Ends of Lava Jato', www.jacobinmag.com/2017/04/brazil-lava-jato-corruption-dilma-rousseff-lula-temer-mani-pulite-italy/ (accessed 13 July 2017).

Hoffmann, R. (2013) 'Transferências de Renda e Desigualdade no Brasil (1995–2011)', in: T. Campello and M. Neri (eds) *Programa Bolsa Família: Uma Década de Inclusão e Cidadania*. Brasília: IPEA.

Hopewell, K. (2016) 'The Accidental Agro-Power: Constructing Comparative Advantage in Brazil', *New Political Economy*, 21 (6), pp. 536–54.

Hurtienne, T. and Sperber, J. (1983) 'The Brazilian Model of Accumulation: Its Origins, Structure, and Crisis', *Latin American Perspectives*, 10 (2–3), pp. 108–27.

Ianni, O. (1988) *Estado e Capitalismo*, 2nd ed. São Paulo: Brasiliense.

IMF [International Monetary Fund] (2002) 'Brazil – Letter of Intent, Memorandum of Economic Policies, and Technical Memorandum of Understanding', 29 August, www.imf.org/external/np/loi/2002/bra/04/index.htm (accessed 5 July 2017).

IMF [International Monetary Fund] (2005b) 'Press Release: IMF Executive Board Completes Final Review Under Brazil's Stand-By Arrangement', www.imf.org/external/np/sec/pr/2005/pr0564.htm (accessed 5 July 2017).

IMF [International Monetary Fund] (2005b) 'Public Information Notice: IMF Executive Board Concludes 2005 Article IV Consultation with Brazil', www.imf.org/en/News/Articles/2015/09/28/04/53/pn0541#P25_355#P25_355 (accessed 20 July 2017).

IPEA [Instituto de Pesquisa Econômica Aplicada] (2010) 'Distribuição Funcional da Renda Pré e Pós-Crise Internacional no Brasil', *Comunicado 47*, repositorio.ipea.gov.br/handle/11058/5261 (accessed 15 July 2017).

IPEA [Instituto de Pesquisa Econômica Aplicada] (2012) *A Dinâmica Recente das Transferências Públicas de Assistência e Previdência Social*, www.ipea.gov.br/portal/images/stories/PDFs/comunicado/120308_comunicadoipea138.pdf (accessed 7 July 2017).

Itoh, M. and Lapavitsas, C. (1999) *Political Economy of Money and Finance*. London: Macmillan.

Jannuzzi, P.M and Sousa, M.F. (2016) 'Pobreza, Desigualdade e Mudança Social no Brasil de 1992 a 2014', in: P.M. Jannuzzi *et al.* (eds) (2016) *Brasil Sem Miséria: Resultados, Institucionalidades e Desafios*. Brasília: Ministério do Desenvolvimento Social e Combate à Fome.

Jessop, B. (2016) *The State: Past, Present, Future*. Cambridge: Polity Press.

Kalecki, M. (1943) 'Political Aspects of Full Employment', *Political Quarterly*, 14 (4), pp. 322–31.

Kaltenbrunner, A. and Painceira, J.P. (2017) 'Subordinated Financial Integration and Financialisation in Emerging Capitalist Economies: The Brazilian Experience', *New Political Economy*, www.tandfonline.com/doi/full/10.1080/13563467.2017.1349089 (accessed 18 July 2017).

Kane, C. and Morisett, J. (1993) 'Who Would Vote for Inflation in Brazil? An Integrated Framework Approach to Inflation and Income Distribution', *World*

Bank Policy Research Working Paper, No.1183, https://ideas.repec.org/p/wbk/wbrwps/1183.html (accessed 5 July 2017).

Karavaev, A. (1987) *Brasil: Passado e Presente do 'Capitalismo Periférico'*. Moscou: Edições Progresso.

Kilsztajn, S. (1996) 'Ancoragem Cambial e Estabilização', in: R.R. Sawaya (ed.) *O Plano Real e a Política Econômica*. São Paulo: Educ.

Kingstone, P.R. (1999) 'Constitutional Reform and Macroeconomic Stability: Implications for Democratic Consolidation in Brazil', in: P. Oxhorn and P.K. Starr (eds) *Markets and Democracy in Latin America: Conflicts or Convergence?* Boulder, CO: Lynne Rienner.

Kinzo, M.A. and Dunkerley, J. (eds) (2003) *Brazil since 1985: Economy, Polity and Society*. London: ILAS.

Kitzberger, P. (2016) 'Media Wars and the New Left: Governability and Media Democratisation in Argentina and Brazil', *Journal of Latin American Studies*, 48 (3), pp. 447–76.

Kormann, L.F. (2015) *Big Business and Brazil's Economic Reforms*. London: Routledge.

Kregel, J. (2014) 'Some Risks and Implications of Financial Globalization for National Policy Autonomy', in: *Economic Development and Financial Instability: Selected Essays*. London: Anthem Press.

Kucinski, B. (1982) *Abertura, a História de Uma Crise*. São Paulo: Brasil Debates.

Kume, H. (1988) 'A Reforma Tarifária de 1988 e a Nova Política de Importação', *Texto para Discussão* No.20, FUNCEX.

Kume, H., Piani, G. and Souza, C.F.B. (2003) 'A Política Brasileira de Importação no Período 1987–1998: Descrição e Avaliação', in: C.H. Corseuil and H. Kume (eds) *A Abertura Comercial Brasileira nos Anos 1990: Impactos Sobre Emprego e Salário*. Brasília. MTE/IPEA.

Lacerda, A.D.F. (2002) 'O PT e a Unidade Partidária como Problema', *Dados*, 45 (1), pp. 39–76.

Lafer, B.M. (1984) *Planejamento no Brasil*. São Paulo: Perspectiva.

Laplane, M.F. (2015) 'Inovação, Competitividade e Reindustrialização no Brasil Pós-Crise', in: N. Barbosa, N. Marconi, M.C. Pinheiro and L. Carvalho (eds) *Indústria e Desenvolvimento Produtivo no Brasil*. Rio de Janeiro: FGV.

Laplane, M.F. and Sarti, F. (1999) 'O Investimento Direto Estrangeiro no Brasil nos Anos 90: Determinantes e Estratégias', in: D. Chudnovsky (ed.) *Investimentos Externos no Mercosul*. Campinas: Papirus.

Lara-Resende, A. (1982) 'A Política Brasileira de Estabilização: 1963/68', *Pesquisa e Planejamento Econômico*, 12 (3), pp. 757–806.

Lassance, A. (2017) 'Para Entender a Lógica e o Timing da Lava Jato', www.cartamaior.com.br/?/Editoria/Politica/Para-entender-a-logica-e-o-timing-da-Lava-Jato/4/38135 (accessed 13 July 2017).

Lavergne, R.F. and Beserra, B. (2016) 'The Bolsa Família Program: Replacing Politics with Biopolitics', *Latin American Perspectives*, 43 (2), pp. 96–115.

Lavinas, L. (2013) '21st Century Welfare', *New Left Review*, 84, pp. 5–40.

Lavinas, L. (2017) *The Brazilian Paradox: The Takeover of Social Policy by Financialization*. London: Palgrave.

Leal, R.P.C. and Silva, A.L.C. (2009) 'O Financiamento Externo no Ciclo Recente da Economia Brasileira', *Texto para Discussão 1384*, IPEA, www.ipea.gov.br/

portal/index.php?option=com_contentandview=articleandid=9706 (accessed 4 July 2017).

Lees, F.A., Botts, J.M and Cysne, R.P. (1990) *Banking and Financial Deepening in Brazil*. London: Macmillan.

Leichsenring, A.R. (2010) 'Precariedade Laboral e o Programa Bolsa Família', in J.A. Castro and L. Modesto (eds.) *Bolsa Família 2003–2010: Avanços e Desafios*, vol.1. Brasília: IPEA.

LEMEP (2016) *Manchetômetro*, www.manchetometro.com.br (accessed 3 July 2017).

Lenin, V.I. (1899) *The Development of Capitalism in Russia*, www.marxists.org/archive/lenin/works/1899/devel/ (accessed 13 July 2017).

Lenin, V.I. (1920) *Left-Wing Communism: An Infantile Disorder*, www.marxists.org/archive/lenin/works/1920/lwc/ (accessed 7 July 2017).

Leonelli, D. and Oliveira, D. (2004) *Diretas Já: 15 Meses que Abalaram a Ditadura*. Rio de Janeiro: Record.

Lesbaupin, I. (ed.) (1999) *O Desmonte da Nação: Balanço do Governo FHC*. Petrópolis: Vozes.

Lessa, C. (1964) 'Fifteen Years of Economic Policy in Brazil', *Economic Bulletin of Latin America*, 9 (2), pp. 153–214.

Lessa, C. and Fiori, J.L. (1991) 'E Houve uma Política Econômica Nacional-Populista?', *Ensaios FEE*, 12 (1), pp. 176–97.

Leubolt, B. (2013) 'Institutions, Discourse and Welfare: Brazil as a Distributional Regime', *Global Social Policy*, 13 (1), pp. 66–83.

Levy, P.M. and Hahn, L.M.D. (1996) 'A Economia Brasileira em Transição: O Período 1993/96', in: IPEA (ed.) *A Economia Brasileira em Perspectiva*. Brasília: IPEA.

Lievesley, G. and Ludlam, S. (eds) (2009) *Reclaiming Latin America: Experiments in Radical Social Democracy*. London: Zed Books.

Lopes, F. (1986) *O Choque Heterodoxo: Combate à Inflação e Reforma Monetária*. Rio de Janeiro: Campus.

Lopes, F. (1989) *O Desafio da Hiperinflação*. Rio de Janeiro: Campus.

Lopes, N. and Maranhão, F. (2016) '7 Fatores que Fizeram a Lava Jato Ser o Que Ela É, Segundo a Força-Tarefa', https://noticias.uol.com.br/politica/listas/7-fatores-que-fizeram-a-lava-jato-ser-o-que-ela-e-segundo-a-forca-tarefa.htm (accessed 13 July 2017).

Loureiro, P. and Saad-Filho, A. (2018) 'The Limits of Pragmatism: The Rise and Fall of the Brazilian Workers' Party (2002–2016)', *Latin American Perspectives* (forthcoming).

Love, J.L. and Baer, W. (eds) (2009) *Brazil under Lula: Economy, Politics, and Society under the Worker-President*. London: Palgrave.

Lula da Silva, L.I. (2002) 'Carta ao Povo Brasileiro', www1.folha.uol.com.br/folha/brasil/ult96u33908.shtml (accessed 8 July 2017).

Lula da Silva, L.I. (2013) 'O Necessário, o Possível e o Impossível: Entrevista concedida a Emir Sader e Pablo Gentili', in: E. Sader (ed.) *10 Anos de Governos Pós-Neoliberais no Brasil: Lula e Dilma*. São Paulo: Boitempo (Kindle edition).

Macedo, R. (1983) 'Wage Indexation and Inflation: the Recent Brazilian Experience', in: R. Dornbusch and M.H. Simonsen (eds) *Inflation, Debt and Indexation*. Cambridge, Mass.: MIT Press.

Machado, G.V. (2002) *A Burguesia Brasileira e a Incorporação da Agenda Liberal nos Anos 90*. MSc dissertation, Instituto de Economia, UNICAMP.

Machado, J. (2003) 'Um Governo Contraditório', *Revista da Sociedade Brasileira de Economia Política*,12, pp. 7–27.

Machado, J. (2005) 'A Crise de 2005 e a Social-Liberalização do Partido dos Trabalhadores', *Outubro*, 13, pp. 105–14.

Machado, J.B.M. and Markwald, R.A. (1997) 'Dinâmica Recente do Processo de Integração do Mercosul', in: J.P.R. Velloso (ed.) *Brasil: Desafios de Um País em Transformação*. Rio de Janeiro: José Olympio.

Maciel, A. (2016) 'Como as Federações Empresariais se Articularam pelo Impeachment', http://apublica.org/2016/08/como-as-federacoes-empresariais-se-articularam-pelo-impeachment/ (accessed 13 July 2017).

Marcelino, P. (2017) 'Neodesenvolvimentismo e Greves no Brasil', *Tempo Social* (forthcoming).

Marconi, N. (2015) 'Estrutura Produtiva e Desenvolvimento Econômico', in: N. Barbosa, N. Marconi, M.C. Pinheiro and L. Carvalho (eds) *Indústria e Desenvolvimento Produtivo no Brasil*. Rio de Janeiro: FGV.

Markoff, J. and Baretta, S.R.D. (1990) 'Economic Crisis and Regime Change in Brazil: The 1960s and the 1980s', *Comparative Politics*, 22 (4), pp. 421–44.

Marques, R.M. (2013) 'Políticas de Transferência de Renda no Brasil e na Argentina', *Revista de Economia Política*, 33 (2), pp. 298–314.

Marques, R.M., Leite, M.G., Mendes, A. and Ferreira, M.R.J. (2009) 'Discutindo o Papel do Programa Bolsa Família na Decisão das Eleições Presidenciais Brasileiras de 2006', *Revista de Economia Política*,29 (1), pp. 114–32.

Marquetti, A., Campos, G.A. and Pires, R. (eds) (2008) *Democracia Participativa e Redistribuição*. São Paulo: Xamã.

Martins, C.E. (ed.) (1977) *Estado e Capitalismo no Brasil*. São Paulo: Hucitec.

Martins, L. (1985) *Estado Capitalista e Burocracia no Brasil Pós-64*. Rio de Janeiro: Paz e Terra.

Martone, C.L. (1970) 'Análise do Plano de Ação Econômica do Governo (PAEG – 1964–1966)', in: B.M. Lafer (ed.) *Planejamento no Brasil*. São Paulo: ed. Perspectiva.

Martuscelli, D.E. (2015) *Crises Políticas e Capitalismo Neoliberal no Brasil*. Curitiba: Editora CRV.

Martuscelli, D.E. (2016) 'As Lutas Contra a Corrupção nas Crises Políticas Brasileiras Recentes', *Crítica e Sociedade*, 6 (2), pp. 4–35.

Marx, K. (1852) *The Eighteenth Brumaire of Louis Bonaparte*, www.marxists.org/archive/marx/works/1852/18th-brumaire/ (accessed 7 July 2017).

Matais, A. and Morais, M. (2017) 'Ação no TSE era para "Encher o Saco" do PT, Disse Aécio a Joesley', http://politica.estadao.com.br/blogs/coluna-do-estadao/acao-no-tse-era-para-encher-o-saco-do-pt-disse-aecio-a-joesley/ (accessed 7 July 2017).

Mattei, L. (2012) 'Políticas Públicas de Combate à Pobreza no Brasil: O Caso do Programa Bolsa Família', *Revista da* Sociedade *Brasileira de Economia Política*, 33, pp. 147–76.

Mattei, L. (2013) 'Gênese e Agenda do Novo Desenvolvimentismo Brasileiro', *Revista de Economia Política*, 33 (1) 130, pp. 41–59.

McCombie, J.S.L. and Thirlwall, A.P. (1994) *Economic Growth and the Balance of Payments Constraint*. New York: St Martin's Press.

McKinnon, R. (1973) *Money and Capital in Economic Development*. Washington: Brookings Institution.

Medeiros, J. (2013) 'O PT e as Classes Sociais no Brasil: Reflexões após Dez Anos de "Lulismo"', https://fpabramo.org.br/wp-content/uploads/2013/05/ed01-fpa-discute.pdf (accessed 20 July 2017).

Medeiros, M., Souza, P.H.G.F. and Castro, F.A. (2015a) 'O Topo da Distribuição de Renda no Brasil: Primeiras Estimativas com Dados Tributários e Comparação com Pesquisas Domiciliares (2006–2012)', *Dados*, 58, pp. 7–36.

Medeiros, M., Souza, P.H.G.F. and Castro, F.A. (2015b) 'The Stability of Income Inequality in Brazil, 2006–2012: An Estimate Using Income Tax Data and Household Surveys', *Ciência and Saúde Coletiva*, 20, pp. 971–86.

Medialdea, B. (2013) 'Brazil: An Economy Caught in a Financial Trap (1993–2003)', *Revista de Economia Política*, 33 (3) 132, pp. 427–45.

Merton, R. (1968) *Social Theory and Social Structure*, enlarged edition. New York: Free Press.

MF [Ministério da Fazenda] (2013) http://politicaemercados.blogspot.co.uk/2013/05/orcamento-2013-mantega-anuncia.html (accessed 15 July 2017).

Michener, G. and Pereira, C. (2016) 'A Great Leap Forward for Democracy and the Rule of Law? Brazil's Mensalão Trial', *Journal of Latin American Studies*, 48, pp. 477–507.

Mir, L. (1994) *A Revolução Impossível*. São Paulo: Editora Best Seller.

Miterhof, M.T., Ferraz, J.C. and Marques, F.S. (2015) 'BNDES: Preenchendo Lacunas, Corrigindo Falhas e Induzindo Externalidades', in: N. Barbosa, N. Marconi, M.C. Pinheiro and L. Carvalho (eds) *Indústria e Desenvolvimento Produtivo no Brasil*. Rio de Janeiro: FGV.

Modenesi, A.M. and Modenesi, R.L. (2012) 'Quinze Anos de Rigidez Monetária no Brasil Pós-Plano Real: Uma Agenda de Pesquisa', *Revista de Economia Política*, 32 (3) 128, pp. 389–411.

Mollo, M.L.R. and Fonseca, P.C.D. (2013) 'Desenvolvimentismo e Novo-Desenvolvimentismo: Raízes Teóricas e Precisões Conceituais', *Revista de Economia Política*, 33 (2) 131, pp. 222–39.

Mollo, M.L.R. and Saad-Filho, A. (2006) 'Neoliberal Economic Policies in Brazil (1994–2005): Cardoso, Lula, and the Need for a Democratic Alternative', *New Political Economy*, 11 (1), pp. 99–123.

Molyneux, M. (2007) 'Two Cheers for CCTs', *IDS Bulletin*, 38 (3), pp. 69–74.

Monthly Review (2007) *Brazil under Lula: An MR Survey*, 58 (9), pp. 15–54.

Moraes, P.B. (1987) 'O Programa de Estabilização de 1964: Balizamento de Preços com Restrições ao Crédito', *Revista Brasileira de Economia*, 41 (2), pp. 137–57.

Morais, L. and Saad-Filho, A. (2003) 'Snatching Defeat from the Jaws of Victory? Lula, the Workers' Party and the Prospects for Change in Brazil', *Capital and Class*, 81, pp. 17–23.

Morais, L. and Saad-Filho, A. (2005) 'Lula and the Continuity of Neoliberalism in Brazil: Strategic Choice, Economic Imperative or Political Schizophrenia', *Historical Materialism*, 13 (1), pp. 3–32.

Morais, L. and Saad-Filho, A. (2011) 'Brazil beyond Lula: Forging Ahead or Pausing for Breath?', *Latin American Perspectives*, 38 (2), pp. 31–44.

Morais, L. and Saad-Filho, A. (2012) 'Neo-Developmentalism and the Challenges of Economic Policy-making under Dilma Rousseff', *Critical Sociology*, 38 (6), pp. 789–98.

Morais, L., Saad-Filho, A. and Coelho, W. (1999) 'Financial Liberalisation, Currency Instability and Crisis in Brazil: Another Plan Bites the Dust', *Capital and Class*, 68, pp. 9–14.

Moreira, M.M. (1991) *Industrialization, Trade and Market Failures: The Role of Government Intervention in Brazil and South Korea.* London: Macmillan.

Moreira, M.M. (2000) 'Capital Nacional na Indústria: Reestruturar para Sobreviver', in: A.C. Lacerda (ed.) *Desnacionalização: Mitos, Riscos e Desafios.* São Paulo: Editora Contexto.

Moreira, M.M. and Correa, P.G. (1998) 'A First Look at the Impacts of Trade Liberalisation on Brazilian Manufacturing Industry', *World Development* 26 (10), pp. 1859–74.

Motoyama, S. (ed.) (1994) *Tecnologia e Industrialização no Brasil.* São Paulo: Editora Unesp.

Munhoz, D. (1988) 'Reflexos Desestabilizadores dos Programas de Ajustamento Externo', in: J.P.Z. Chahad and R. Cervini (eds) *Crise e Infância no Brasil: O Impacto das Políticas de Ajustamento Econômico.* São Paulo: IPE-USP.

Nakatani, P. (1999) 'Capital Especulativo Parasitário, Capital Fictício e Crise no Brasil'. Unpublished manuscript.

Nassif, A. (2013) 'Estagnação: Reflexões e Sugestões', www.portaldoeconomista. org.br/comunicacao/noticias_detalhes.php?notId=1051 (accessed 4 July 2017).

Nassif, A., Feijó, C.A. and Araújo, E.C. (2015a) 'Structural Change and Economic Development: Is Brazil Catching Up or Falling Behind?', *Cambridge Journal of Economics*, 39 (5), pp. 1307–32.

Nassif, A., Feijó, C.A. and Araújo, E.C. (2015b) 'Overvaluation Trend of the Brazilian Currency in the 2000s: Empirical Estimation', *Revista de Economia Política*, 35 (1), 138, pp. 3–27.

Nassif, L. (2008) 'Há Evidências de Desindustrialização no Brasil?', *Revista de Economia Política* 28 (1), pp. 72–96.

Nassif, M.I. (2015) 'O Problema Não Foi o Que Aconteceu no Dia 15 de março', www.cartamaior.com.br/?/Especial/A-direita-nas-ruas/O-problema-nao-foi-o-que-aconteceu-no-dia-15-de-marco/196/33075 (accessed 8 July 2017).

Nembhard, J.G. (1996) *Capital Control, Financial Regulation, and Industrial Policy in South Korea and Brazil.* Westport, Conn.: Praeger.

Nepomuceno, E. (2015) 'Afinal, do que se trata? Simples: destituir Dilma e liquidar o PT', http://cartamaior.com.br/?/Especial/A-direita-nas-ruas/Afinal-do-que-se-trata-Simples-destituir-Dilma-e-liquidar-o-PT-/196/33055 (accessed 3 July 2017).

Neri, M. and Considera, C. (1996). 'Crescimento, Desigualdade e Pobreza: O Impacto da Estabilização', in: IPEA (ed.) *A Economia Brasileira em Perspectiva.* Brasília: IPEA.

Neumann, D. (2016) 'Empresários Explicam Por Que Defendem Saída de Dilma', www.valor.com.br/cultura/4524317/empresarios-explicam-por-que-defendem-saida-de-dilma (accessed 8 July 2017).

Nobre, M. (2013) *Imobilismo em Movimento: Da Abertura Democrática ao Governo Dilma.* São Paulo: Companhia das Letras.

Nobre, M. (2017) '1988+30', *Novos Estudos*, 35 (2), pp. 135–49.

Nobre, M. (2017) 'Como Governistas e Opositores Trabalham o Pós-Temer', www.nexojornal.com.br/entrevista/2017/05/20/Como-governistas-e-opositores-trabalham-o-p%C3%B3s-Temer-segundo-este-fil%C3%B3sofo-da-Unicamp (accessed 2 July 2017).

Nobre, M. and Rodriguez, J.R. (2011) 'Judicialização da Política: Déficits Explicativos e Bloqueios Normativistas', *Novos Estudos*, 91, pp. 5–20.

Nogueira Batista Jr, P. (1996) 'Plano Real: Estabilização Monetária e Desequilíbrio Externo', *Cadernos Temáticos* 2, Sindicato dos Engenheiros do Rio de Janeiro.

Nozaki, W. (2015) 'Qual é a Crise Política Brasileira Hoje?, http://plataformapolitica social.com.br/qual-e-a-crise-politica-brasileira-hoje/ (accessed 7 July 2017).

O'Donnell, G. (1989) 'Situaciones: Micro-Escenas de la Privatizacion de lo Publico en São Paulo', *Kellogg Institute Working Paper No. 121*, https://kellogg.nd.edu/publications/workingpapers/WPS/121.pdf (accessed 4 July 2017).

O'Donnell, G. (1992) 'Transitions, Continuities, and Paradoxes', in: S. Mainwaring, J.S. Valenzuela and G. O'Donnell (eds) *Issues in Democratic Consolidation*. Notre Dame, IN: University of Notre Dame Press.

O'Donnell, G.A. (1982) *1966–1973, El Estado Burocrático Autoritário: Triunfos, Derrotas y Crisis*. Buenos Aires: Belgrano.

Oliveira, F. (1977) *A Economia da Dependência Imperfeita*. Rio de Janeiro: Graal.

Oliveira, F. (1978) *Um Estudo da Reforma Tributária de 1966*. MSc dissertation, IFCH UNICAMP.

Orair, R.O. (2015) 'Notas sobre a Trajetória do Investimento Público no Brasil', in: G.C. Squeff (ed.) *Dinâmica Macrossetorial Brasileira*. Brasília: IPEA.

Oreiro, J.L. (2015) 'Muito Além do Tripé', in: N. Barbosa, N. Marconi, M.C. Pinheiro and L. Carvalho (eds) *Indústria e Desenvolvimento Produtivo no Brasil*. Rio de Janeiro: FGV.

Oreiro, J.L. and Feijó, C.A. (2010) 'Desindustrialização: Conceituação, Causas, Efeitos e o Caso Brasileiro', *Revista de Economia Política* 30 (2), pp. 219–32.

Paes De Barros, R., Camargo, J.M. and Mendonça, R. (1998) 'A Estrutura do Desemprego no Brasil', in: IPEA (ed.) *A Economia Brasileira em Perspectiva*. Brasília: IPEA.

Paes de Barros, R., Grosner, D. and Mascarenhas, A. (2012) *Vozes da Classe Média: Desigualdade, Heterogeneidade e Diversidade*. Brasília: Presidência da República.

Palma, G. (1998) 'Three and a Half Cycles of 'Mania, Panic and [Asymmetric] Crash: East Asia and Latin America Compared', *Cambridge Journal of Economics*, 22: 789–808.

Palma, G. (2015) 'Why Corporations in Developing Countries are Likely to be even More Susceptible to the Vicissitudes of International Finance than their Counterparts in the Developed World', *Cambridge Working Paper in Economics* No.1539, available at www.econ.cam.ac.uk/research/repec/cam/pdf/cwpe1539.pdf (accessed 7 July 2017).

Palmer, B. (2014) 'Reconsiderations of Class: Precariousness as Proletarianization', in: L. Panitch, G. Albo and V. Chibber (eds) *Socialist Register*. London: Merlin Press.

Panitch, L. and Gindin, S. (2012) *The Making of Global Capitalism: The Political Economy of American Empire*. London: Verso.

Panizza, F. (2004) 'Brazil Needs to Change: Change as Iteration and the Iteration of Change in Brazil's 2002 Presidential Election', *Bulletin of Latin American Research*, 23 (4), pp. 465–82.

Parkin, V. (1991) *Chronic Inflation in an Industrialising Economy: the Brazilian Experience*. Cambridge: Cambridge University Press.

Paula, J.A. (ed.) (2005) *Adeus ao Desenvolvimento: A Opção do Governo Lula*. Belo Horizonte: Autentica Editora.

Paula, L.F. (1996) 'Liquidez e Zeragem Automática: Crítica da Crítica', *Estudos Econômicos*, 26 (3), pp. 411–39.

Paula, L.F. (2011) *Financial Liberalization and Economic Performance: Brazil at the Crossroads*. London: Routledge.

Paula, L.F. (2013) 'Financiamento, Crescimento Econômico e Funcionalidade do Sistema Financeiro: Uma Abordagem Pós-Keynesiana', *Estudos Econômicos*, 43 (2), pp. 363–96.

Paula, L.F. and Oreiro, J.L. (2013) 'Estrutura do Setor Bancário e o Ciclo Recente de Expansão do Crédito: O Papel dos Bancos Públicos Federais', *Nova Economia*, 23 (3), pp. 473–520.

Paula, L.F. and Pires, M. (2017) 'Crise e Perspectivas para a Economia Brasileira', *Estudos Avançados*, 31 (89), pp. 125–44.

Paulani, L.M. (1997) 'Teoria da Inflação Inercial: Um Episódio Singular na História da Ciência Econômica Brasileira', in: M.R. Loureiro (ed.) *50 Anos de Ciência Econômica no Brasil*. Petrópolis: Vozes.

Paulani, L.M. (2003) 'Brasil *Delivery*: A Política Econômica do Governo Lula', *Revista de Economia Política*, 23 (4), 92, pp. 58–73.

Paulani, L.M. (2017) 'A Experiência Brasileira entre 2003 and 2014: Neodesenvolvimentismo?', *Cadernos do Desenvolvimento*, 12 (20), pp. 135–55.

Pereira, A.W. (2016a) 'The US Role in the 1964 Coup in Brazil: A Reassessment', *Bulletin of Latin American Research*, http://onlinelibrary.wiley.com/doi/10.1111/blar.12518/full (accessed 17 July 2017).

Pereira, A.W. (2016b) 'Is the Brazilian State "Patrimonial" ?', *Latin American Perspectives*, 43 (2), pp. 135–52.

Pereira, A.W. and Mattei, L. (eds) (2016) *The Brazilian Economy Today*. London: Palgrave.

Pinheiro, A.C. and Fukasaku, K. (eds) (2000) *A Privatização no Brasil: O Caso dos Serviços de Utilidade Publica*. Rio de Janeiro: BNDES.

Pinto, E.C. *et al.* (2017) 'A Guerra de Todos contra Todos: A Crise Brasileira', *Texto para Discussão* No.6–2017, I.E.-UFRJ, www.ie.ufrj.br/index.php/listar-td/textos-para-discussao-2017/a-guerra-de-todos-contra-todos-a-crise-brasileira (accessed 8 July 2017).

Pinto, E.C., Filgueiras, L. and Gonçalves, R. (2015) 'Governo Dilma, PT, Esquerda e Impeachment: Três Interpretações da Conjuntura Econômica e Política', *Texto para Discussão* No.15–2015, www.ie.ufrj.br/images/pesquisa/publicacoes/discussao/2015/TD_IE_015_2015_PINTO_FILGUEIRAS_GONALVES.pdf (accessed 8 July 2017).

Pizzolatto, R. (2016) 'Relatório P.A. Corte Especial No 0003021-32.2016.4.04.8000/RS', https://s.conjur.com.br/dl/lava-jato-nao-seguir-regras-casos.pdf (accessed 16 July 2017).

Pochmann, M. (1999) *O Trabalho sob Fogo Cruzado: Exclusão, Desemprego e Precarização no Final do Século*. São Paulo: Contexto.

Pochmann, M. (2003) 'Sobre a Nova Condição de Agregado Social no Brasil', *Revista Paranaense de Desenvolvimento*, 105, pp. 5–23.

Pochmann, M. (2006) 'Mercado Geral de Trabalho: O Que Há de Novo no Brasil?', *Parcerias Estratégicas*, 22, pp. 121–44.

Pochmann, M. (2010) 'Estrutura Social no Brasil: Mudanças Recentes', *Serviço Social and Sociedade*, 104, pp. 637–49.

Pochmann, M. (2011) 'Políticas Sociais e Padrão de Mudanças no Brasil durante o Governo Lula', *SER Social*, 13 (28), pp. 12–40.

Pochmann, M. (2012) *Nova Classe Média? O Trabalho na Base da Pirâmide Social Brasileira*. São Paulo: Boitempo, 2012.

Pochmann, M. (2013) 'Políticas Públicas e Situação Social na Primeira Década do Século XXI', in: E. Sader (ed.) *10 Anos de Governos Pós-Neoliberais no Brasil: Lula e Dilma*. São Paulo: Boitempo (Kindle edition).

Pochmann, M. (2016) *Brasil sem Industrialização: A Herança Renunciada*. Ponta Grossa: Editora UEPG.

Pochmann, M. (2017) 'Reforma para um Novo Ciclo Político', www.brasil247. com/pt/colunistas/marciopochmann/273952/Reforma-para-um-novo-ciclo-pol%C3%ADtico.htm (accessed 8 July 2017).

Pomar, V. (2013) *Debatendo Classes e Luta de Classes no Brasil*, www.scribd.com/ document/116459858/Caderno-SRI-Debatendo-Classes-e-Luta-de-Classes-No-Brasil (accessed 3 July 2017).

Pomar, V. (2014) *A Estrela na Janela: Ensaios Sobre o PT e a Situação Internacional*. São Paulo: Fundação Perseu Abramo.

Portugal, M.S. (1994) 'As Políticas Brasileiras de Comércio Exterior – 1947–88', *Ensaios FEE*, 15 (1), pp. 234–52.

Prates, D.M. and Freitas, M.C.P. (2001) 'A Abertura Financeira no Governo FHC: Impactos e Conseqüências', *Economia e Sociedade*, 17, pp. 81–111.

Proner, C. *et al.* (eds) (2016) *A Resistência ao Golpe de 2016*. Bauru: Canal 6 Editora.

PT (1998) *Partido dos Trabalhadores: Resoluções de Encontros e Congressos*. São Paulo: Fundação Perseu Abramo.

Purcell, S.K. and Roett, R. (eds) (1997) *Brazil under Cardoso*. Boulder, CO: Lynne Rienner.

Ramalho, V. (1995) 'Zeragem Automatica no Mercado Aberto e Controle Monetário', *Estudos Econômicos*, 25 (1), pp. 25–52.

Ramos, L. and Almeida Reis, J.G. (1998) 'Emprego no Brasil nos Anos 90', in: IPEA (ed.) *A Economia Brasileira em Perspectiva*. Brasília: IPEA.

Revista Consultor Jurídico (2016) 'Sem Freios: "Lava jato" não precisa seguir regras de casos comuns, decide TRF-4', www.conjur.com.br/2016-set-23/lava-jato-nao-seguir-regras-casos-comuns-trf (accessed 16 July 2017).

Ribeiro (2014) 'An Amphibian Party? Organisational Change and Adaptation in the Brazilian Workers' Party, 1980–2012', *Journal of Latin American Studies*, 46, pp. 87–119.

Ribeiro Jr, A. (2011) *A Privataria Tucana*. São Paulo: Geração Editorial.

Ribeiro, C.G. and Novaes, H.T. (2014) 'Da "Lei do Petróleo" ao Leilão de Libra: Petrobras de FHC a Dilma', *Revista da Sociedade Brasileira de Economia Política*, 39, pp. 34–58.

Ricci, R. (2012) 'Classe Média Tradicional se Incomoda com Classe C', http://rudaricci.blogspot.co.uk/2012/09/classe-media-tradicional-se-incomoda.html (accessed 3 July 2017).

Ridenti, M. (2016) 'The Debate over Military (or Civilian-Military?) Dictatorship in Brazil in Historiographical Context', *Bulletin of Latin American Research*, http://onlinelibrary.wiley.com/wol1/doi/10.1111/blar.12519/full (accessed 17 July 2017).

Robaina, R. (2003) *A Socialdemocracia, o Estado e o PT: As Perspectivas do Governo Lula*. Porto Alegre: MES.

Rocha, B.L. (2017) 'Os Ataques Sofridos em Escala Internacional pelas Empresas Líderes da Engenharia Brasileira: Uma Análise por Esquerda', www.ihu.unisinos.br/563619-os-ataques-sofridos-em-escala-internacional-pelas-empresas-lideres-da-engenharia-brasileira-uma-analise-por-esquerda (accessed 8 July 2017).

Rodrik, D. (1998) 'Globalisation, Social Conflict and Economic Growth', *The World Economy*, 21 (1), pp. 143–58.

Rollemberg, D. (2003) 'Esquerdas Revolucionárias e Luta Armada', in: J. Ferreira and L.A.N. Delgado (eds) *O Brasil Republicano: O Tempo da Ditadura*. Rio de Janeiro: Civilização Brasileira.

Rolnik, R. (2015) *Guerra dos Lugares - A Colonização da Terra e da Moradia na Era das Finanças*. São Paulo: Boitempo.

Rose, R.S. (2006) *The Unpast: Elite Violence and Social Control in Brazil, 1954–2000*. Athens, OH: Ohio University Press.

Rossi, P. (2016) *Taxa de Câmbio e Política Cambial no Brasil*. Rio de Janeiro: FGV Editora.

Rossi, P. and Mello, G. (2016) 'Componentes Macroeconômicos e Estruturais da Crise Brasileira: o Subdesenvolvimento Revisitado', *Brazilian Keynesian Review*, 2 (2), pp. 252–63.

Rossi, P. and Mello, G. (2017a) 'Choque Recessivo e a Maior Crise da História: A Economia Brasileira em Marcha à Ré', *Nota do Cecon, I.E.-UNICAMP*, No.1, http://brasildebate.com.br/wp-content/uploads/NotaCecon1_Choque-recessivo-2.pdf (accessed 8 July 2017).

Rossi, P. and Mello, G.S. (2017b) 'A Restauração Neoliberal sob o (Des)Governo Temer', http://brasildebate.com.br/a-restauracao-neoliberal-sob-o-desgoverno-temer/ (accessed 13 July 2017).

Rousseff, D. (2016) 'Discurso de Defesa no Senado', www12.senado.leg.br/noticias/materias/2016/08/29/veja-a-integra-do-discurso-de-defesa-de-dilma-no-senado (accessed 8 July 2017).

Rousseff, D. (2017) 'Entrevista exclusiva: Dilma Rousseff sem censura, ou quase' www.pagina13.org.br/revista-esquerda-petista/entrevista-exclusiva-dilma-rousseff-sem-censura-ou-quase/#.WWB6LYSrphF (accessed 8 July 2017).

Rovai, R. (2013) 'Jantar com empresários: Campos percebeu que o ponto fraco do governo Dilma é a boca', www.revistaforum.com.br/blogdorovai/2013/03/16/jantar-com-empresarios-campos-percebeu-que-o-ponto-fraco-do-governo-dilma-e-a-boca/ (accessed 3 July 2017).

Rugitsky, F. (2016) 'Milagre, Miragem, Antimilagre: A Economia Política dos Governos Lula e as Raízes da Crise Atual', *Fevereiro* 9, www.revistafevereiro.com/pag.php?r=09andt=03 (accessed 3 July 2017).

Saad Filho, A. (2000) '"Vertical" versus "Horizontal" Economics: Systems of Provision, Consumption Norms and Labour Market Structures', *Capital and Class*, 72, pp. 209–14.

Saad-Filho, A. (2003a) 'New Dawn or False Start in Brazil? The Political Economy of Lula's Election', *Historical Materialism*, 11 (1), pp. 3–21.

Saad-Filho, A. (2003b) 'Introduction', in: *Anti-Capitalism: A Marxist Introduction*. London: Pluto Press.

Saad-Filho, A. (2005) 'The Political Economy of Neoliberalism in Latin America', in: A. Saad-Filho and D. Johnston (eds) *Neoliberalism: A Critical Reader*. London: Pluto Press.

Saad-Filho, A. (2007a) 'There is Life beyond the Washington Consensus: An Introduction to Pro-Poor Macroeconomic Policies', *Review of Political Economy*, 19 (4), pp. 513–37.

Saad-Filho, A. (2007b) 'Monetary Policy in the Neoliberal Transition: A Political Economy Review of Keynesianism, Monetarism and Inflation Targeting', in: R. Albritton, B. Jessop and R. Westra (eds) *Political Economy and Global Capitalism: The 21st Century, Present and Future*. London: Anthem Press.

Saad-Filho, A. (2011) 'Crisis *in* Neoliberalism or Crisis *of* Neoliberalism?', in: L. Panitch, G. Albo and V. Chibber (eds) *Socialist Register*. London: Merlin Press.

Saad-Filho, A. (2013) 'Mass Protests under Left Neoliberalism: Brazil, June-July 2013', *Critical Sociology*, 39 (5), pp. 657–69.

Saad-Filho, A. (2014a) 'Brazil: Development Strategies and Social Change From Import-Substitution to the "Events of June"', *Studies in Political Economy*, 94 (1), pp. 3–29.

Saad-Filho, A. (2014b) 'The "Rise of the South": Global Convergence at Last?', *New Political Economy*, 19 (4), pp. 578–600.

Saad-Filho, A. (2015a) 'Social Policy for Neoliberalism: The Bolsa Família Programme in Brazil', *Development and Change*, 46 (6), pp. 1227–52.

Saad-Filho, A. (2015b) 'Brazilian Democracy in Distress: Unpacking Dilma Rousseff's Impeachment', www.socialistproject.ca/bullet/1201.php (accessed 8 July 2017).

Saad-Filho, A. (2016a) 'Social Policy beyond Neoliberalism: From Conditional Cash Transfers to Pro-Poor Growth', *Journal of Poverty Alleviation and International Development*, 7 (1), pp. 67–94.

Saad-Filho, A. (2016b) 'A Coup in Brazil?', www.jacobinmag.com/2016/03/dilma-rousseff-pt-coup-golpe-petrobras-lavajato/ (accessed 8 July 2017).

Saad-Filho, A. (2016c) 'Dilma Rousseff's Impeachment Would Not Clean Up Corruption in Brazil', http://fortune.com/2016/03/14/brazil-dilma-rouseffs-impeachment/?iid=sr-link3 (accessed 8 July 2017).

Saad-Filho, A. (2016d) 'Democracy in the Crucible: Impeachment or Coup d'État in Brazil?', www.e-ir.info/2016/01/14/democracy-in-the-crucible-impeachment-or-coup-detat-in-brazil/ (accessed 8 July 2017).

Saad-Filho, A. (2017) 'Fora Temer – Eleições Diretas Já! Brazil's Political Rupture and the Left's Opportunity', www.opendemocracy.net/alfredo-saad-filho/fora-temer-elei-es-diretas-j-brazils-political-rupture-and-lefts-opportunity (accessed 8 July 2017).

Saad-Filho, A. (2017) 'Neoliberalism', in: D. M. Brennan, D. Kristjanson-Gural, C. Mulder, E. Olsen (eds) *The Routledge Handbook of Marxian Economics*. London: Routledge.

Saad-Filho, A. and Boito, A. (2016) 'Brazil: The Failure of the PT and the Rise of the New Right', in: L. Panitch and G. Albo (eds) *Socialist Register*. London: Merlin Press.

Saad-Filho, A. and Boito, A. (2017) 'Brazil's Crisis of Hegemony', www.jacobinmag.com/2017/05/temer-corruption-impeachment-pt-jbs-lava-jato (accessed 8 July 2017).

Saad-Filho, A. and Johnston, D. (eds) (2005) *Neoliberalism: A Critical Reader*. London: Pluto Press.

Saad-Filho, A. and Maldonado-Filho, E. (1998) 'Economia Brasileira: da Heterodoxia ao Neomonetarismo', *Indicadores Econômicos*, 26 (3), pp. 87–103.

Saad-Filho, A. and Mollo, M.L.R. (2002) 'Inflation and Stabilization in Brazil: A Political Economy Analysis', *Review of Radical Political Economics*, 34 (2), pp. 109–35.

Saad-Filho, A. and Morais, L. (2000) 'The Costs of Neomonetarism: The Brazilian Economy in the 1990s', *International Papers in Political Economy*, 7 (3), pp. 1–39.

Saad-Filho, A. and Morais, L. (2002) 'Neomonetarist Dreams and Realities: A Review of the Brazilian Experience', in: P. Davidson (ed.) *A Post Keynesian Perspective on 21st Century Economic Problems*. Cheltenham: Edward Elgar.

Saad-Filho, A. and Morais, L. (2004) 'The Costs of Neomonetarism: The Brazilian Economy in the 1990s', in: P. Arestis and M. Sawyer (eds) *Neo-Liberal Economic Policy: Critical Essays*. Cheltenham: Edward Elgar.

Saad-Filho, A. and Morais, L. (2014) 'Mass Protests: Brazilian Spring or Brazilian Malaise', in: L. Panitch, G. Albo and V. Chibber (eds) *Socialist Register*. London: Merlin Press.

Saad-Filho, A., Iannini, F. and Molinari, E. (2007) 'Neoliberalism and Democracy in Argentina and Brazil', in: P. Arestis and M. Sawyer (eds) *Political Economy of Latin America: Recent Issues and Performance*. London, Palgrave.

Sabóia, J. (1991) 'Política Salarial e Distribuição de Renda: 25 Anos de Desencontros', in: J.M. Camargo (ed.) *Distribuição de Renda no Brasil*. Rio de Janeiro: Paz e Terra.

Sachs, J. and Zini, A.A. (1996) 'Brazilian Inflation and the *Plano Real*', *The World Economy*, 19 (1), pp. 13–37.

Sader, E. (2003) *A Vingança da História*. São Paulo: Boitempo.

Sader, E. (2004) 'Política Nacional', in: L.T. Soares *et al.* (eds) *Governo Lula: Decifrando o Enigma*. São Paulo: Viramundo.

Sader, E. (2005) 'Taking Lula's Measure', *New Left Review*, 33, pp. 59–80.

Sader, E. (2013) 'A Construção da Hegemonia Pós-Neoliberal', in: E. Sader (ed.) *10 Anos de Governos Pós-Neoliberais no Brasil: Lula e Dilma*. São Paulo: Boitempo (Kindle edition).

Sader, E. and Silverstein, K. (1991) *Without Fear of Being Happy: Lula, the Workers' Party and Brazil*. London: Verso.

Saes, D. (2001) *República do Capital: Capitalismo e Processo Político no Brasil*. São Paulo: Boitempo.

Saes, D. (2016) 'Aliança entre PMDB e PSDB Não Tem Futuro', http://brasileiros. com.br/2016/07/alianca-pmdb-psdb-nao-tem-futuro-diz-cientista-politico/ (accessed 2 July 2017).

Safatle, V. (2012) 'O Filho Bastardo', www1.folha.uol.com.br/fsp/opiniao/64413-0-filho-bastardo.shtml (accessed 3 July 2017).

Sallum, Jr, B. and Kugelmas, E. (2004) 'Sobre o Modo Lula de Governar', in: B. Sallum Jr (ed.) Brasil e Argentina Hoje: Política e Economia. Bauru-SP: USC.

Salm, C., Saboia, J. and Carvalho, P.G.M. (1997) 'Produtividade na Indústria Brasileira: Uma Contribuição ao Debate', in: L. Carleial and R. Valle (eds) Reestruturação Produtiva e Mercado de Trabalho no Brasil. São Paulo: Hucitec-ABET.

Sampaio, A. (2014) 'Brazil's Angry Middle Class', Survival, 56 (4), pp. 107–18.

Sampaio, P.A. (2009) 'Para Além da Ambigüidade: Uma Reflexão Histórica sobre a CF/88', in: J.C. Cardoso Jr (ed.) A Constituição Brasileira de 1988 Revisitada. Brasília: IPEA.

Sampaio Jr, P.A. (2017) Crônica de Uma Crise Anunciada: Crítica à Economia Política de Lula e Dilma. São Paulo: SG-Amarante.

Sánchez-Ancochea, D. and Mattei, L. (2011) 'Bolsa Família, Poverty and Inequality: Political and Economic Effects in the Short and Long-Run', Global Social Policy, 11 (2–3), pp. 299–318.

Santana, M.A. (2003) 'Trabalhadores em Movimento: O Sindicalismo Brasileiro nos Anos 1980–1990', in: J. Ferreira and L.A.N. Delgado (eds) O Brasil Republicano: O Tempo da Ditadura. Rio de Janeiro: Civilização Brasileira.

Santos, C.H. and Gentil, D.L. (2009) 'A CF/88 e as Finanças Públicas Brasileiras', in: J.C. Cardoso Jr (ed.) A Constituição Brasileira de 1988 Revisitada. Brasília: IPEA.

Santos, C.H., Amitrano, C.R., Pires, M.C.C., Carvalho, S.C., Ferreira, E., Esteves, F.H.A., Zagbai, K., Yannick, J. and Lima, L.S. (2016a) 'A Natureza da Inflação de Serviços no Brasil: 1999–2014', Textos para discussão do IPEA No.2169, repositorio.ipea.gov.br/handle/11058/3817 (accessed 7 July 2017).

Santos, C.H., Modenesi, A.M., Squeff, G., Vasconcelos, L., Mora, M., Fernandes, T., Moraes, T., Summa, R. and Braga, J. (2016b) 'Revisitando a Dinâmica Trimestral do Investimento no Brasil: 1996–2012', Revista de Economia Política, 36 (1), pp. 190–213.

Santos, C.H., Orair, R.O., Gobetti, S.W., Ferreira, A.S., Rocha, W.S., Silva, H.L. and Britto, J.M. (2012) 'Estimativas Mensais da Formação Bruta de Capital Fixo Pública no Brasil (2002–2010)', Economia Aplicada, 16 (3), pp. 445–73.

Santos, D.R.P. (2017) 'O Que se Esconde Por Trás do Congelamento dos Gastos?', http://brasildebate.com.br/o-que-se-esconde-por-tras-do-congelamento-dos-gastos/ (accessed 8 July 2017).

Santos, J. (2001) 'Mudanças na Estrutura de Posições e Segmentos de Classe no Brasil', Dados, 44 (1), available at: www.scielo.br/scielo.php?script=sci_arttextandpid=S0011-52582001000100005 (accessed 3 July 2017).

Sarti, F. (2015) 'Padrão de Crescimento e Desenvolvimento Industrial', in: N. Barbosa, N. Marconi, M.C. Pinheiro and L. Carvalho (eds) Indústria e Desenvolvimento Produtivo no Brasil. Rio de Janeiro: FGV.

Sawaya, R. (2014) 'Poder Econômico , Desenvolvimento e Neoliberalismo no Brasil', Revista da Sociedade Brasileira de Economia Política, 39, pp. 124–49.

Schapiro, M.G. (2017) 'O Estado Pastor e os Incentivos Tributários no Setor Automotivo', *Revista de Economia Política*, 37 (2) 147, pp. 437–55.

Schneider, A.M. (2016) 'Legislative Efforts against Impunity in the 1979 Amnesty Debate in Brazil', *Bulletin of Latin American Research*, http://onlinelibrary.wiley. com/wol1/doi/10.1111/blar.12521/full (accessed 18 July 2017).

Schneider, B.R. (2015) 'The Developmental State in Brazil: Comparative and Historical Perspectives', *Revista de Economia Política*, 35 (1) 138, pp. 114–32.

Schymura, L.G. (2015) 'Apresentação', in: N. Barbosa, N. Marconi, M.C. Pinheiro and L. Carvalho (eds) *Indústria e Desenvolvimento Produtivo no Brasil*. Rio de Janeiro: FGV.

Seabra, C. (2009) 'Presa Durante a Ditadura, Dilma Pediu Indenização a 3 Estados', www1.folha.uol.com.br/folha/brasil/ult96u578599.shtml (accessed 14 July 2017).

Secco, L. (2011) *História do PT*, 4th ed. Cotia: Ateliê Editorial.

Seekings, J. (2012) 'Pathways to Redistribution: The Emerging Politics of Social Assistance across the Global South', *Journal für Entwicklungspolitik*, 28 (1), pp. 14–34.

SEP-PPS (2016) *Austeridade e Retrocesso - Finanças Públicas e Política Fiscal no Brasil*, by GT de Macro da Sociedade Brasileira de Economia Política (SEP) and Plataforma Política Social. São Paulo: Fórum 21 and Friedrich Ebert Stiftung.

Serrano, F. and Summa, R. (2015) 'Aggregate Demand and the Slowdown of Brazilian Economic Growth from 2011–2014', *CEPR Papers*, http://cepr.net/ documents/Brazil-2015-08.pdf (accessed 7 July 2017).

Shaw, E.S. (1973) *Financial Deepening in Economic Development*. Oxford: Oxford University Press.

Sicsú J., Paula, L.F. and Michel, R. (eds) *Novo-Desenvolvimentismo: um Projeto Nacional de Crescimento com Eqüidade Social*. Rio de Janeiro: Fundação Konrad Adenauer.

Sicsú, J. (1996) 'A URV e Sua Função de Alinhar Preços Relativos', *Revista de Economia Política*, 16 (2) 62, pp. 71–85.

Sicsú, J. (2006) 'Rumos da Liberalização Financeira Brasileira', *Revista de Economia Política*, 26 (3), pp. 507–15.

Silva, A.C., Carvalho, L.O. and Medeiros, O.L. (2009) *Dívida Pública: A Experiência Brasileira*. Brasília: Secretaria do Tesouro Nacional.

Silva, A.M. (1979) 'Evolução Recente da Economia Brasileira', *Estudos Econômicos*, 9 (3), pp. 7–59.

Silva, F.C.T. (2003) 'Crise da Ditadura Militar e o Processo de Abertura Política no Brasil, 1974–1985', in: J. Ferreira and L.A.N. Delgado (eds) *O Brasil Republicano: O Tempo da Ditadura*. Rio de Janeiro: Civilização Brasileira.

Silva, H.C.M. (2003) 'Deterioração dos Termos de Intercâmbio, Substituição de Importações, Industrialização e Substituição de Exportações: A Política de Comércio Exterior Brasileira de 1945 ad 1979', *Revista Brasileira de Política Internacional*, 46 (1), pp. 39–65.

Silva, J.A. (2016) 'O Crescimento e a Desaceleração da Economia Brasileira (2003–2014) na Perspectiva dos Regimes de Demanda Neokaleckianos', *Revista da Sociedade Brasileira de Economia Política*, 44, pp. 113–38.

Silva, M.L.F. and Andrade, J.P. (1996) 'Alternative Theoretical Interpretations of the Brazilian Inflationary Process', *Annals of ANPEC*.

Simões, J. (2013) 'Mais Médicos Abre Debate Sobre Racismo e Xenofobia', https://oestrangeiro.org/2013/09/16/mais-medicos-abre-debate-sobre-racismo-e-xenofobia/ (accessed 16 July 2017).

Simonsen, M.H. (1994) 'Avaliação do Plano Real', in: J.P. dos Reis Velloso (ed.) *Estabilidade e Crescimento: Os Desafios do Real*. Rio de Janeiro: José Olympio Editora.

Simonsen, M.H. and Barbosa, F. (eds) (1989). *Plano Cruzado: Inércia x Inépcia*. Rio de Janeiro: Globo.

Singer, A. (2009) 'Raízes Sociais e Ideológicas do Lulismo', *Novos Estudos*, 85, pp. 83–102.

Singer, A. (2010) 'A Segunda Alma do Partido dos Trabalhadores', *Novos Estudos*, 88, pp. 89–111.

Singer, A. (2012) *Os Sentidos do Lulismo*. São Paulo: Companhia das Letras.

Singer, A. (2014) 'Rebellion in Brazil: Social and Political Complexion of the June Events', *New Left Review*, 85, pp. 18–37.

Singer, A. (2015a) 'Cutucando Onças Com Varas Curtas: O Ensaio Desenvolvimentista no Primeiro Mandato de Dilma Rousseff (2011–2014)', *Novos Estudos*, 102, pp. 43–71.

Singer, A. (2015b) 'PT Precisa Mudar Rápido', www1.folha.uol.com.br/ilustrissima/2015/03/1605819-pt-precisa-mudar-rapido-afirma-cientista-politico-andre-singer.shtml (accessed 3 July 2017).

Singer, P. (1978). *A Crise do 'Milagre'*. Rio de Janeiro: Paz e Terra.

Singer, P. (1981) *Dominação e Desigualdade: Estrutura de Classes e Repartição da Renda no Brasil*. Rio de Janeiro: Paz e Terra.

Skidmore, T. (1973) 'Politics and Economic Policy Making in Authoritarian Brazil, 1937–71', in A. Stepan (ed.) *Authoritarian Brazil: Origins, Policies and Future*. New Haven, CT: Yale University Press.

Skidmore, T.E. (1988) *The Politics of Military Rule in Brazil, 1964–1985*. Oxford: Oxford University Press.

Snider, T. (2017) 'What's Happening in Brazil? Exactly What the Coup Leaders Said Would Happen', www.truth-out.org/news/item/39711-what-s-happening-in-brazil-exactly-what-the-coup-leaders-said-would-happen (accessed 13 July 2017).

Soares, P. (2013) 'Inflação Dispara em Janeiro e Acende Alerta no Banco Central', www1.folha.uol.com.br/mercado/2013/02/1227959-inflacao-dispara-em-janeiro-e-acende-alerta-no-banco-central.shtml (accessed 20 July 2017).

Soares, S., Souza, P., Osório, R. and Silveira, F.G. (2010) 'Os Impactos do Benefício do Programa Bolsa Família sobre a Desigualdade e a Pobreza, in: J.A. Castro and L. Modesto (eds) *Bolsa Família 2003-2010: Avanços e Desafios*, vol.1. Brasília: IPEA.

Solnik, A. (1987) *Os Pais do Cruzado Contam Por Que Não Deu Certo*. Porto Alegre: LandPM Editora.

Souza, F.E.P. (2015) 'Por Que a Indústria Parou?', in: N. Barbosa, N. Marconi, M.C. Pinheiro and L. Carvalho (eds) *Indústria e Desenvolvimento Produtivo no Brasil*. Rio de Janeiro: FGV.

Squeff, G.C. (2015) 'Rigidez Produtiva e Importações no Brasil: 1995–2009', in: *Dinâmica Macrossetorial Brasileira*. Brasília: IPEA.

Standing, G. (2011) *The Precariat: The New Dangerous Class*. London: Bloomsbury Publishing.

Ste. Croix, G. de (1984) 'Class in Marx's Conception of History', *New Left Review*,146, pp. 94–111.

Stepan, A. (ed.) (1989) *Democratising Brazil*. New York: Oxford University Press.

Studart, R. (1995) *Investment Finance in Economic Development*. London: Routledge.

Studart, R. and Hermann, J. (2001) 'Estrutura e Operação dos Sistemas Financeiros no MERCOSUL: Perspectivas a Partir das Reformas Institucionais dos Anos 1990', *Texto para Discussão No.799, Escritório da Cepal no Brasil*.

Summa, R. and Serrano, R. (2015) 'Distribution and Cost-Push Inflation in Brazil under Inflation Targeting, 1999–2014', *Centro Sraffa Working Paper* No.14, www.centrosraffa.org/cswp_details.aspx?id=15 (accessed 18 July 2017).

Suzigan, W. and Villela, A.V. (1997) *Industrial Policy in Brazil*. Campinas: Unicamp.

Tardelli, B. (2017) 'Muita Convicção, Nenuma Profa: Raio-X da Sentença de Moro no "Caso Triplex"', https://br.noticias.yahoo.com/muita-conviccao-nenhuma-prova-o-raio-x-da-sentenca-de-moro-no-caso-triplex-192344519.html (accessed 24 July 2017).

Tauile, J.R. (2001) *Para (Re)construir o Brasil Contemporâneo: Trabalho, Tecnologia e Acumulação*. Rio de Janeiro: Contraponto.

Tavares, L. (2003) *O Debate sobre o Gasto Social do Governo Federal, ou 'Os Economistas da Fazenda Atacam Outra Vez'*, www.proppi.uff.br/revista economica/o-debate-sobre-o-gasto-social-do-governo-federal-ou-os-econom istas-da-fazenda-atacam-outra-vez (accessed 7 July 2017).

Tavares, M.C. (1978) *Da Substituição de Importações ao Capitalismo Financeiro*. Rio de Janeiro: Zahar.

Tavares, M.C. (1999) *Destruição Não Criadora*. Rio de Janeiro: Record.

Théret, B. (1993) 'Hyperinflation de Producteurs et Hyperinflation de Rentiers: le Cas du Brésil', *Révue Tiers Monde*, 34 (133), pp. 37–67.

Thorp, R. (1992) 'A Reappraisal of the Origins of Import-Substituting Industrialisation, 1930–1950', *Journal of Latin American Studies*, 24 (quincentenary supplement), pp. 181–95.

Tible, J. (2013) '¿Una Nueva Clase Media en Brasil? El Lulismo Como Fenómeno Político-Social', http://nuso.org/articulo/una-nueva-clase-media-en-brasil-el-lulismo-como-fenomeno-politico-social/ (accessed 3 July 2017).

Torras, M. (2001) 'Welfare Accounting and the Environment: Reassessing Brazilian Economic Growth, 1965–1993', *Development and Change*, 32, pp. 205–29.

Torres, R.L. and Cavalieri, H. (2015) 'Uma Crítica aos Indicadores Usuais de Desindustrializacao no Brasil', *Revista de Economia Política*, 35 (4), pp. 859–77.

Troster, R.L. and Solimeo, M. (eds) (1997) *Plano Real: Para ou Continua?*. São Paulo: Makron Books.

Trubek, D.M., Coutinho, D.R. and Schapiro, M.G. (2013) 'Toward a New Law and Development: New State Activism in Brazil and the Challenge for Legal Institutions', *World Bank Legal Review*, 4, pp. 281–314.

Urani, A. (1998) 'Ajuste Macroeconômico e Flexibilidade do Mercado de Trabalho no Brasil: 1981/95', in: IPEA (ed.) *A Economia Brasileira em Perspectiva*. Brasília: IPEA.

Valença, M.M. (2002) 'The Politics of Giving in Brazil: The Rise and Demise of Collor (1990–1992)', *Latin American Perspectives*, 29 (1), pp. 115–52.

Valle Baeza, A. and Martínez González, G. (2011) *México, Otro Capitalismo Fallido.* Buenos Aires: Ediciones RyR.

Van Dijk, T.A. (2016) 'Como a Rede Globo Manipulou o Impeachment da Presidente do Brasil, Dilma Rousseff', www.cartamaior.com.br/?/Editoria/ Midia/Como-a-Rede-Globo-manipulou-o-impeachment-da-presidente-do-Brasil-Dilma-Rousseff/12/37490 (accessed 13 July 2017).

Varaschin, J. (2015) 'Para Além do Populismo: Governo João Goulart e a Crise do Modelo Trabalhista de Política Econômica', *Revista da Sociedade Brasileira de Economia Política*, 42, pp. 122–46.

Végh, C.A. (1992) 'Stopping High Inflation', *IMF Staff Papers*, 39 (3), pp. 626–95.

Versiani, F.R. and Mendonça de Barros, J.R. (1978) *Formação Econômica do Brasil: A Experiência da Industrialização.* Rio de Janeiro: Saraiva.

Villela, A.V. (1984) *Empresas do Governo como Instrumento de Política Econômica.* Rio de Janeiro: IPEA.

Weeks, J. (2000) 'Latin America and the High Performing Asian Economies: Growth And Debt', *Journal of International Development*, 12, pp. 635–54.

Weffort, F. (1980) *O Populismo na Política Brasileira*, 2nd ed. Rio de Janeiro: Paz e Terra.

Wood, E.M. (1998) *The Retreat from Class: A New 'True' Socialism.* London: Verso.

World Bank (2006) *Brazil: Interest Rates and Intermediation Spreads*, Report No. 36628-BR, siteresources.worldbank.org/EXTLACOFFICEOFCE/Resources/ 36628oBR.pdf (accessed 5 July 2017).

World Bank (2016) *The Path to Inclusion Growth and Sustainability*, Brazil systematic country diagnostic report No. 101431-BR, https://openknowledge. worldbank.org/handle/10986/23954 (accessed 5 July 2017).

Wu, V. (2010) 'Por Que a Grande Mídia e a Oposição Resolveram Jogar Sujo', www. cartamaior.com.br/?/Editoria/Politica/Por-que-a-grande-midia-e-a-oposicao-resolveram-jogar-sujo/4/16108 (accessed 5 July 2017).

Zysman, J. (1983) *Governments, Markets and Growth: Financial Systems and the Politics of Industrial Change.* Oxford: Martin Robertson.

Index

Printed in Great Britain
by Amazon

65672611R00154